CiTY·SMaRT™
GUIDEBOOK

Baltimore

Joe Sugarman

D1408918

John Muir Publications
A Division of Avalon Travel Publishing

John Muir Publications
A division of Avalon Travel Publishing
5855 Beaudry Street, Emeryville, CA 94608

Printed in the United States of America.
First edition. First printing April 2000

ISBN: 1-56261-518-1
ISSN: 1527-375-X

Editors: Peg Goldstein, Sarah Baldwin, Kate Willis
Graphics Editor: Ann Silvia
Production: Janine Lehmann
Design: Janine Lehmann
Cover Design: Suzanne Rush
Maps: Julie Felton, Chris Alvarez
Typesetter: Diane Rigoli
Printer: Publishers Press
Front cover: © Gisele Damm/Leo de Wys, Inc.—Inner Harbor
Back cover: © Andre Jenny/Unicorn Stock Photos—Inner Harbor

Distributed to the book trade by
Publishers Group West
Emeryville, California

CONTENTS

MAP CONTENTS

Restaurants, hotels, museums and other facilities marked by the
♿ symbol are wheelchair accessible.

See Baltimore the CiTY·SMaRT™ Way

The Guide for Baltimore Natives, New Residents, and Visitors

In *City•Smart Guidebook: Baltimore*, local author Joe Sugarman tells it like it is. Residents will learn things they never knew about their city, new residents will get an insider's view of their new hometown, and visitors will be guided to the very best Baltimore has to offer—whether they're on a weekend getaway or staying a week or more.

Opinionated Recommendations Save You Time and Money

From shopping to nightlife to museums, the author is opinionated about what he likes and dislikes. You'll learn the great and the not-so-great things about Baltimore's sights, restaurants, and accommodations. So you can decide what's worth your time and what's not; which hotel is worth the splurge and which is the best choice for budget travelers.

Easy-to-Use Format Makes Planning Your Trip a Cinch

City•Smart Guidebook: Baltimore is user-friendly—you'll quickly find exactly what you're looking for. Chapters are organized by travelers' interests and needs, from Where to Stay and Where to Eat to Sights and Attractions, Kids' Stuff, Sports and Recreation, and even Day Trips from Baltimore.

Includes Maps and Quick Location-Finding Features

Every listing in this book is accompanied by a geographic zone designation (see the following pages for zone details) that helps you immediately find each location. Staying in Fells Point and wondering about nearby sights and restaurants? Look for the Southeast label in the listings and you'll know that that statue or café is not far away. Or maybe you're looking for the National Aquarium. Along with its address, you'll see a Downtown label, so you'll know just where to find it.

All That and Fun to Read, Too!

Every City•Smart chapter includes fun-to-read (and fun-to-use) tips to help you get more out of Baltimore, city trivia (did you know there are catacombs beneath Federal Hill?), and illuminating sidebars (to learn how to speak "Bawlmerese," see page 12). And well-known local residents provide their personal "Top Ten" lists, guiding readers to the city's best art and architecture, best offbeat shopping spots, and more.

BALTIMORE ZONES

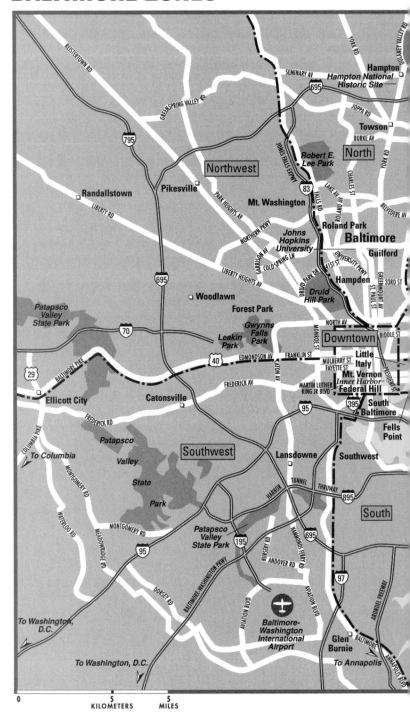

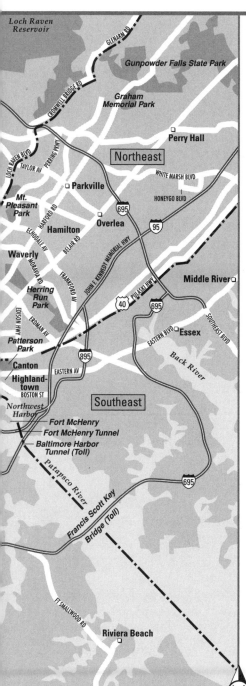

BALTIMORE ZONES

DT—Downtown Baltimore
Bounded on the west by Martin Luther King Jr. Blvd., on the east by S. President St. and I-83, on the north by North Ave., and on the south by Key Hwy. Includes the Inner Harbor and Mount Vernon.

SE—Southeast Baltimore
Bounded on the north by Orleans St./Pulaski Hwy. (U.S. 40) and on the west by S. President St. Includes Little Italy, Fells Point, Canton, and Highlandtown.

S—South Baltimore
Bounded on the west by I-395, on the east by the Inner Harbor, and on the north by Key Hwy. Includes Federal Hill and South Baltimore.

SW—Southwest Baltimore
Bounded on the north by Edmondson Ave./Baltimore National Pike (U.S. 40) and on the east by Baltimore Annapolis Blvd. Includes Union Square/ Hollins Market (SoWeBo) and Historic Ellicott City.

NE—Northeast Baltimore
Bounded on the west by Loch Raven Blvd. and on the south by Orleans St./Pulaski Hwy. (U.S. 40). Includes Parkville, Waverly, and White Marsh.

N—North Baltimore
Bounded on the west by Falls Rd., on the east by Loch Raven Blvd., and on the south by North Ave. Includes Hampden, Charles Village, Roland Park, and Towson.

NW—Northwest Baltimore
Bounded on the east by Falls Rd. and on the south by Edmondson Ave./Baltimore National Pike (U.S. 40). Includes Mount Washington, Pikesville, Reisterstown, and Owings Mills.

Baltimore Area CVA

1

WELCOME TO BALTIMORE

Thirty years ago, you wouldn't have been caught dead reading a guidebook to Baltimore. It was a place tourists passed *through*, a glorified rest stop on the way to New York or Washington. Race relations were tense; unemployment somewhere in the stratosphere. Nightlife meant a trip to "the Block," a line of go-go bars that featured a stripper named Blaze Starr who claimed to have slept with JFK. In his sardonic ode "Baltimore," Randy Newman called the city that "hard town by the sea," not even taking the time to learn that Baltimore sits 150 miles from the sea—on a river.

A lot has changed in 30 years. The Inner Harbor, once a mess of sea shanties and dilapidated wharves, attracts more than 13.4 million visitors annually to its waterfront museums, shopping plazas, and restaurants. Urban developers plan a $350 million revitalization of western downtown, and another $1 billion in development will be pumped into the Inner Harbor by 2001. The city has some of the best medical facilities in the country, an excellent symphony, and several fine art museums.

Still, many wait in frustration for the successes of the waterfront to spread to their own neighborhoods. In the 1990s, nearly 100,000 people fled from Baltimore, fed up with unsafe public schools, rampant open-air drug markets, and a homicide rate that's regularly one of the highest in the country. In one of his Tonight Show monologues, Jay Leno even suggested renaming the city "Balti-sore" to better reflect its formidable rates of venereal disease. So why do people stay?

Travel writers adventurous enough to stop in Baltimore during the 1960s and 1970s called it a city of "hidden gems." Local promoters labeled it "Charm City, U.S.A." Both of these sentiments remain true to this day. It's a city of a thousand quirky footnotes and almost as many obscure firsts. Edgar Allan Poe died here. The first umbrella in the United States was raised here. The city produced the first monuments to George Washington,

Christopher Columbus, and Adam and Eve. It's the beehive-hairdo capital of the world.

Despite a population of 650,000, Baltimoreans call their city a "big small town." Spend a night on the town, and you'll bump into a half dozen people you know. Work downtown and you'll see the same faces during lunch. The pace is slower here than in most East Coast cities. Baltimoreans take their time, get to know one another. Strangers call you "Hon."

Looking for local color? Baltimore is thick with it. This is the town responsible for producing the irascible journalist H. L. Mencken, a duchess of Windsor, rocker Frank Zappa, a disgraced U.S. vice president, and a 300-pound transvestite named Divine. People born here tend to stay. As one of our more famous (infamous?) residents, movie director John Waters, once wrote: "I would never want to live anywhere but Baltimore. You can look far and wide, but you'll never discover a stranger city with such extreme style."

Welcome to Charm City, hon.

Washington monument, the first to memorialize George Washington

Baltimore Area CVA

Getting to Know Baltimore

Geographically, Baltimore City is a five-sided shape—kind of like a rectangle with a clumsily formed 90-degree triangle glued to its southern side. That well-publicized but often misidentified body of water that constitutes the city's southwestern border is not the Atlantic Ocean nor the Chesapeake Bay but the northwestern branch of the Patapsco River. Baltimore County, which actually pre-dates Baltimore itself, borders the city on every side. Interstate 695, Baltimore's beltway, surrounds the whole enchilada in a ring of concrete and steel.

Baltimore is a city of neighborhoods. As immigrants arrived they tended to settle in ethnic enclaves that remain today. All of these neighborhoods seem to have several things in common: the corner bar, the local place of worship, a ball field or park, and row upon row of little redbrick houses with polished white marble steps.

Settlement of Baltimore began around the water, and that's where you'll find some of the city's oldest neighborhoods: funky Fells Point, gentrifying Canton, and Federal Hill, which describes both the mound of earth just south of the harbor and the surrounding neighborhood of Federal-era homes. Mount Vernon—not *the* Mount Vernon where George Washington lived, but the site of the first monument memorializing him—was once home to Baltimore's social elite. Its magnificent townhomes remain, although many have been divided into apartments and offices. These days, the wealthy tend to reside in sprawling Victorian homes in northern areas of the city—Guilford, Homeland, Mount Washington, and Roland Park.

Baltimore's working classes remain ensconced in the eastern sections of the city and in eastern Baltimore County—in Highlandtown, Essex, and Dundalk—close to jobs at Baltimore's port.

Poor neighborhoods, marked by rundown, abandoned row houses, can be found in all-too-many quadrants of the city. Thankfully, many of the high-rise housing projects constructed during the 1960s have been torn down, and affordable, low-rise townhomes are being built in their place.

A Brief History of Baltimore

Susquehanock Indians were the first tourists to enjoy Baltimore's Inner Harbor. They lived mainly in northern Maryland but would venture south seasonally to hunt bear and deer and camp along the Patapsco, which modern-day anthropologists think meant "backwater" or the even more unflattering "tidewater covered with froth" in the native tongue.

Captain John Smith was the first European to see the potential of the spot when he journeyed up Chesapeake Bay in 1608. Settlers arrived in the 1660s, including David Jones, who would later get a polluted river (Jones Falls) and a congested highway (Jones Falls Expressway or I-83) named after him.

Baltimore was officially established in 1729 by a group of tobacco planters. They named it "Baltimore Town" after the Lords Baltimore, a.k.a. the Calvert family, who had charted the colony of Maryland in 1632 after coming to realize that despite great fishing, their first colony—Newfoundland—was just too darn cold.

The fledgling town got off to a rocky start in the tobacco trade and didn't really prosper until 1750, when an immigrant by the name of John Stevenson, the Bill Gates of his day, exported the first cargo of flour. Thereafter, Baltimore's prosperity became linked with wheat rather than tobacco.

Baltimore merchants abhorred oppressive British taxes and trade policies, and many eagerly joined colonial militias to fight during the

TRIVIA

Something about living in Baltimore just brings out the writer in a person. Several well-known scribes who have called Baltimore home over the years include Edgar Allan Poe, F. Scott Fitzgerald, Emily Post, H. L. Mencken, Dashiell Hammett, Gertrude Stein, Upton Sinclair, Ogden Nash, and Anne Tyler.

Historic Battle Monument

Revolutionary War. When the Continental Congress feared attack in Philadelphia, the seat of government moved to Baltimore for 68 days, from December 20, 1776, to February 27, 1777.

Using fast, agile schooners—precursors to the famous Baltimore clipper ships—Baltimoreans privateered numerous British vessels throughout the war, a tactic the city would pay for forty years later during the War of 1812, when vengeful British admirals declared the city and its "nest of pirates" a doomed town. In September of 1814, the British bombed Fort McHenry, a precarious outpost that guarded the city's harbor. The successful defense of Fort McHenry and its "rockets red glare" inspired a young American lawyer named Francis Scott Key, who watched the battle from the beam of a British ship. His scribblings on the back of an envelope would eventually become "The Star-Spangled Banner."

After the war, Baltimore and its busy port prospered. By 1830 the city's population topped 80,000—second only to New York City. On July 4, 1828, 90-year-old Charles Carroll of Carrollton, Baltimore's leading citizen and the only patriot to add his address to his signature on the Declaration of Independence, ceremoniously broke ground for the Baltimore & Ohio Railroad. By 1853 trains journeyed from Baltimore to the Ohio River Valley, delivering cans of Chesapeake Bay oysters and tomatoes from Maryland's Eastern Shore.

On the eve of the Civil War, Maryland, a borderline state just below the Mason-Dixon line, was divided: She had her pocketbook firmly aligned with the merchants of the North, but her heart—and the opinions of most of the population—lay with the South. Maryland was also home to the largest population of free blacks in the country. These explosive conditions ignited when a pro-secessionist mob attacked a band of Union troops trying to change trains in Baltimore. After order was restored, the first casualties of the Civil War had been recorded: four members of the Sixth Massachusetts Infantry and 12 civilians. A month later, citizens awoke one morning to see a makeshift garrison atop Federal Hill and six cannons trained upon the city. The Union occupation of Baltimore would last throughout the Civil War.

The late nineteenth and early twentieth centuries saw a huge influx of immigrants from Poland, Italy, Russia, Ireland, and Greece. At one time, Baltimore's immigrant stations at Locust Point recorded almost as many new arrivals as those at New York's Ellis Island. The same B&O trains that transported cargo now conveyed thousands of thick-accented immigrants to the Midwest as well.

Disaster occurred in 1904, when a warehouse fire wiped out 70 blocks and 1,500 buildings downtown. Miraculously, nobody was killed. Although the Great Fire leveled most of the city, it gave planners an opportunity to rebuild Baltimore, which was acquiring a reputation for its filth. A new sewage system was installed, cows were banned within city limits, and men were ticketed for spitting on the streets.

When the 18th Amendment made it illegal to consume or sell alcohol, a writer for the *Sunpapers* drafted a tongue-in-check editorial called "The Maryland Free State," which promoted the idea that the time was finally right for Maryland to secede. The state didn't, but it did pick up "The Free State" as its new motto. For years, rumor had it that thirsty Baltimoreans

The Allure of a Baltimore Woman

Many know of the shocking marriage of England's King Edward VIII to Baltimore divorcée Wallis Warfield Simpson, but fewer are aware that a century before, Jerome Bonaparte, against the wishes of his elder brother Napoleon, married Betsy Patterson, daughter of wealthy Baltimore merchant William Patterson. Unlike the Duke and Duchess of Windsor's marriage, however, this scandalous romance did not have a happy ending. Not long after the wedding, Napoleon lured Jerome back to France, quickly annulling his brother's "illegitimate union" and marrying him off to a princess. Brokenhearted and bitter, Betsy spent much of her remaining life fighting for her son's accession to the French throne. She didn't succeed, but her grandson Charles Joseph did serve as attorney general under President Theodore Roosevelt. Patterson died at age 94 and lies buried in Green Mount Cemetery under an epitaph that reads: "After life's fitful fever, she sleeps well."

BALTIMORE TIME LINE

1100s–1660s Susquehanock Indians use present-day Baltimore as hunting grounds. They are later wiped out by disease and war with Iroquois Indians and European settlers.

1608 Captain John Smith sails up Chesapeake Bay to the Patapsco River and makes note of Federal Hill.

1632 King Charles I grants Maryland charter to Cecil Calvert, second Lord Baltimore.

1661 Settler David Jones moves onto 380 acres along a stream that would later bear his name, Jones Falls.

1729 Baltimore Town is formally established by a group of planters.

1776–1777 Baltimore's Congress Hall serves as temporary home to the Continental Congress.

1814 British troops invade North Point by land and bombard Fort McHenry by sea. Inspired by the Baltimoreans' victory, Francis Scott Key writes "The Defense of Fort McHenry," later known as "The Star-Spangled Banner."

1815 City lottery raises $250,000 to build country's first monument to George Washington. Completed in 1826.

1828 Ground is broken for construction of Baltimore & Ohio Railroad.

1833 Resident Edgar Allan Poe earns $50 prize and first public note for "Ms. Found in a Bottle."

1849 Edgar Allan Poe dies in a Baltimore hospital and is buried in a graveyard on Greene and Fayette Streets, later known as Westminster Cemetery.

1853 B&O Railroad links Baltimore to the Ohio River Valley in Wheeling, West Virginia.

1861 First casualties of the Civil War are recorded in Baltimore after unruly mob attacks Union troops transferring trains in town.

1867 Businessman Johns Hopkins donates nearly all of his $7 million estate to establish a university and hospital in his name. University opens in 1876; hospital opens in 1889.

1886 Enoch Pratt Free Library is built with $833,000 donated by merchant Enoch Pratt.

were so thrilled with the repeal of the 18th Amendment that they built a monument in Druid Hill Park to commemorate the occasion.

The Great Depression hit the city hard—one in six families was on relief—but residents took a break from the soup lines to applaud the surprise wed-

Fire destroys 70 city blocks and 1,500 buildings.	1904
Pitcher Babe Ruth wins 14 games for the Baltimore Orioles of the International League.	1914
Babe Ruth and three other players sold to the Boston Red Sox for $25,000.	1915
University of Maryland Law School opens to African Americans after NAACP attorney Thurgood Marshall sues.	1935
Baltimore Colts win their first National Football League championship.	1958
Baltimore Orioles win first World Series, sweeping the Los Angeles Dodgers in four games.	1966
Riots follow in the aftermath of the assassination of Dr. Martin Luther King. National Guard called to restore order.	1968
First city fair held downtown; 300,000 people show up. Hope for downtown renewed. Orioles win World Series, beating the Cincinnati Reds.	1970
Tall ships welcomed by thousands for U.S. Bicentennial. Maryland Science Center opens with front facade facing *away* from Inner Harbor.	1976
Harborplace shopping pavilions open.	1980
National Aquarium opens.	1981
Baltimore Orioles beat Philadelphia Phillies in six games for World Series title.	1983
Baltimore Colts owner Robert Isray moves team to Indianapolis under cover of night.	1984
City councilman Clarence "Du" Burns becomes Baltimore's first African American mayor.	1986
Oriole Park at Camden Yards opens.	1992
NAACP moves headquarters from New York City to Baltimore.	1995
PSINet Stadium opens for Baltimore Ravens football games.	1998
City proposes $350 million plan to revitalize historic Hippodrome Theatre and west side of downtown.	1999

ding of twice-divorced Baltimorean Wallis Warfield Simpson to England's King Edward VIII, who abdicated his throne just to get hitched. Simpson would go on to utter smarmy statements like, "One can never be too rich or too thin" (later used in an advertisement for Slender-alls pantyhose).

West 34th Street residents cover their houses with holiday lights.

Baltimore's post–World War II years were marked by prosperity and huge losses in population to the suburbs. Both blacks and whites traded decaying rowhomes and mounting urban ills for two-car garages and half-acre lawns—a trend, unfortunately, that continues in many parts of the city today.

The 1970s brought a successful city fair that helped heal race relations after the 1968 riots and went a long way toward convincing cynical citizens that Baltimore's downtown was worth saving. The 1980s saw a realization of those dreams in the opening of twin shopping pavilions, creation of a world-class aquarium, and election of an eccentric mayor named William Donald Schaefer, who jumped in the aquarium's seal pool to settle a bet. The 1990s witnessed the building of two swanky professional sports stadiums, an additional $1 billion in Inner Harbor redevelopment, and the promise of more urban renewal.

The People of Baltimore

At 60 percent of the population, African Americans constitute the city's largest "minority" and have contributed much to local politics, arts, and culture. Abolitionist and statesman Frederick Douglas, former U.S. Supreme Court Justice Thurgood Marshall, and such jazz greats as Eubie Blake, Cab Calloway, and Billie Holliday all called Baltimore home at one time.

European immigrants flocked to Baltimore for its manufacturing jobs and helped the city grow from its earliest days. Germans were among the first to arrive and worked as grain farmers and millers on the frontier and butchers and brewers within the town limits.

Irish immigrants settled in Old Town along East Lombard Street and near

Mount Clare Station and were instrumental in building the B&O Railroad. Lithuanian and Polish immigrants settled in Southwest and East Baltimore respectively and took jobs at oyster canneries and in sweatshops. In fact, Eastern Avenue was once known as "Polish Wall Street" because so many Poles did their banking there.

Greeks settled in East Baltimore around St. Nicholas Church. Visit Greektown today and you'll see men sipping demitasse and playing cards in coffeeshops with signs only in Greek. In Little Italy, Old World Italians discuss politics from their front stoops or play boccie on the courts next to St. Leo's Parochial School every Friday night.

Northwest Baltimore is home to a thriving Jewish community and contains the largest population of Orthodox Jews outside of New York City. On Friday and Saturday, groups of bearded men dressed in black walk to the neighborhood's many synagogues.

Koreans, Latinos, Indians, and Russians are among the city's newest immigrants, all of whom celebrate their ethnic heritage with huge festivals every summer.

Weather

Before visiting Baltimore during the summer, you should be familiar with one weather-related cliché: "It's not the heat, it's the humidity." (Read: You're gonna have a bad hair day.) While not approaching the summertime soupiness of, say, Miami, Baltimore has its share of hazy, hot, and humid days, with temperatures reaching well into the 90s during July and August. Most disturbing are the several dozen "code red" days each summer, when air quality drops below safe levels and people with respiratory problems are cautioned to stay indoors. Listen to radio or TV news for advisories.

A Miracle on West 34th Street

Hollywood may have its movies about a miracle on 34th Street, but Baltimore has the real thing. Every year, just after Thanksgiving, all the residents of West 34th Street, in the working-class neighborhood of Hampden, literally envelop their houses in holiday lights. Strands of lights run across the street, neon reindeer take to the roofs, and carloads of gawking visitors slow down to take it all in. If you're in town during the eight nights of Hanukkah, check out the "Hanukkah House" at 6211 Park Heights Avenue for an equally mind-boggling display of holiday spirit.

Baltimore Climate Chart

	Avg. High Temps (°F)	Avg. Low Temps (°F)
January	42	28
February	45	30
March	55	38
April	66	48
May	77	58
June	85	67
July	89	72
August	87	70
September	80	63
October	68	51
November	57	42
December	46	32

Winters are relatively mild in Baltimore, despite the panic that accompanies even the thinnest possibility of snowfall. Schools close before even the first flakes hit the ground and supermarkets are stripped naked of bread, milk, and toilet paper. (Stay off the roads; Maryland drivers are notoriously skittish when the white stuff falls.) Temperatures are often below freezing but average in the mid-30s January through March.

Spring and autumn are both pleasant times of the year, with highs in the 60s during the day and lows in the 40s at night. These shoulder seasons don't last as long as they do even two hours north in Philadelphia, and Baltimoreans savor the mild days and crisp nights before the soggy blanket of summer returns.

Dressing in Baltimore

To put it bluntly, Baltimoreans are not known for their sense of style. *Sun* columnist Dan Rodericks once described the city's fashion ethos as "hairdos from hell, rampant polyester, guys with long sideburns, women in white go-go boots." And that was in 1990! Despite its location on the stuffy East Coast, most Baltimoreans remain casual, unpretentious dressers even as more of us exchange blue collars for white. We may wear dressy skirts and jackets and ties to work, but we throw on jeans and T-shirts as soon as we get home. Of course, there are the fashion-conscious among us, but they're usually from out of town. For that reason, plan on wearing nicer duds when visiting touristy restaurants near the Harbor or when dining in Little Italy.

Summer is an especially casual time of year, with shorts and collared shirts acceptable for most restaurants during lunch and only slightly more dressiness required for dinner. If you're planning to eat crabs at any of Baltimore's authentic crab houses, definitely wear something you can afford to get messy. During the summer, a jacket—without a tie—is fine for a night at the opera or symphony, but you might want to spruce things up in the winter. If you're conducting business in Baltimore, a nice suit or dress is appropriate any time of the year.

When to Visit

During Orioles baseball season—roughly early April through September (and, we always hope, into October)—Baltimore swells like a beach town. Hotel rates nearly double, long lines form at the best restaurants, and traffic along Pratt Street moves like a diamondback terrapin. Despite all these nuisances and the sticky weather, summer remains the most popular season to check out Charm City. Ethnic festivals proliferate. Artscape, a three-day circus-like celebration of the fine and performing arts, occurs every July. And fat, tasty blue-claw crabs are available fresh at every seafood restaurant in town.

Autumn means Ravens football at the Inner Harbor, changing leaves

A Town by Any Other Name Just Wouldn't Be Baltimore—or Would It?

- *Charm City, U.S.A.*: *Originally a marketing slogan from the mid-1970s meant to help boost city pride and promote tourism. Despite its untimely debut during the height of a citywide garbage strike, the name stuck.*
- *Mobtown*: *A reference to Baltimore's long history of gang violence, most infamously the mob that attacked the Sixth Massachusetts infantry as it made its way through town, resulting in the first casualties of the Civil War.*
- *The Monumental City*: *A reference to Baltimore's many marble statues, most notably the Washington Monument, the first to memorialize George Washington.*
- *The City That Reads*: *A slogan first uttered by former Mayor Kurt L. Schmoke and derided every time another underfunded city library is forced to close.*

How to Speak Bawlmerese

An amused writer from National Geographic *magazine once described the "Bawlamer" dialect as sounding something like "Pennsylvania Dutch, West Virginian Southern, Brooklynese, and a pinch of Cockney." Here are a few phrases—and translations—to help you get by:*

- *What it sounds like: "Dese aigs are right tasty!"*
- *What it means: "I am enjoying this omelet very much."*

- *What it sounds like: "Where's the rostrum, hon? Ah gotta use the tawlit."*
- *What it means: "Excuse me, sir. Where is your bathroom?"*

- *What it sounds like: "I've never been to Drooslem or Yerp, but Ah've got a cuzin in Napolis."*
- *What it means: "I've never been out of Maryland."*

- *What it sounds like: "How 'bout dem O's?"*
- *What it means: "My, those Baltimore Orioles sure are playing well, aren't they?"*

- *What it sounds like: "Wanna go down de oshun, hon?"*
- *What it means: "Would you care to take a trip to Ocean City, Maryland?"*

in western Maryland, and rockfish runs in Chesapeake Bay. Nights begin to cool down and the lines at the National Aquarium become easier to negotiate.

In December, the Inner Harbor ice rink opens, "Miracle on West 34th Street"—the area's most unusual holiday-light display—illuminates the night, and old-world Ellicott City, bedecked in holiday wreaths, looks like something from a Dickens novel. Rates for accommodations, so inflated in the summer, drop to all-time lows in January and February. And more often than not, the Baltimore Museum of Art or the Walters Art Gallery opens a blockbuster exhibit, providing plenty of options for indoor activities.

TIP

To check the exact dates of any special events occurring in Baltimore, contact the Baltimore events hotline at 410/342-7469 or check www.bop.org.

Spring arrives in Baltimore when *The Sun* begins prognosticating the Orioles' chances for the upcoming season. By opening day, daffodils are beginning to sprout in Roland Park. A month later dogwood and cherry trees fill St. Paul Street with pink and white blossoms, and 80,000 brilliant tulips bloom at Sherwood Gardens. The Baltimore Waterfront Festival means graceful sailboats at the Inner Harbor and sinewy racehorses (and drunken revelers) at the Preakness Stakes.

Calendar of Events

JANUARY
Edgar Allan Poe Birthday Celebration

FEBRUARY
Baltimore on Ice Winterfest, Inner Harbor

MARCH
Maryland Home and Flower Show; St. Patrick's Day Parade, Inner Harbor

APRIL
Billie Holiday Vocal Competition; Maryland Hunt Cup

MAY
Baltimore Waterfront Festival, Inner Harbor; Towsontown Spring Fair; Preakness Stakes, Pimlico Race Track; Flower Mart, Mount Vernon Square; Harborplace Concert Series begins

TRIVIA

H. L. Mencken once said, "If the true purpose of living is to be born in comfort, to live happily and to die at peace, the average Baltimorean is infinitely better off than the average New Yorker."

JUNE
Greek Festival, Greektown; Latino Festival, various locations; Polish Festival, Patterson Park; HonFest, Cafe Hon; Federal Hill FunFest, Federal Hill; City Sand, Harborplace; SoWeBohemian Festival, Hollins Market area; St. Anthony Festival, Little Italy

JULY
Baltimore's Fourth of July Celebration, Inner Harbor; Artscape, Cultural Center; Lexington Market's Ice Cream Festival

AUGUST
Hispanic Festival, various locations; India Day, various locations; Maryland Renaissance Festival, Crownsville; Maryland State Fair, Timonium Fairgrounds; American Indian Pow-Wow, various locations; St. Gabriel Festival, Little Italy

SEPTEMBER
AFRAM, Druid Hill Park; Maryland State Fair, Timonium Fairgrounds; Maryland Renaissance Festival, Crownsville; Korean Festival, various locations; Irish Festival, Maryland Fifth Regiment Building; Baltimore Book Festival, Mount Vernon Square

OCTOBER
German Festival, Carroll Park; Lexington Market's Chocolate Festival; Zoo-Boo, Baltimore Zoo; Haunted Factory on the Harbor, Museum of Industry

NOVEMBER
Thanksgiving Day Parade, Inner Harbor; Zoo Lights, Baltimore Zoo; Inner Harbor Ice Rink opens

Fourth of July fireworks

© The Rouse Company

On the Virtues of an Unpretty City

"The astounding, the incredible, the downright fabulous ugliness of Baltimore . . . is distinctly a positive quality. The amazed newcomer to the city is almost persuaded that she has studied ugliness, practiced it long and toilsomely, made a philosophy of ugliness and raised it to a fine art, so that in the end it has become a work of genius more fascinating than a spick-and-span tidiness could ever be."
—Century Magazine, *May 1928*

DECEMBER
Parade of Lighted Boats, Inner Harbor; Miracle on West 34th Street; A Monumental Occasion, Washington Monument Holiday Lighting; New Year's Eve Extravaganza, Inner Harbor

Business and Economy

The key to Baltimore's early financial successes was its port. As the westernmost port on the East Coast, it allowed for goods to be transferred by water further into the interior of the country, cutting down travel time on more expensive modes of transport. Baltimore's port remains the fifth busiest in the United States and is still an important, albeit lesser, economic engine for the city. Like most cities built on an industrial foundation, Baltimore has seen its manufacturing jobs replaced by positions in the service industry. Banking and biotechnology are the railroads and canneries of today.

By far the city's largest single private-sector employer is Johns Hopkins University, with more than 20,000 workers; Hopkins's outstanding medical system employs another 11,500. Other nationally known businesses with headquarters in Baltimore include Helix Heath, Northrop Grumman, T. Rowe Price, Legg Mason, USF&G Corp, Black and Decker, Sylvan Learning Systems, McCormick & Co. Spices, Cienna Corp, and Jos. A Bank Clothiers.

Despite the revitalization of downtown, many of Baltimore's other neighborhoods continue to flounder economically: Unemployment remains high compared to the rest of the state (7 versus 3.3 percent in September 1999), and approximately one out of every five residents lives below the poverty line. The median income for city residents is $23,018. Factor in the wealthier suburbs and that number jumps to $30,533.

Generally, Baltimore's cost of living is below average for an East Coast city, which makes living in Baltimore and enduring the commute to pricier Washington, D.C., a popular option for many. The average dinner for two runs about $30 to $40 without a bottle of wine. Movies are just beginning to cross the dreaded $8 barrier, but most run $7 or $7.50 at area theaters. Prices for a five-mile cab ride average about $5 to $6, depending on how long you get stuck in traffic. If you want to read the news of the day, you'll have to sacrifice 50 cents for a *Baltimore Sun*, or pick up the alternative *Baltimore City Paper* for free. If you want milk, it'll cost you $2.65 a gallon.

Housing

Most of Baltimore's distinctive row houses were built during periods of large population spurts, after the Civil War and the two World Wars. "On a modest working-man's income you may live in a delightful toy-like little redbrick house with fresh paint, green shutters, and the whitest of white steps," said a writer in *Harper's Weekly* in 1928. Fast and easy to construct, the houses' trademark steps were a symbol of pride, to be kept white using various recipes usually involving bleach. In a strategy for urban renewal that made headlines in the 1970s, dozens of crumbling row houses in Baltimore's run-down neighborhoods were sold for $1 each, with the caveat that buyers restore the structures to meet city codes.

These days, housing in Baltimore is a bit more expensive. The average sale price in 1998 was $55,524—still low for the East Coast and actually lower than 10 years ago. However, in hot real estate areas such as Federal Hill and Canton row houses sell for easily double or triple that figure. If you include the entire metropolitan area, the average selling price for a home jumps to $101,000. Meanwhile, rents remain reasonable in most parts of Baltimore, averaging $490 citywide.

TRIVIA

The Great Fire of 1904 burned so bright that flames could be seen 35 miles away in Washington. When fire engines arrived from Philadelphia and Washington, they were forced to watch Baltimore burn, since their hoses did not fit the attachment on the city's fire hydrants. One good thing did come of the disaster: Fire hydrants and hose nozzles were standardized throughout the country to ensure the mishap would never happen again.

Schools

Perhaps nowhere else do residents of a city identify so strongly with their schools. At social gatherings and business functions, when someone asks, "What school did you go to?" they don't mean what college, they mean what *high school.* (This, of course, probably has something to do with the fact that native Baltimoreans never leave.)

Improving Baltimore City public schools has been the scourge of many a school superintendent, and radical solutions, like independent management and custodianship by the state of Maryland, have met with frustratingly little success. The city does have several excellent magnet schools, such as Polytechnic Institute, for budding engineers, and the Baltimore City School for the Arts, where scenes from the movie *Fame* are reenacted every day. If they can afford them, many parents send their children to one of Baltimore's 130 private schools, most of which are concentrated in the city's posh northern neighborhoods.

Baltimore has its share of outstanding colleges and universities, and the city was ranked 10th in the nation for higher education in the 1997 edition of *Places Rated Almanac.* Johns Hopkins University and its medical school are certainly the best known of the lot, but the University of Maryland's medical and dental schools are also well regarded. Other institutions of higher learning include Loyola College, Goucher College, University of Baltimore, Towson University, Morgan State University, Coppin State College, College of Notre Dame of Maryland, St. Mary's Seminary, Baltimore International College (hotel management and restaurant training), and the Maryland Institute College of Art, the oldest independent art college in the United States.

Joe Sugarman

2

GETTING AROUND BALTIMORE

.From the 27th-floor observation deck of the Inner Harbor's World Trade Center, Baltimore sprawls below in miniature, a three-dimensional map from which to gain your bearings. You'll see that most of downtown's office buildings cluster just north of the Inner Harbor basin. Baltimore is not a particularly tall city; its highest building, the William Donald Schaefer Tower, is about one-third the height of New York's Empire State Building. The names of city neighborhoods—Seton Hill, Mount Vernon, Druid Hill—would seem to indicate that Baltimore is a city of steep inclines. Perhaps in the days of horse-drawn carriages, and before so many buildings occupied these hills, the rise and fall of Baltimore streets was more perceptible. Today, looking from the top of the World Trade Center, only to the far west and northwest can you glean that Baltimore indeed was built on a piedmont, as the rise of the land becomes evident toward the mountains of Frederick County. The eastern half of the city, in particular, lies low, its row houses lined up like models from a toy train set.

To the north, the Jones Falls Expressway (I-83) winds through town like a concrete snake above and along the Jones Falls, a polluted river that's been mercifully concealed south of Penn Station. (In Baltimore, rivers and streams are called "falls" and "runs," words used by the pioneering millers who tapped the rushing waters.) To the southeast, beyond the black Inner Harbor basin, the Patapsco River, lined with the port's marine terminals and huge cranes, flows out to the Francis Scott Key Bridge and eventually into Chesapeake Bay. Meanwhile, South Baltimore, behind Federal Hill, forms a peninsula, surrounded by the middle and northwest branches of the Patapsco.

All told, Baltimore is only 12 miles long and 10 miles wide, but as Tony Hiss, a writer for the *New Yorker,* once pointed out, the city seems far wider than long, since no expressways link the east and west sides of town. It's a city you should find fairly easy to negotiate. Most attractions lie some-where near the water's edge, accessible via the Inner Harbor's redbrick promenade or by water taxi. Buses, underground metro, and above-ground light-rail cars service other parts of the city.

Baltimore's Layout

Baltimore's downtown streets follow a fairly rigid grid, without too many tricks. The city's main artery is, and has been for years, Charles Street, which runs one-way north through the city until just south of Cold Spring Lane, from where it accommodates two-way traffic. Charles Street is the Y, or north-south, axis of the grid while Baltimore Street, albeit a less major thorough-fare, is its X, or east-west, axis. All street names to the east of Charles Street begin with "East," and all those to the west start with "West"—West 21 Street, East 21st Street, West Biddle Street, East Biddle Street, and so on. By the same logic, all downtown streets north of Baltimore Street begin with "North," while all streets below start with "South." Therefore, north of Bal-timore Street, Charles Street is called North Charles Street; south of Balti-more Street, it's considered South Charles Street. Got it?

Other major downtown arteries are Calvert Street, which runs north one

Don't Try Driving Your Car Down Here

In 1909, Baltimore's Department of Public Works boasted a brand-new sewer system. But before sewage flooded the pipes, a Balti-more photojournalist named Sadie Miller—accompanied by her husband and four friends—decided to investigate the new system by driving their turn-of-the-century automobile through the 12-foot-wide main tunnel. The trip took them around sharp curves and through "a regular London fog," as Mrs. Miller later wrote. The out-ing was fairly uneventful until the party reached the end of the line, at which point they discovered that their vehicle was too large to turn around. Mr. Miller was forced to maneuver the automobile through six curving miles—in reverse! After changing a flat tire and spending more than four hours under the streets of Baltimore, the party emerged, startling a work crew at the exit. Mrs. Miller later published an account of the expedition, accompanied by pho-tographs, in Frank Leslie's Illustrated Weekly.

Cyclists and Pedestrians Take Note

Unless you're a fearless bicycle messenger or a die-hard green commuter, you don't want to bike in Baltimore. Very few roads anywhere in the city have designated bicycle lanes, and none of them can be found downtown. If you want to take the two-wheeler for a cruise, explore the Northern Central Railroad or the Baltimore-Annapolis trails, both profiled in Chapter 10, Sports and Recreation.

Hometown motorists generally respect the rights of pedestrians, but you never know if there's a New Yorker behind the wheel. Pedestrians have it good around the Inner Harbor: Skywalks link several major downtown hotels and the convention center with Harborplace, meaning visitors never have to touch the asphalt. Best of all, the redbrick promenade that rings the Inner Harbor wall will one day link the Canton Waterfront to the Baltimore Museum of Industry in South Baltimore.

way, and St. Paul Street, which runs south one way before morphing into Light Street at Lombard Street. Speaking of Lombard, it's the main western route through downtown, while Pratt Street is the major eastern thoroughfare (both run one way). Provided you don't try driving while reading this book, you shouldn't have much trouble navigating Baltimore.

Public Transportation

All forms of local public transportation—bus, metro, and light rail—fall under the aegis of the Maryland Mass Transit Administration or MTA. The folks at MTA make things easy for riders by charging the same fares for all modes of transport: $1.35 for a one-way trip, $2.70 for a round-trip pass, and $3.00 for all-day travel. Seniors and people with disabilities get a bargain at 45¢ for one-way travel and $1 for an all-day pass. For automated information and customer service, call MTA at 410/539-5000 or 800/543-9809, or check their Web site at www.mtamaryland.com.

Buses

Baltimore's lumbering blue-and-white buses cover 51 routes that crisscross the city and spread into Baltimore, Anne Arundel, and Howard Counties.

Ed Kane's Water Taxi service also offers an Inner Harbor trolley service that runs east along Pratt Street and west along Lombard Street, linking sights west of downtown, like the B&O Railroad Museum, with sights east of downtown, like Port Discovery children's museum. Stops are few and far between on Lombard and Pratt. Look for signs. Trolleys run daily in summer from 10 a.m. to 5 p.m. and weekends only in spring and fall. Ed Kane's Water Taxi tickets are good for transportation on trolleys.

They generally afford a safe and reliable means of transportation, and they're a necessity for city dwellers without automobiles. Blue-and-white signs at bus stops indicate the route number serviced by the bus. Schedules are not posted at stops, but are available at Penn Station, BWI Airport, metro stations, and by calling MTA. Hotel concierges often have a stack of schedules as well. Remember that the machines on buses take exact change only—any combination of coins (except pennies) and dollar bills that add up to $1.35—and no haggling with the driver. Press the yellow strip above the windows to alert the driver of your stop.

Metro

Yes, Baltimore does have a metro system, although the fact may come as a shock even to lifelong city residents. The route cuts a narrow path from its northwestern terminus of Owings Mills in Baltimore County, through downtown to Johns Hopkins Hospital in East Baltimore. It makes 14 stops along the way and takes about half an hour to run its 15-mile length. Key tourist stops include Lexington Market (at Eutaw Street), Charles Center (several blocks between the Inner Harbor and Mount Vernon), and Shot Tower/Market Place (behind Port Discovery children's museum). Trains run approximately every 8 minutes during rush hour and creep along every 10 to 20

Stuck at BWI Airport with some time to kill? Check out the Observation Gallery located between Piers B and C on the ticketing concourse. You can watch the planes land and listen to the air-traffic controllers jabber, and the kids can pretend they're landing a jet behind the controls of a mock cockpit. Serious aviation buffs can park their cars at the Thomas A. Dixon Jr. Aircraft Observation Area off Dorsey Road and watch the big metal birds soar just overhead.

Options for Transportation to and from BWI Airport

- **Automobile:** The trip between BWI and downtown takes approximately 20 to 25 minutes. From Baltimore to BWI, take either I-95 or Baltimore-Washington Parkway (I-295) south to I-195 east. From BWI to Baltimore, take I-195 west to either I-95 or the Baltimore-Washington Parkway north.

- **Light Rail:** This service transports riders in trolley-like cars between BWI's international pier and points throughout the city. Tickets cost $1.35 per person one way and can be purchased at ticket machines at the station. The trip between the airport and the Inner Harbor takes 35 minutes, 45 minutes to Penn Station.

- **MARC's Penn Line Train:** A free shuttle bus links BWI terminal to BWI Rail Station, where you can connect with Amtrak trains or with MARC, a commuter line that runs weekdays only, 5 a.m. to 11 p.m. Ask for schedule information at the airport or call 800/325-RAIL. The trip between BWI and Baltimore's Penn Station costs $3.25 one way and takes about 20 minutes. MARC trains also run to Washington's Union Station, a 35-minute ride.

- **Amtrak Train:** Amtrak trains are more expensive than MARC trains, but they are faster and run on weekends. Expect to pay $9 for the 10-minute trip to Penn Station. Amtrak trains also run to Washington's Union Station. Call 800/USA-RAIL for more information.

- **Taxi:** A cab ride between downtown and BWI costs approximately $20, plus tip.

- **SuperShuttle:** This van service accepts reservations for pickups between any of the area's three airports and your residence or hotel. A ride between Baltimore and BWI costs $16, plus $5 for each additional person. Call 800/258-3826 for reservations.

- **Limousine:** Limo service can be a surprisingly economical option, particularly if you're traveling with several passengers. They charge a flat rate depending on how far you need to go, plus a 15-percent gratuity. Call 410/519-0000 for more information.

- **Hotel Shuttle:** Most hotels and motels near BWI offer complimentary shuttle service for their guests. Some in downtown Baltimore do as well. Check when reserving a room.

minutes at other times. Hours of operation are weekdays from 5 a.m. to midnight and Saturday from 6 a.m. to midnight. Trains do not run on Sunday.

Light Rail

Baltimore's newest form of public transport carries passengers in clean, above-ground, trolleylike cars. A northern terminus in Hunt Valley connects with Cromwell Station in Glen Burnie, about five miles, as the crow flies, south of the city line. The route skirts along the western edge of downtown, conveniently intersecting many of the city's attractions: PSINet Stadium, Oriole Park at Camden Yards (get off here to visit the Inner Harbor), Lexington Market, and the Cultural Center (Meyerhoff Symphony Hall and Lyric Opera House). It also stops at Penn Station, where you can link up with Amtrak trains, as well as making a loop to BWI Airport. Unfortunately, it's a slow, prodding affair between the train station and the airport, with frequent stops and a travel time of 45 minutes, compared to a 30-minute drive. Still, it's by far the cheapest mode of public transportation between the city and the airport. Light rail operates weekdays from 6 a.m. to 11 p.m., Saturday from 8 a.m. to 11 p.m., and Sunday from 11 a.m. to 7 p.m. Trains depart every 17 minutes.

Taxis

Yellow taxi cabs cruise the city's main arteries and Inner Harbor hotels looking for a fare at all hours of the day. In areas outside of downtown, you should call one of the below-listed cab companies and arrange for a pick-up. All cabs have meters and charge a base rate of $1.40, plus 20¢ per one-eighth of a mile after that. Per-mile rates double if you leave Baltimore City, and tips are expected. Flat rates are illegal in Maryland, but you might find a

---

Nine Charming Things about Charm City
by William Donald Schaefer, Baltimore mayor 1971–1987

1. The neighborhoods
2. Camden Yards
3. Inner Harbor
4. Baltimore Zoo
5. Maryland Science Center
6. Churches and synagogues
7. Fort McHenry
8. A new mayor*
9. Little Italy

*Mr. Schaefer compiled this list after Mayor Kurt L. Schmoke announced he would not seek office for a fourth term and before a new mayor had been elected.

---

cabby offering to take you to the airport for a predetermined price. Use your own discretion—if they want to charge more than $20 to $25 from downtown, forget it. Cab companies include Yellow and Checkered Cab (410/685-1212), County Cab (410/788-8000), Mini-Star Cab (410/461-7777), and Valley Cab, serving the northwest suburbs (410/486-4000).

Water Taxis

One cool thing about a city with its downtown located on the water is that you can take a boat to get from point A to point B. Two competing water transportation companies vie for your cruising dollars: the blue and white boats of Ed Kane's Water Taxi (410/563-3901) and the Harbor Shuttle's red, black, and white boats (410/675-2900). Both offer stops at sights ringing the Harbor—Fort McHenry, Fells Point, Museum of Industry, the Canton waterfront, American Visionary Art Museum, and many more. But before boarding, it's very important to ask the boat operator where he or she is heading, since not every boat stops at every landing all the time. From May through September, boats run about every 15 to 18 minutes at the most popular landings, such as Harborplace and Fells Point. From the more obscure stops—Captain James Landing, Harris Creek, and Canton Waterfront Park—you may have to call for a pickup. Tickets for Ed Kane's Water Taxi cost $4.50 per person and are valid for all-day transportation. Harbor Shuttle's all-day passes cost $4 per person.

Driving in Baltimore

Driving in Baltimore isn't nearly as frustrating nor as hazardous as driving in other East Coast cities like New York or Washington. Traffic usually moves

Water taxis can take you to sites around the harbor.

Baltimore Area CVA

at a robust clip; however, there are frequent exceptions, most notably when sporting events tie up traffic downtown and, of course, during rush hour, from 8 to 9 a.m. and from 4:30 to 6 p.m. Rush hour brings routine traffic snarls in both directions along the Baltimore Beltway (I-695), most frequently where it meets I-83. Other trouble spots include I-95 at Fort McHenry and I-895 at the Harbor Tunnel. Listen to any radio station for traffic updates during these times. You should know that Baltimoreans are notorious for running red lights, to such an extreme that the city has erected traffic cameras at key intersections to record the license plate numbers of violators. So if you get a ticket in the mail three weeks after your visit to Baltimore, you'll know why.

Parking

City law-enforcement agents get a lot of flack for failing to shut down the city's open-air drug markets, but they're vigilant when it comes to enforcing parking laws—especially around the Inner Harbor. Most parking meters that ring the harbor require a constant feeding of quarters, 24 hours a day. (One quarter gets you only 15 minutes.) Once they expire, it's almost as if they silently send a signal to the nearest meter maid. Parking in garages is a safer option. Most downtown garages charge $10 to $12 for up to 12 hours or overnight. As a general rule, the farther away from the water's edge, the cheaper the parking. Many garages offer $5 rates for evening Orioles games and special events.

Parking in Fells Point isn't as expensive as parking downtown—just a lot more difficult. On Friday and Saturday nights the streets fill, and you'll simply have to circle the blocks looking for an empty spot. Two pay lots on Thames Street, west of Broadway, offer spaces but fill up fast.

Air Travel

Baltimore-Washington International Airport, a.k.a. BWI (800/I FLY BWI, www.bwiairport.com) is a major hub on the East Coast but tends to get overshadowed by Reagan National Airport and Dulles Airport, both outside of Washington and at least an hour's drive from Baltimore. That's fine with Baltimoreans, because BWI is a far easier airport to negotiate than those two behemoths. Also, flights are often cheaper in and out of BWI, particularly on US Airways and Southwest Airlines, which use the airport as a hub. In 1997, BWI completed a $425 million upgrade that included the opening of an international pier, serviced by British Airways, Air Jamaica, El Al Israel, and Icelandair. The airport's four domestic piers contain the usual fast-food eateries, a pub or two, newsstands, and shops selling last-chance Maryland souvenirs.

Long-term parking costs seven dollars per day in the color-coded "blue" and "green" satellite lots along Aviation Boulevard (Route 170); tack on 15 minutes or so for the shuttle service between the parking lot and the airport. Park for the short term in the five-story garage adjacent to the main terminal. The garage charges by the hour, but the first half-hour is free.

Major Airlines Serving Baltimore

Air Aruba: 800/882-7822
Air Jamaica: 800/523-5585
Air Ontario/Air Canada: 800/776-3000
America West: 800/235-9292
American Airlines: 800/433-7300
British Airways: 800/247-9297
Continental Airlines: 800/525-0280
Delta Air Lines: 800/221-1212
El Al Israel Airlines: 800/223-6700
Frontier Airlines: 800/432-1359
Icelandair: 800/223-5500
Midway: 800/446-4392
Northwest Airlines: 800/225-2525
Southwest Airlines: 800/435-9792
Trans World Airlines: 800/221-2000
United Airlines: 800/241-6522
US Airways: 800/428-4322

Rail Service

F. Scott Fitzgerald called Baltimore's Pennsylvanian Station (1500 N. Charles St., 800/USA-RAIL) "Athenian," and indeed there is something Grecian about the beaux arts structure completed in 1911. Inside, Sicilian marble walls, terrazzo floors, and green ceramic tiles add to the aura of antiquity. Unfortunately, unlike Washington's Union Station and Philadelphia's 30th

Take a MARC train from Penn Station.

Baltimore Area CVA

Lost downtown? Ask one of the men or women in the purple hats and jackets for directions. Downtown Partnership sponsors these guides to help keep the city "safe and clean"—and point you in the right direction.

Street Station, both built around the same time, Baltimore's Penn Station has nothing more than a poorly stocked newsstand and a coffee shop to wile away the time waiting for your train.

Amtrak trains service Penn Station along the company's Northeast Direct and Metroliner routes between Boston and Washington, D.C. You can stow your car in a recently completed lot at the station.

Light rail stops here, as do Penn Line MARC commuter trains that run weekdays between Baltimore and Washington, D.C. (A round-trip ticket from Baltimore to Washington's Union Station costs $10.25.) MARC trains also run from Camden Station next to Oriole Park at Camden Yards to Washington, but they operate less frequently and do not connect with BWI Airport. If you're staying in Baltimore and want to take a weekday excursion to Washington, D.C. (see Chapter 13, Day Trips), MARC commuter trains are a convenient way to travel.

Regional Bus Service

Greyhound buses (800/231-2222) stop at 210 West Fayette Street, about 12 blocks west of the Inner Harbor, at a small, outdated depot with few amenities to keep travelers amused and even fewer places to sit. Buses also stop at the Baltimore Travel Plaza (5623 O'Donnell Street, 410/633-7146), a sprawling, well-lit travel hub with numerous fast-food restaurants, free parking, and a 100-room Best Western hotel for weary travelers, about a 15-minute drive southeast of downtown. In addition to Greyhound, Peter Pan (800/237-8747) and a variety of other tour companies service this stop.

Burtnett Studios

3

WHERE TO STAY

Back in the nineteenth century, Baltimore was known for its grand hotels and swanky hotel restaurants. A visitor could mention she stayed at the Fountain Inn or Barnum's or ate canvasback duck at the Rennert, and even her friends back in New York City would nod approvingly.

Baltimore still has some fine roosts, but these days they go by the somewhat less glamorous-sounding names of Hyatt, Marriott, and Hilton. Most of the city's ritzier hotels are perched around the Inner Harbor or downtown, while more affordable options ring the Baltimore Beltway (I-695) and lie within hearing distance of the sonic booms at BWI Airport.

Generally, the closer you are to the water, the more you'll have to pay, with prices topping $200 per night during peak season for rooms with harbor views. "Peak season" means Orioles baseball season (early spring through early fall); key weekends, such as those for the Preakness Stakes and the Baltimore Waterfront Festival, often fill up even before baseball season begins. On top of your quoted room rate, you'll also have to cover Baltimore City's 7.5 percent occupancy tax as well as an additional 5 percent state tax.

Baltimore is a big—and growing—convention town, and you'll see plenty of badge-wearing folks in business suits scurrying along the Inner Harbor skywalks during the week, particularly in spring and fall; convention traffic drops off somewhat during summer months.

Alternatives to chain hotels—B&Bs, campgrounds, youth hostels, and small inns—are relatively scarce in Baltimore and therefore fill quickly. Proposals

Price-rating symbols:
$	Under $50
$$	$51 to $100
$$$	$101 to $150
$$$$	$151 and up

for new high-rise hotels are announced seemingly every other day, and soon the current dearth of rooms could become a glut, meaning better prices for you.

Note that two price ratings in a listing indicate a substantial difference between peak season (late spring through early fall) and off-season (winter) rates.

DOWNTOWN

Hotels

BALTIMORE HILTON AND TOWERS
20 W. Baltimore St.
Baltimore
410/539-8400 or 800/HILTONS
www.hilton.com
$$–$$$$

When this facility was built, in 1928, it was the fourth tallest building in Baltimore and, as early brochures boasted, included "A Radio in Every Room!" Known as the Lord Baltimore Hotel, it was the last of the city's grand hotels to be constructed before the decline of downtown after World War II. The venerable building retains some 1920s panache in its gold-plated revolving doors, high-ceilinged lobby, and original gold-leaf clock that's been ticking since FDR was president. All the rooms have undergone recent renovations and include hair dryers, coffee makers, and free HBO, but none have harbor views. Children under 18 stay for free when they occupy the same room as their parents or grandparents. 👤 (Downtown)

BALTIMORE MARRIOTT INNER HARBOR
110 S. Eutaw St.

Baltimore
410/962-0202 or 800/228-9290
www.marriotthotels.com
$$–$$$$

If you've got a very strong arm, you might be able to throw a baseball from the Marriott to the gates of Oriole Park at Camden Yards. The ballpark is just a block south of this snazzy Inner Harbor hotel. You can choose from parlor rooms, kings, doubles, mini-suites, and concierge rooms that feature continental breakfast and happy-hour treats in an exclusive lounge. A "leisure rate" includes breakfast for guests staying on weekends only. In addition to the typical top-of-the-line amenities in all rooms, the hotel also has an indoor pool and Jacuzzi, a health club, and two restaurants on the premises. Parking is $8 per day or $12 if you get someone else to do it for you. Since the hotel is so close to the ballpark, room rates tend to shoot up when the O's are in town. 👤 (Downtown)

BILTMORE SUITES
205 W. Madison St.
Baltimore
410/728-6550
$$–$$$

If you like quirky accommodations, you'll like the Biltmore. The Norman Gothic structure, with long windows and a gambrel roof, must have been quite the hotel when it opened in 1880. These days, the floors slant, the carpet's lumpy, and not every light goes on when you flick the switch, but the joint still has its charms. The Biltmore has 15 suites with electric stoves and refrigerators as well as 25 regular guest rooms serviced by an ancient gold-painted elevator that's literally the size of a telephone booth. Continental breakfast is offered in the homey common area, and guests

DOWNTOWN BALTIMORE

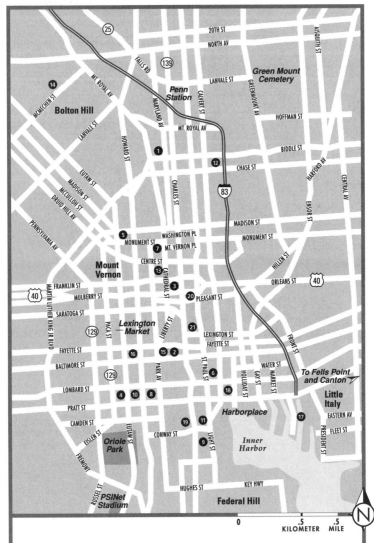

Where to Stay Downtown

1 Abacrombie Badger B&B
2 Baltimore Hilton and Towers
3 Baltimore International Hostel
4 Baltimore Marriott Inner Harbor
5 Biltmore Suites
6 Brookshire Inner Harbor Suite Hotel
7 Clarion Hotel at Mount Vernon Square

8 Days Inn Inner Harbor
9 Harbor Court Hotel
10 Holiday Inn Inner Harbor
11 Hyatt Regency
12 The Inn at Government House
13 Mount Vernon Hotel
14 Mr. Mole Bed and Breakfast
15 Omni Inner Harbor Hotel
16 Paramount Inner Harbor Hotel

17 Pier 5 Hotel
18 Renaissance Harborplace Hotel
19 Sheraton Inner Harbor Hotel
20 The Tremont Hotel
21 Tremont Plaza

Baltimore's most expensive hotel room is the 2,600-square-foot presidential suite at the Harbor Court Hotel. It has three rooms, a working fireplace, a wet bar, a baby grand piano, an all-marble bathroom, a full kitchen, and a dining room table that seats 14.

Numerous kings, queens, and heads of state have slept there, as well as Hollywood types like Frank Sinatra, Jodie Foster, and Faye Dunaway. The price? A mere $3,000 a night.

park at a nearby hospital for a very reasonable $2.50 per night. Avoid the queen suites in the inn's second building; quirky charm only goes so far. (Downtown)

BROOKSHIRE INNER HARBOR SUITE HOTEL
120 E. Lombard St.
Baltimore
410/625-1300
$$–$$$$
www.harbormagic.com
$$-$$$$

A 1999 renovation jazzed up the previously dowdy interior of the Brookshire, which occupies a good location a block north of the waterfront. The compact lobby follows an art deco theme, with plush purple and green couches and eye-catching statuary. The one- and two-bedroom suites—some with harbor views—are attractive, but decorated much more conservatively than the lobby. All rooms have wet bars, some have pullout couches, none have cooking facilities. Rates include a hot buffet breakfast served in the airy Cloud Club on the building's 12th floor. A tiny exercise room holds stationary bicycles and treadmills. Valet parking costs $20 per night. &. (Downtown)

CLARION HOTEL AT MOUNT VERNON SQUARE
612 Cathedral St.
Baltimore
410/727-7101 or 800/292-5500
www.sunbursthospitality.com
$$–$$$

Ideally located right on grassy Mount Vernon Square, this historic hotel was built in 1928, and most of its east-facing rooms have wonderful views of the Washington Monument. The 103-room property was originally a boarding house; it has since been spruced up with modern amenities like mini-refrigerators, dataports, and hairdryers in all the king, queen, and double rooms. All-marble bathrooms with towel warmers add a nice touch of luxury. Courtesy shuttles transport hotel guests to the Inner Harbor, Johns Hopkins Hospital, and Fells Point. &. (Downtown)

DAYS INN INNER HARBOR
100 Hopkins Pl.
Baltimore
410/576-1000 or 800/942-7543
www.daysinn.com
$$$

This 250-room, family-friendly establishment is in a good location across East Pratt Street from the Baltimore Convention Center and two blocks

Harbor Court Hotel's lobby

from Inner Harbor attractions. These digs don't provide fancy amenities, just clean rooms and a kidney-shaped outdoor pool. If you want to exercise, ask the concierge for a free pass to a nearby athletic club. The hotel's restaurant, Ashley's, serves up breakfast, lunch, and dinner, but it doesn't provide room service. Feel free to bring back a doggie bag, however; "micro-refrigerators" are standard in most rooms. ⑤ (Downtown)

HARBOR COURT HOTEL
550 Light St.
Baltimore
410/234-0550 or 800/824-0076
www.harborcourt.com
$$$$
Step into the lobby at the Harbor Court and you'll soon realize why this hotel is considered Baltimore's classiest. Note the spiraling teak-wood staircase, the huge vases of fresh flowers, the doorman sporting a top hat. Hallways are wide and airy, and all rooms have dataports, fax machines, and even small televisions in

the bathrooms. The decor is meant to evoke a sea-travelers home: old paintings in gilded frames, a large wooden globe in the lobby, and a book-lined sitting room that looks like something out of a captain's cabin. Of course, you'll also find a complete fitness room, a raquetball court, an indoor pool, two outdoor tennis courts, a tanning salon, massage therapists, and aerobics classes. The hotel is host to two restaurants: airy Brighton's and the esteemed Hampton's, consistently rated one of Baltimore's best—and most expensive (see Chapter 4, Where to Eat). ⑤ (Downtown)

HOLIDAY INN INNER HARBOR
301 W. Lombard St.
Baltimore
410/685-3500 or 800/HOLIDAY
www.holiday-inn.com
$$–$$$
A year after it was constructed, the Beatles stayed at this Holiday Inn, which is just a couple of blocks from the Inner Harbor and Oriole Park. The

hotel's exterior still evokes the days of Nehru jackets and lava lamps, but its lobby and guest rooms have been completely renovated. That enormous flying saucer–like object on the roof once housed North America's first revolving restaurant. (Now it just holds a revolving schedule of meetings.) If you're a baseball fan, ask for a south-facing room on one of the upper floors: You'll be able to see home plate at the ballpark. The hotel also has a sizeable indoor pool, a fitness center, and bargain parking at six dollars a day for hotel guests. ♿ (Downtown)

HYATT REGENCY
300 Light St.
Baltimore
410/528-1234 or 800/233-1234
www.hyatt.com
$$$–$$$$

The Hyatt was the first hotel to open at Baltimore's fledgling Inner Harbor, back in 1981, and in doing so it claimed some choice waterfront real estate. The building's fantastic six-story, glass-enclosed lobby is located a block off the water, behind the Harborplace shopping pavilions. (Kids will love riding the glass-enclosed elevators.) A quarter of all the rooms have harbor views. A complete renovation in 1996 spruced things up, with business-plan rooms getting oversized desks, dataports, and fax machines. The hotel also offers a very complete fitness center (with daily aerobics classes) and a business center. The sixth-floor terrace is home to an outdoor pool with deckside service, two tennis courts, a basketball hoop, and—could it be? Yes, it is!—a putting green. The casual Bistro 300 offers breakfast and lunch, while Pisces (see Chapter 4, Where to Eat) serves up sweeping views and fresh seafood. ♿ (Downtown)

THE INN AT GOVERNMENT HOUSE
1125 N. Calvert St.
Baltimore
410/539-0566
$$$

As the official inn of Baltimore City, Government House is where dignitaries (and not so dignitaries) stay for free when visiting on official city business. Your room will have all the same amenities—private bath, iron, refrigerator—but will cost you just under 150 bucks a night. The inn is actually several buildings, a circa-1889 Victorian mansion and two row houses. The mansion—with its exquisite entrance hall, grand staircase, and woody library with stained-glass windows—is a popular site for weddings. Guests of the inn have access to all this Old World opulence and eat

TIP

If you want to save a few bucks and don't care if your room has a water view, try booking a room at a hotel in the Mount Vernon neighborhood. The hotels average about $50 less per room than the Inner Harbor facilities, yet many are still within walking distance of Inner Harbor attractions. And you'll get to explore historic Mount Vernon to boot.

The Victorian-style Inn at Government House was built by Baltimore banker John S. Gilman and later occupied by a very wealthy inventor and businessman named William Painter, who made a lot of dough on an ordinary item we take for granted today—the bottle cap.

continental breakfast around a magnificent hundred-year-old table. On the down side, some of the front rooms face noisy North Calvert Street, and the hotel is a long (and not particularly safe) walk to any attractions. If it's a special occasion, ask for the bridal suite, the nicest room in the house for only $10 more than a queen suite. (Downtown)

MOUNT VERNON HOTEL
24 W. Franklin St.
Baltimore
410/576-8400
$$–$$$

Built in 1909 in the Renaissance Revival style, this hotel doesn't look like it housed a YMCA for 50-odd years. But, sure enough, the Olympic-size swimming pool has been replaced by an Olympic-size parking lot, and a large lobby filled with Victorian furniture now occupies the space where athletes perhaps once lifted weights. Run by the Baltimore International College, the hotel is used as a training ground for hotelier wannabes. Its rooms and hallways are basic and clean, and since it operates as a nonprofit, its rates are outstanding—particularly considering its choice location a block from Walters Art Gallery (inquire about package deals) and other neighborhood sights. Students train at its ground-floor restaurant, the Washington Inn, open for breakfast and lunch. & (Downtown)

OMNI INNER HARBOR HOTEL
101 W. Fayette St.
Baltimore
410/752-1100 or 800/THE-OMNI
$$$–$$$$

Baltimore's largest hotel, the Omni is comprised of two towers and 707 rooms that loom over downtown. Despite the hotel's 23 floors, none of the rooms feature views of the water three blocks east and two blocks south. The towers sit in Charles Center, near the Morris Mechanic Theatre (see Chapter 11, Performing Arts) and the Baltimore Arena. With 30,000 square feet of meeting space, the Omni attracts hoards of businessfolk, meaning it'll usually be cheaper for you to stay here on weekends or when there's not a big convention in town. Shula's Steakhouse (see Chapter 4, Where to Eat), a meat-eater's paradise and part of a chain owned by former Baltimore Colts and Miami Dolphins coach Don Shula, is just off the lobby. & (Downtown)

PARAMOUNT INNER HARBOR HOTEL
8 N. Howard St.
Baltimore
410/539-1188 or 800/948-6418
www.by1.com/md/paramounthotel
$$

Built in 1888, burned in the great fire of 1904, and rebuilt in 1907, the Paramount is Baltimore's oldest continuously operating hotel. It's also one of the cheapest places to stay downtown, with rates topping off at $100 a night during summer months and dropping to $78 during the winter. Most of the counter staff are veterans of the Baltimore hotel scene and know their way around downtown. Unfortunately, the hotel, which is just two blocks from the convention center and five blocks from the Inner Harbor, is stuck in a somewhat dicey area. Exercise caution at night. Parking is available across the street for $8 a night. (Downtown)

PIER 5 HOTEL
711 Eastern Ave.
Baltimore
410/843-7711
www.harbormagic.com
$$$–$$$$

From the outside this place looks like a well-manicured brick condominium. Inside, it's a wonderland of overstuffed couches in purples, greens, and mustard yellows; handsome triangular lights; dark-wood accents; and colorful art rimming the lobby. The deco theme is carried into the rooms, which come complete with complimentary bottled water, minibars, and scenic water views. The hotel is in a great location—behind the defunct Columbus Center; you can visit the National Aquarium and the Power Plant without even crossing a street. Plus, with only 65 rooms, this place seems a world away from the bustling high-rise hotels nearby. If you get hungry, the upscale seafood emporium McCormick and Schmick's is located right next door. ᔕ (Downtown)

RENAISSANCE HARBORPLACE HOTEL
202 E. Pratt St.
Baltimore
410/547-1200 or 800/468-3571

www.renaissancehotels.com
$$$–$$$$

This upscale roost has basically all you could possibly want in a waterfront hotel: spacious rooms (many with water views), an attractive restaurant and bar, a fitness center, an indoor pool, and a skywalk to the Pratt Street Pavilion right across the street. The hotel's lobby is connected to the Gallery at Harborplace (see Chapter 9, Shopping), so you can shop the day away if you so desire. Club Level room rates include continental breakfast and happy-hour hors d'oeuvres. Note: Summer weekends fill very fast. ᔕ (Downtown)

SHERATON INNER HARBOR HOTEL
300 S. Charles St.
Baltimore
410/962-8300 or 800/325-3535
www.sheraton.com
$$–$$$$

Located just two blocks away from Oriole Park at Camden Yards, the Sheraton bills itself as the "official hotel of the Baltimore Orioles." (Players from visiting teams often bunk here.) The hotel is also the closest to the Baltimore Convention Center and during the week crowds with conventioneers. Despite its location behind the Hyatt, the hotel has some rooms with harbor views. An outpost of the Chicago-based Morton's Steakhouse is on the premises, as is an additional restaurant that serves up breakfast and lunch buffets. Parking is provided in an underground lot for $12 a day. Inquire about special "baseball packages" that include room, parking, tickets, and drinks at the hotel's Orioles Bar. ᔕ (Downtown)

THE TREMONT HOTEL
8 E. Pleasant St.

Baltimore
410/576-1200
$$–$$$

The Tremont Hotel's claim to fame is that it was Baltimore's first all-suite hotel when it opened in 1984. (Wait, it gets better.) In 1999, the hotel underwent a much-needed top-to-bottom renovation and now has all-new furniture in its two sizes of suites, plus updated kitchenettes with microwaves, electric stoves, and enough kitchen gadgets to host a cooking show. Smaller and less sophisticated than its cousin, the Tremont Plaza, it attracts mainly vacationing families and folks visiting patients at Johns Hopkins Hospital. (Ask about the patient rate if you're in town to visit the hospital.) Continental breakfast is included with your stay, and a restaurant off the lobby serves dinner six nights a week. Valet parking is available at $12 a night. ⛨ (Downtown)

TREMONT PLAZA
222 St. Paul Pl.
Baltimore
410/727-2222
$$$

Sleep at the Tremont Plaza and you could be sleeping in the bed where Johnny Depp slept. Or Kevin Bacon. Or any number of the Hollywood stars who camp in these downtown digs when shooting films for several weeks or months. The Tremont, a towering 37-story former apartment building, was turned into 222 efficiency suites in 1984. Since then, it's lobby has undergone a dramatic renovation, and its rooms are slated to be spruced up soon. Each suite has a kitchenette, a sitting area, and a queen- or king-size bed. It's popular with families and anyone who needs to spend more than a few days in

The 19th-century Abacrombie Badger B&B

Charm City. The location is good—lower Mount Vernon, about six blocks from the harbor. The hotel has an informal restaurant, a deli, a swimming pool, a sparsely equipped fitness room, and men's and women's saunas. Parking is by valet only, at $12 per night. ⛨ (Downtown)

Other Accommodations

ABACROMBIE BADGER B&B
58 W. Biddle St.
Baltimore
410/244-7227 or 888/9BADGER
www.badger-inn.com
$$–$$$

This nineteenth-century row house once belonged to a Colonel Biddle—his portrait still hangs over the living room's mantle. It's directly across the street from Meyerhoff Symphony Hall (see Chapter 11, Performing Arts) and a block away from light rail's Cultural Center stop, which runs to Camden Yards, Raven's Stadium, and BWI Airport. The inn offers 12 uniquely furnished guest rooms, free parking, and Dutch-style continental breakfast in an airy, yellow dining room. Each room has a private bathroom and a yellow rubber duckie by the tub. Make reservations at least two weeks in advance. (Downtown)

BALTIMORE INTERNATIONAL HOSTEL
17 W. Mulberry St.
Baltimore
410/576-8880
$

Baltimore's lone hostel, housed in an 1880s brownstone, was due (at press time) to receive a $750,000 top-to-bottom makeover in early 2000. The renovation promises to make the hostel "world-class," including all new bunks and an updated kitchen and common area. Dorm-style rooms will accommodate 6 to 10 people, and several private rooms should be available as well. The hostel will also be wheelchair-accessible. Its location is good: a block from North Charles Street and the heart of Mount Vernon and six blocks north of the Inner Harbor. The bus station is within walking distance, but the train station is a schlepp. Call first to see if the hostel has reopened for business. & (Downtown)

MR. MOLE BED AND BREAKFAST
1601 Bolton St.
Baltimore
410/728-1179
$$$–$$$$

Baltimore's only four-star B&B offers discriminating travelers accommodations in a Civil War–era home with towering 14-foot ceilings, bay windows, and marble fireplaces. Each of the five suites is decorated with eighteenth- and nineteenth-century antiques, and all come complete with

modern amenities. Two of the suites have two bedrooms and can accommodate up to three people. Single-bedroom suites have queen beds and sitting areas. Mr. Mole is located in the historic Bolton Hill neighborhood, on the outskirts of downtown and approximately four blocks from public transportation. "Well-mannered" children over 10 are welcome. (Downtown)

NORTH

Hotels and Motels

BURKSHIRE GUEST SUITES AND CONFERENCE CENTER
10 W. Burke Ave.
Towson
410/324-8100 or 800/435-5986
www.marriott.com
$$

Owned by Towson University but run by Marriott, the Burkshire has 119 guest suites with full kitchens, washer/dryers, and balcony views of the university or the Towson business district. (Opt for the wooded views of the university.) Suites are either one-bedroom or one-bedroom with a den. Weekend rates are lower than weekday rates, and discounts are given to Towson University alumni, staff, and faculty. The hotel has a restaurant and a sports pub with a Towson Tigers theme. It also has a fitness room, but the weight room, basketball courts, and tennis courts at the university—available to guests for free—are certainly more comprehensive. Parking is free for overnight guests. & (North)

DAYS INN BALTIMORE EAST
8801 Loch Raven Blvd.
Towson

410/882-0900 or 800/235-DAYS
www.daysinn.com
$–$$
Not only are the room rates reasonable here, but you also get a full breakfast, with choice of five entrees. If you're coming from the north, you'll like the location, too—Exit 29B off the Baltimore Beltway, 12 miles from downtown. The hotel attracts mainly vacationing families, tour groups on weekends, and a corporate crowd during the week. Amenities are few, but there is a low-key restaurant and lounge on the premises. Oh, and if you crave liver and onions in the middle of the night, the classic Bel-Loc Diner is located across the street (see Chapter 4, Where to Eat). ⅙ (North)

DOUBLETREE INN AT THE COLONNADE
4 W. University Pkwy.
Baltimore
410/235-5400 or 800/222-TREE
www.doubletreehotels.com
$$–$$$

This is the accommodation of choice for many of the bigwigs who visit the Johns Hopkins University Homewood campus, located just across the street. Its 125 attractive rooms—all with two telephones, dataports, on-command video, irons and ironing boards, and coffeemakers—occupy the first three floors of a luxury condominium. The inn also contains arguably Baltimore's best-looking hotel pool, housed under a glass dome next to two whirlpool baths. The Polo Grill (see Chapter 4, Where to Eat), one of Baltimore's top restaurants, is located off the lobby. Courtesy shuttles whisk guests to Inner Harbor attractions 10 minutes away. ⅙ (North)

EMBASSY SUITES–HUNT VALLEY
213 International Circle
Hunt Valley
410/584-1400
$$$

This establishment is popular among people doing business in Hunt Valley, a suburb about 25 minutes north of downtown. It's an all-suites hotel with

Embassy Suites, located in Hunt Valley

Beware: On weekends when the dreaded New York Yankees are scheduled to come to town, hotels have been known to sell out a year in advance. Check the baseball schedule to see if the Orioles are playing at home. Chances are you'll have an easier time finding a room (and pay less for it) when they're not.

a pleasant atrium of tropical plants and a waterfall. All rooms have king or double beds, separate living rooms, galley-style kitchens, and queen-size pullout sofa beds. Complimentary breakfast and happy-hour hors d'oeuvres are served daily in the hotel's atrium restaurant, the Hunt Valley Grill. While the hotel isn't completely cut off from the city—the northernmost light rail stop is less than a mile away—if you don't have a car, you'll feel pretty stranded out here. Kids under 18 stay free with their parents or grandparents. ♿ (North)

SHERATON BALTIMORE NORTH
903 Dulaney Valley Rd.
Towson
410/321-7400 or 800/433-7614
www.sheraton.com/baltimore
$$$–$$$$
For a suburban hotel located 20 minutes north of downtown, this place is surprisingly genteel, with polished brass, green Italian marble, and twinkling chandeliers in its lobby. Its 284 newly renovated rooms have all the standard amenities, including coffee makers, ironing boards, and phones with dataports. The hotel attracts mainly a corporate crowd during the week and parents visiting students at nearby Goucher College and Towson

University on the weekends. It has a restaurant, an indoor pool, and a fitness room on the premises (guests also have access to a nearby Bally's Fitness Club). The hotel is attached via walkway to Towson Town Center Mall (see Chapter 9, Shopping), a good bet in case you need a last-minute present for that newly minted graduate. ♿ (North)

Bed-and-Breakfasts

HOPKINS INN
3404 St. Paul St.
Baltimore
410/235-8600
$$$
Here's a unique accommodation. Located in the earthy Charles Village neighborhood, near the Johns Hopkins Homewood campus and about 10 minutes from downtown, this former 1920s apartment complex features 25 newly refurbished rooms decorated in Victorian-era antiques and period reproductions. The place has a homey feel, courtesy of friendly innkeeper Peggy Trapp and her even friendlier black Labrador Sam. (The dog—as well as three cats—are kept away from guests who are allergic to animals.) Each morning Peggy whips up an "expanded" continental breakfast of muffins, cereal, juice, and

GREATER BALTIMORE

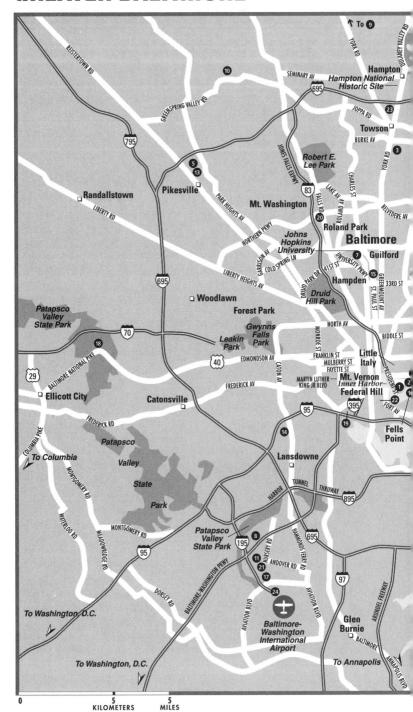

To 9

REISTERTOWN RD

795

GREENSPRING VALLEY RD

SEMINARY AV

695

Hampton
Hampton National
Historic Site

YORK RD

DULANEY VALLEY RD

JOPPA RD

23

Towson

BURKE AV

YORK RD

3

Randallstown

LIBERTY RD

Pikesville

5
13

PARK HEIGHTS AV

JONES FALLS EXPWY

Robert E.
Lee Park

83

Mt. Washington

FALLS RD

LAKE AV

ROLAND AV

CHARLES ST

BELVEDERE AV

Roland Park

20

Johns
Hopkins
University

NORTHERN PKWY

GARRISON AV

COLD SPRING LN

Baltimore

7

Guilford

UNIVERSITY PKWY

41ST ST

GREENMOUNT AV

ST PAUL ST

15

33RD ST

Hampden

695

LIBERTY HEIGHTS AV

DRUID PARK DR

Druid
Hill Park

Woodlawn

Forest Park

Patapsco
Valley
State Park

70

Gwynns
Falls
Park

Leakin
Park

NORTH AV

MONROE ST

BIDDLE ST

18

40

EDMONDSON AV

CATON AV

FRANKLIN ST
MULBERRY ST
FAYETTE ST

Little
Italy

29

BALTIMORE NATIONAL PIKE

FREDERICK AV

MARTIN LUTHER
KING JR BLVD

Mt. Vernon
Inner Harbor
Federal Hill

PRESIDENT ST

1
2

Ellicott City

Catonsville

95

395

FORT AV

22

Fells
Point

FREDERICK RD

14

19

To Columbia

COLUMBIA PIKE

MONTGOMERY RD

Patapsco

Valley

State

Park

Lansdowne

HARBOR

TUNNEL

THRUWAY

895

WATERLOO RD

MONTGOMERY RD

95

Patapsco
Valley
State Park

195

8

NURSERY RD

HAMMONDS FERRY RD

695

MEADOWRIDGE RD

11
21

ANDOVER RD

17

97

DORSEY RD

BALTIMORE-WASHINGTON PKWY

24

AVIATION BLVD

AVIATION BLVD

Baltimore-
Washington
International
Airport

ARUNDEL FREEWAY

Glen
Burnie

BALTIMORE

ANNAPOLIS BLVD

To Washington, D.C.

To Washington, D.C.

To Annapolis

0   5   5
   KILOMETERS   MILES

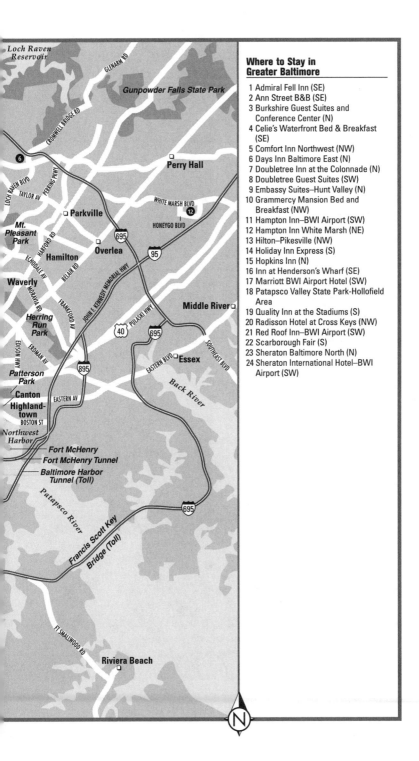

Where to Stay in Greater Baltimore

1 Admiral Fell Inn (SE)
2 Ann Street B&B (SE)
3 Burkshire Guest Suites and Conference Center (N)
4 Celie's Waterfront Bed & Breakfast (SE)
5 Comfort Inn Northwest (NW)
6 Days Inn Baltimore East (N)
7 Doubletree Inn at the Colonnade (N)
8 Doubletree Guest Suites (SW)
9 Embassy Suites–Hunt Valley (N)
10 Grammercy Mansion Bed and Breakfast (NW)
11 Hampton Inn–BWI Airport (SW)
12 Hampton Inn White Marsh (NE)
13 Hilton–Pikesville (NW)
14 Holiday Inn Express (S)
15 Hopkins Inn (N)
16 Inn at Henderson's Wharf (SE)
17 Marriott BWI Airport Hotel (SW)
18 Patapsco Valley State Park-Hollofield Area
19 Quality Inn at the Stadiums (S)
20 Radisson Hotel at Cross Keys (NW)
21 Red Roof Inn–BWI Airport (SW)
22 Scarborough Fair (S)
23 Sheraton Baltimore North (N)
24 Sheraton International Hotel–BWI Airport (SW)

coffee. The hotel attracts mainly visitors to Hopkins and even accommodated a foreign princess in 1998, as a plaque outside the entrance boasts. (North)

NORTHEAST

Hotels and Motels

HAMPTON INN WHITE MARSH
8225 Town Center Dr.
White Marsh
410/931-2200 or 800/HAMPTON
www.hamptoninn.com
$$
If you're traveling south along I-95 to Baltimore and you happen to run out of gas (literally or figuratively), this chain motel makes for a good stopover. The 127-room establishment is located near White Marsh Mall (see Chapter 9, Shopping) in a booming suburb of the same name. Most rooms have either double- or king-size beds. The inn has an outdoor swimming pool and a small exercise room, and it serves complimentary continental breakfast. ♿ (Northeast)

NORTHWEST

Hotels and Motels

COMFORT INN NORTHWEST
10 Wooded Way
Pikesville
410/484-7700 or 800/732-2458
www.sunbursthospitality.com
$$
This facility doesn't look like your everyday Comfort Inn because half of it used to be an apartment complex. Its 87 apartment suites are fully furnished and have two bedrooms, living rooms, and full kitchens; they can be rented weekly or nightly, depending on availability. An additional 103 clean hotel rooms feature king and queen beds, plus access to an outdoor pool and "deluxe" continental breakfasts in the morning. The location isn't bad, either: about 20 minutes from down-

Hilton Pikesville

Hilton Pikesville

> The cheapest time to stay in Baltimore is during January, when the best rates for Inner Harbor hotels drop below $100 a night.

town. The hotel is close to Pimlico Race Course, and rooms fill quickly during the Preakness Stakes in mid-May. ♿ (Northwest)

HILTON–PIKESVILLE
1726 Reisterstown Rd.
Pikesville
410/653-1100 or 800/283-0333
www.hilton.com
$$$

Located just off the Baltimore Beltway (Exit 20), this spartan Hilton is in the heart of Baltimore's Jewish community. In addition to its proximity to good knishes, this establishment offers complimentary local shuttle service, an outdoor pool, free parking, and access to OptiFit fitness center and its six-court tennis barn. (If you forget your tennis outfit, Optifit rents clothes, rackets, balls—even a partner.) Room service is available from San Marcos, a Mediterranean restaurant, or Gabby's, a sports bar with a menu of 60 different beers. Continental breakfast is included with certain room packages. The hotel also has well-designed rooms for people with handicaps, including big bathrooms with massive roll-in showers. ♿ (Northwest)

RADISSON HOTEL AT
CROSS KEYS
5100 Falls Rd.
Baltimore
410/532-6900 or 800/333-3333
www.radisson.com/baltimoremd
$$$

Recently absorbed and refurbished by the Radisson Hotel chain, this inn/hotel is a unique accommodation in the middle of the Village at Cross Keys, an upscale shopping plaza of specialty shops (see Chapter 9, Shopping). Its 146 guest rooms have a French country decor, coffeemakers, free newspapers, and windows that actually open (a rarity for hotels these days). The hotel also has a lovely outdoor swimming pool, an indoor tennis facility, a complete fitness center and tanning rooms, his-and-hers saunas, and free parking. Scheduled shuttles run to the Inner Harbor daily. Room service is available from the hotel restaurant, Crossroads. ♿ (Northwest)

Bed-and-Breakfasts

GRAMERCY MANSION BED AND
BREAKFAST
1400 Greenspring Valley Rd.
Stevenson
410/486-2405 or 800/533-3404
www.gramercymansion.com
$$–$$$$

Railroad magnate Alexander Cassatt (brother of Impressionist painter Mary Cassatt), presented this fantastic Tudor mansion to his daughter as a wedding gift in 1902. Evoking the days of robber barons and Early American industrialist wealth, the inn is an exceedingly romantic destination set on 45

Gramercy Mansion Bed and Breakfast, p. 43

Gramercy Mansion Bed and Breakfast

wooded acres in the middle of Maryland horse country. City life seems a world away, yet the inn is just 25 minutes from downtown. Breakfasts are superb and feature ingredients handpicked from the on-site organic vegetable garden. Rooms that share a common bath go for less than $100 for double occupancy (ask for the Toy Room); rooms with private baths start at $165 per night. Be sure to inquire whether a wedding is taking place; the noise can be a disturbance. (Northwest)

SOUTH

Hotels and Motels

HOLIDAY INN EXPRESS
1401 Bloomfield Ave.
Baltimore
410/646-1700 or 800/HOLIDAY
www.holiday-inn.com
$$
Just three miles south of the Inner Harbor, this establishment is a good bet if you'd like to be close to the sights and attractions of Baltimore without paying the big bucks for a harborside room. Rooms are basic but clean, and the hotel has an outdoor pool. Continental breakfast is included with your stay. (South) &

QUALITY INN AT THE STADIUMS
1701 Russell St.
Baltimore
410/727-3400 or 800/221-2222
$$
Stay at this Quality Inn and you'll have better access to the southbound ramps of I-95 and the Baltimore-Washington Parkway than anyone else staying downtown. Not that that's necessarily a good thing. The motel is located in an industrial area about a tenth of a mile from the busy highways' on-ramps, and, well, merging traffic just doesn't make for pleasant scenery. Oriole Park is located about a mile's walk away through a rundown semi-industrial part of town. Inside, the rooms are basic and clean. & (South)

Bed-and-Breakfasts

SCARBOROUGH FAIR
1 E. Montgomery St.
Baltimore
410/837-0010
www.scarborough-fair.com
$$$
Located in Federal Hill, this B&B is the only one within walking distance of the Inner Harbor, and it's a homey alternative to the big waterside hotels. The Federal-era 1801 structure was built by a bricklayer and in 1997 was transformed into a bed-and-breakfast by congenial owners Ellen and Ashley Scarborough. The building has six rooms with private baths, decorated mainly in antiques. Four rooms have gas fireplaces and two have Jacuzzis. Guests get free parking in a nearby lot, keys to the front door, and a full-service breakfast featuring French toast, frittatas, or curried eggs. Ashley, who was born just down the street, can provide all sorts of insider recommendations on where to eat and what to do. The B&B has a two-night minimum stay on weekends during peak season. Book well in advance. (South)

SOUTHEAST

Hotels and Motels

ADMIRAL FELL INN
888 S. Broadway
Baltimore
410/522-7377 or 800/292-4667
www.admiralfell.com
$$–$$$$
Located in the heart of historic Fells Point, this now-stylish inn once accommodated, for 35 cents a night, turn-of-the-century seamen on leave. These days the Federal-era lodging is your best bet for exploring the area's antiques stores by day and its crowded pubs by night. Rooms are tastefully decorated with period furnishings, and the two-story luxury suite has a fireplace and a Jacuzzi. The inn offers free parking—a big plus in Fells Point—and courtesy van service to the Inner Harbor. & (Southeast)

INN AT HENDERSON'S WHARF
1000 Fell St.
Baltimore
410/522-7777 or 800/522-2088
www.hendersonswharf.com
$$$–$$$$
In 1893, the B&O Railroad built a warehouse on the wharf of marine merchant John Henderson and from there shipped headhogs of tobacco all over the world. The brick building was in shambles after the B&O went bust, but it was renovated and turned into classy residences and an attractive ground-floor inn. This place is close to the shopping and restaurants of Fells Point but far enough off the main drag that you won't be bothered by traffic and drunken revelers through the night. Rooms are large with views of either the water or a tidy courtyard. Parking is available onsite, and you can even park your boat at the adjacent marina. & (Southeast)

Bed-and-Breakfasts

ANN STREET B&B
804 S. Ann St.
Baltimore
410/342-5883
$$
If it weren't for the set of blocks on a front windowsill that spell out "B AND B," passersby would have no clue that this eighteenth-century

Reservation Services

You could call each of Baltimore's B&Bs individually to locate a vacant room, or you could have Amanda's Bed & Breakfast Reservation Service, 443/535-0008 or 800/899-7533, do the work for you. After finding a suitable inn and checking for vacancies, Amanda's will book the room with a one-night deposit from you. (Checks or credit cards are accepted.) The convenience will cost you a $5 reservation fee. Looking for life after Baltimore? They'll also book any B&B in Maryland for you, plus selective sites in six surrounding states.

Room Finders USA, 800/473-7829, is a national organization that helps you locate vacant rooms in most American cities. You provide the dates, and they book the rooms. There is no additional charge for this useful service, but keep in mind that they don't have room rates for all the hotels and inns in town. As with all reservation services, make sure you locate the hotel on a map and ask for an unbiased opinion before you commit.

row house is an inn. Hosts Joanne and Andrew Mazurek offer relaxed accommodations in just three guest rooms in this building a block off the water and across the street from the Wharf Rat Pub (see Chapter 12, Nightlife). Two of the three rooms have fireplaces, and all have private baths, double poster beds, hardwood floors, and "not too stuffy" Colonial decor. Full breakfasts are served daily. This is one of the least expensive places to stay in Fells Point, with rates topping off at about $100 per night. For that reason, it's also one of the most popular: Make reservations two months in advance for summer weekends. (Southeast)

**CELIE'S WATERFRONT
BED & BREAKFAST**
1714 Thames St.
Baltimore
410/522-2323 or 800/432-0184
$$–$$$
This unpretentious B&B is right in the thick of Fells Point. A great deck overlooks the rooftops of East Baltimore and the Recreation Pier, former home to the police station on TV's *Homicide*. Most rooms are furnished in period reproductions. If you're a heavy sleeper, opt for one of the two harborfront rooms that feature fireplaces and Jacuzzis. Continental breakfast is served. The inn's six rooms fill fast—book for summer weekends at least six weeks in advance. ఉ (Southeast)

SOUTHWEST

Hotels and Motels

DOUBLETREE GUEST SUITES
1300 Concourse Dr.
Linthicum
410/850-0747 or 800/222-TREE
$$–$$$
A bright, airy atrium gives this airport-area hotel some instant class. Pullout couches, wet bars, refrigerators, and microwaves are standard in many rooms; indoor and outdoor pools, a Jacuzzi, and a fitness center are available to all. Babysitting services and free shuttle rides to the airport are other pluses. If you're a paying guest, you can ditch your car in the hotel's parking lot for free while you travel to other cities and then return. The hotel, which crowds with businesspeople during the week, can be a bargain on weekends, when rates drop by almost half. & (Southwest)

HAMPTON INN–BWI AIRPORT
829 Elkridge Landing Rd.
Linthicum
410/850-0600 or 800/HAMPTON
www.hamptoninn.com
$$
What can you say about a Hampton Inn? The rooms are clean, you get free cable TV, and the air conditioning works. At this surprisingly attractive Hampton Inn, however, you also get complimentary continental breakfast and free shuttle rides to the airport. & (Southwest)

MARRIOTT BWI AIRPORT HOTEL
1743 W. Nursery Rd.
Linthicum
410/859-8300 or 800/228-9290
www.marriotthotels.com
$$–$$$$
This is a good bet for travelers who are looking for upscale accommodations near the airport. The glass-enclosed swimming pool is stunning and has a cascading waterfall next to a comfortable hot tub. The lobby has a sleek black baby grand piano, on which you can serenade fellow guests if you so choose. Rooms are attractively decorated and have all the usual modern amenities. Moniker's Grill is open for breakfast, lunch, and dinner, and you can watch "dem O's" at Champions, a sports bar. Shuttle service to the airport is complimentary, as is coffee in the lobby every morning from 5:00 to 8:30. The hotel attracts a corporate crowd during the week, and rates often drop under $100 on Friday and Saturday nights. & (Southwest)

RED ROOF INN–BWI AIRPORT
827 Elkridge Landing Rd.
Linthicum
410/850-7600 or 800/THEROOF
www.redroof.com
$$
At least you can count on consistency when staying at the Red Roof Inn; this motel looks the same in Linthicum, Maryland, as it does in Toledo, Ohio. Yep, the roof is red and there's a cardboard stand-up of celebrity spokesperson Martin Mull in the lobby. The Red Roof offers free shuttle service to the airport, as well as complimentary coffee and newspaper. & (Southwest)

SHERATON INTERNATIONAL HOTEL–BWI AIRPORT
7032 Elm Rd.
Linthicum
410/859-3300
www.sheraton.com
$$–$$$
The Sheraton is so close to BWI Airport that it was built only two stories

tall so it wouldn't interfere with the views from the airport's traffic tower. Luckily, due to the miracle of sound-proofing, the only time you'll hear the jets soaring overhead is when you're lounging at the hotel's outdoor pool. Even louder than the jets, however, might be the sonic booms emanating from the adjacent tropical-theme nightclub, Hurricanes. Shuttle buses run the five-minute trip to the airport terminal 24 hours a day, and two electronic displays—just like the ones at BWI—broadcast arrival and departure information. Room service is available from Michener's Restaurant and Lounge. &. (Southwest)

Campgrounds

PATAPSCO VALLEY STATE PARK–HOLLOFIELD AREA
8020 Baltimore National Pike
Ellicott City
410/461-5005
$
The only campground in the Baltimore area is located three miles off the Beltway and about 20 minutes from downtown. Set on 12 semi-wooded acres within Patapsco Valley State Park (see Chapter 8, Parks, Gardens, and Recreation Areas), the Hollofield campground contains 75 sites with flush and pit toilets, a playground, picnic areas, nature trails, fishing, and a dump station. The campground is convenient to Historic Ellicott City (see Chapter 5, Sights and Attractions). Open Apr–Oct only. Pets welcome. (Southwest)

Evan Cohen

4

WHERE TO EAT

Philadelphia has its cheesesteaks, Chicago has its deep-dish pizza, and Baltimore has its crab. The numerous ways Baltimoreans prepare and eat crab read like dialogue from the movie Forrest Gump: crab cakes, crab soup, cream of crab, deviled crab, crab stew, crab salad, crab imperial, and so on. Only in Baltimore does a crab mallet get a space in the silverware drawer, a blue-and-yellow container of peppery Old Bay seasonings its own place next to the salt and pepper shakers. Truth be told, fewer and fewer crabs come from Chesapeake Bay these days, and Baltimoreans are forced to rely on imports from North Carolina, Texas, or Louisiana. But where they're from doesn't seem to matter as much as who cooks them. (Yes, there are proper ways to steam a crab.)

Baltimore has a lot of good restaurants but few on the culinary cutting edge. (Remember, director Barry Levinson called his Baltimore-set movie Diner, not Bistro.) You can eat some excellent meals here, but the most memorable will probably involve a combination of the aforementioned crustaceans, a pitcher of beer, and a sheet of brown paper serving as a tablecloth. Snotty celebrity chefs with rarified culinary styles are about as common as Beluga caviar. The city, with its significant Polish and German population, is at heart a sausage-and-potatoes town.

Indeed, Baltimore's immigrant enclaves have created pockets of fine ethnic eats. A dozen restaurants in Little Italy perfume the streets nightly with garlic. (But be warned: In addition to breath mints, you'll need a wallet full of cash

Price-rating symbols:
$ Under $10
$$ $11 to $15
$$$ $16 to $20
$$$$ $21 and up

to afford the neighborhood's best.) Greektown, along Eastern Avenue in East Baltimore, has Old World lamb dishes, moussaka, and ouzo. Corned Beef Row, along East Lombard Street, isn't quite the deli dreamland it used to be, but it still gives Baltimore's Jewish population a taste of knishes and kugels like mom used to make. Several restaurants in the Little Korea neighborhood near North Charles and West 21st Street prepare exotic dishes such as cuttlefish and raw jellyfish. And the burgeoning Latino community in Upper Fells Point promises to produce some great Latin American restaurants. Not surprisingly, many of these ethnic groups have contributed to the city's vast repertoire of crab recipes.

This chapter begins with a list of restaurants organized by cuisine type. Each restaurant name is followed by an abbreviated zone designation and the page where the restaurant is described. The restaurant descriptions are organized alphabetically within each zone. The following price-rating symbols indicate the average cost of a dinner entrée.

RESTAURANTS BY TYPE OF CUISINE

Afghan/Indian
Ambassador Dining Room (N), p. 60
Bombay Grill (DT), p. 51
Cafe Bombay (DT), p. 53
The Helmand (DT), p. 55

American/Steakhouses
BOP (SE), p. 75
The Cheesecake Factory (DT), p. 53
The Prime Rib (DT), p. 56
Regi's (S), p. 71
Ruth's Chris Steak House (DT), p. 57
Shula's Steakhouse (DT), p. 57

Trolley Stop (SW), p. 82
Wayne's Bar-B-Que (DT), p. 60

Asian/Pacific Rim
Ban Thai (DT), p. 51
Cafe Zen (NE), p. 62
Kawasaki (DT), p. 55
Matsuri (S), p. 70
Nam Kang (N), p. 64
Ten-O-Six (S), p. 71

Cafés/Coffeehouses
City Café (DT), p. 53
Donna's Coffee Bar and Café (DT), p. 54
Funk's Democratic Coffee Spot (SE), p. 76
Golden West Café (N), p. 62
Louie's Café (DT), p. 55
Margaret's Café (SE), p. 79
One World Café (S), p. 71
The Strand (DT), p. 59
Woman's Industrial Exchange Tea Room (DT), p. 60
Ze Mean Bean Café (SE), p. 81

Continental/New American
Atlantic (SE), p. 74
Brass Elephant (DT), p. 53
The Brewer's Art (DT), p. 53
Charleston (SE), p. 76
Corks (S), p. 69
Ethel and Ramone's (NW), p. 68
Gertrude's (N), p. 62
Hamilton's (SE), p. 77
Hampton's (DT), p. 54
Helen's Garden Restaurant (SE), p. 77
Joy America Cafe (S), p. 70
Maison Marconi (DT), p. 56
Peter's Inn (SE), p. 80
Pier Point (SE), p. 80
Pisces (DT), p. 56
Polo Grill (N), p. 65
The Ruby Lounge (DT), p. 57
Sobo Cafe (S), p. 71
Spike & Charlie's (DT), p. 59
Zodiac (DT), p. 60

Crabhouses/Seafood
Bertha's (SE), p. 74
Bo Brooks (SE), p. 75
Captain Harvey's (NW), p. 68
G&M (SW), p. 81
Gunning's Crabhouse (S), p. 70
Henninger's Tavern (SE), p. 77
Kali's Court (SE), p. 78
Kelly's (SE), p. 78
Obrycki's (SE), p. 79

Diners/Delicatessens
Attman's Delicatessen (SE), p. 74
Bel-Loc Diner (NE), p. 65
Café Hon (N), p. 60
Jimmy's Restaurant (SE), p. 78
Paper Moon Diner (N), p. 64
Pete's Grille (N), p. 65
Rallo's Restaurant (S), p. 71
Sip & Bite Restaurant (SE), p. 81

French
Jeannier's (N), p. 63
Tersiguel's (SW), p. 81

Greek
The Black Olive (SE), p. 75
Ikaros (SE), p. 78

Italian
Amici's (SE), p. 72
Angelina's (NE), p. 65
Boccaccio (SE), p. 75
Caesar's Den (SE), p. 76
Dalesio's (SE), p. 76
Da Mimmo Ristorante (SE), p. 76
La Tavola (SE), p. 79
Sotta Sopra (DT), p. 59
Vaccaro's (SE), p. 81
Vespa (S), p. 72

Latin American/Spanish
Restaurante San Luis (SE), p. 80
Tio Pepe (DT), p. 59

Mexican/Southwestern
Holy Frijoles (N), p. 62
Loco Hombre (N), p. 63

Nacho Mama's (SE), p. 79

Soul
Micah's Cafeteria (NW), p. 68

Vegetarian Friendly
Ban Thai (DT), p. 51
Bombay Grill (DT), p. 51
Café Bombay (DT), p. 53
Café Zen (N), p. 62
Funk's Democratic Coffee Spot (SE), p. 76
The Helmand (DT), p. 55
Liquid Earth (SE), p. 79
Margaret's Cafe (SE), p. 79
One World Cafe (S), p. 71
Sobo Cafe (S), p. 71

DOWNTOWN

BAN THAI
340 N. Charles St.
Baltimore
410/2-0125
$
Traditional Thai dishes like pad Thai chicken with basil and lemongrass soup are well done at this North Charles Street restaurant with the pink interior. The food's a real bargain, too; lunch specials top off at $6.50, and very few dinner entrées exceed $10. Lunch, dinner. (Downtown)

BOMBAY GRILL
2 E. Madison St.
Baltimore
410/837-2937
$$
You can't go wrong with the comforting vegetable and potato samosas, the blood-red tandoori chicken, or the *rogan josh*—cubes of tender lamb in a delicate curry. Finish your meal with a cooling yogurt-mango *lhasi*. Lots of vegetarian options are available, too. Lunch, dinner. ქ (Downtown)

DOWNTOWN BALTIMORE

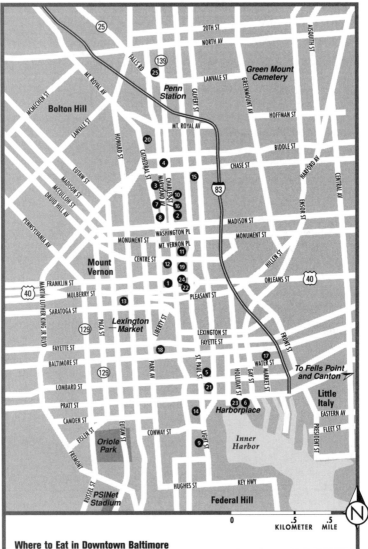

Where to Eat in Downtown Baltimore

1 Ban Thai
2 Bombay Grill
3 Brass Elephant
4 The Brewer's Art
5 Cafe Bombay
6 Cheesecake Factory
7 City Cafe
8 Donna's Coffee Bar and Café
9 Hampton's
10 The Helmand
11 Kawasaki

12 Louie's Café
13 Maison Marconi
14 Pisces
15 The Prime Rib
16 Ruby Lounge
17 Ruth's Chris Steak House
18 Shula's Steak House
19 Sotto Sopra
20 Spike & Charlie's Restaurant and Wine Bar
21 The Strand
22 Tio Pepe

23 Wayne's Bar-B-Que
24 Woman's Industrial Exchange Tea Room
25 Zodiac

THE BREWER'S ART
1106 N. Charles St.
Baltimore
410/547-6925
www.belgianbeer.com
$$$

The brewing of Belgian beers is brought to an art here (see Chapter 12, Nightlife), and the food—when it succeeds—is almost good enough to hang on the walls too. Set in a spectacular Mount Vernon townhouse, Brewer's Art offers a menu that changes by the season. Summer might feature grilled halibut filet with a blue crab sauce over saffron rice, grilled duck, or fusilli with Japanese eggplant, kalamata olives, and feta cheese. The atmosphere looks upscale—deep wood accents, walls of hardback books—but you'll feel as comfortable dressed down for a movie as you would dressed up for the symphony. Dinner only. (Downtown)

BRASS ELEPHANT
924 N. Charles St.
Baltimore
410/547-8485
$$$$

Lavishly decorated with teak and oak woodwork, marble fireplaces, and seemingly more crystal chandeliers than Versailles, this nineteenth-century town house sets the mood for diners celebrating birthdays, anniversaries, and other special events. Choose from a menu of continental cuisine—filet mignon, grilled rockfish, veal scallopini. If all you want to do is celebrate the end of the work week, head upstairs to the Tusk Lounge (see Chapter 12, Nightlife) for equally eye-catching decor, light appetizers, and moderately priced entrées. Dinner. &. (Downtown)

CAFE BOMBAY
114 E. Lombard St.
Baltimore
410/539-2233
www.bombaygrill.com
$

This reasonably priced Indian restaurant is just a quick walk from the water's edge. It's run by the same people who own Bombay Grill, but it serves southern Indian cuisine in addition to the more common curries and tandoori preparations of northern India. The strictly vegetarian southern Indian offerings include *dosas* (Indian crepes stuffed with vegetables) and *vada* (spiced lentils shaped like a donut and prepared in a variety of ways). Cafe Bombay also offers Balti cooking, which originated in Baltistan (a province of Pakistan) and involves stir-frying chicken, lamb, seafood, or vegetables. Lunch, dinner. &. (Downtown)

CHEESECAKE FACTORY
Pratt Street Pavilion
201 E. Pratt St.
Baltimore
410/234-3990
www.cheesecake.com
$$

Let's look at the numbers: The meatloaf is a pound and a half, the burrito is 12 inches long, and the "Factory Burger" has three layers. Of course, lunch or dinner at this popular chain would not be complete without a slice of one of the 35 different cheesecakes. The menu—no, it's a book—comes complete with tacky advertisements for nearby shops. Expect a wait. Lunch, dinner; brunch Sun. &. (Downtown)

CITY CAFE
1001 Cathedral St.
Baltimore

410/539-4252
$$

Is it a grab-and-go coffee shop with great desserts? A trendy restaurant with original art on its walls and dissonant jazz on its sound system? Or a cool, intimate bar with 20 different kinds of martinis? City Cafe is actually all three, though the standouts are definitely the martinis and the desserts—think mango-coconut mousse, caramel-walnut torte, and white chocolate pie. The food is generally good, and the menu features everything from inexpensive salads, pastas, and sandwiches to $20 dinner entrées. It's a popular destination for pre- and post-theater crowds, as well as the neighborhood's gay community. Breakfast, lunch, dinner; weekend brunch. & (Downtown)

DONNA'S COFFEE BAR AND CAFE
2 W. Madison St.
Baltimore
410/385-0180
$$

Hometown girl Donna Crivello cor-nered the coffee market before any outside behemoth could seize Baltimore's caffeine-loving heart. Donna's goes one up on the big boys with the green logo by offering full lunch and dinner menus of designer salads, fresh pastas, and sandwiches on focaccia. Go ahead and finish things off with a double decaf mocha, but avoid the large tea at—gulp—$3.50 a cup. Breakfast, lunch, dinner; brunch Sun. & (Downtown)

HAMPTON'S
Harbor Court Hotel
550 Light St.
Baltimore
410/347-9744
$$$$

Candlelight and fresh flowers. Huge half-moon windows and Bruce Willis at the next table. Hampton's is the restaurant of choice for many visiting celebrities and other high rollers who come for the four-star food, impeccable service, and elegant atmosphere. Chef Michael Forster changes his menu seasonally; offerings might in-

Hampton's

Harbor Court Hotel

clude sea bass swimming in a white-bean puree or a half-pound Maine lobster flamed in Glenmorangie single-malt scotch. Romantic? Yes. Expensive? Oh, yes: Entrées start in the low $30s. Dinner; brunch Sun. & (Downtown)

THE HELMAND
806 N. Charles St.
Baltimore
410/752-0311
$

One of Baltimore's best restaurants is also one of its best bargains; most of the Afghan dinner entrées hover around $10. The vegetarian options, in particular, are sublime: Try the *dolma murch*—bell pepper stuffed with vegetables, beans, and rice—or the *mantwo*—pastry filled with rice, lentils, and beans and topped with a sauce of corn, carrots, and yellow split peas. Meat eaters should skip the fish and order a plate of *sabzy challow*—sautéed spinach and beef served on a bed of Afghan rice. You'll never look at Halloween the same way after sampling the famous *kaddo borawni*—pumpkin in a garlic-yogurt sauce. Dinner. & (Downtown)

KAWASAKI
413 N. Charles St.
Baltimore
410/659-7600
$$

Some cigar bars have private humidors that smokers can rent on a yearly basis. At Kawasaki, for $20 you can stash your personal chopsticks in a giant lacquered cabinet for the remainder of your sushi-eating life. Actor Tom Berenger did it. So did Richard Gere, Nicholas Cage, and the Orioles' Brady Anderson. Sushi is the name of the game here, with the usual assortment of yellowtail, tuna, salmon, eel, conch, and snapper, plus more exotic specialties like live scallop. Entrées include tempura platters and teriyaki dinners of beef, chicken, or salmon. Lunch, dinner. (Downtown)

LOUIE'S CAFÉ
518 N. Charles St.
Baltimore
410/962-1224
$$

Louie's, a bastion of Baltimore hipness for many years, closed briefly in the fall of 1999 and reopened looking much the same but feeling, somehow, more grown-up. The space is just as grand as ever, with towering red walls and huge paintings, but the avant-garde bookstore has been banished to the basement in favor of comfy chairs and café tables. The wait staff is now comprised of a decidedly older, post-nose-ring crowd. Thankfully, talented musicians from neighboring

Peabody Conservatory still serenade diners with jazz or classical music nightly. The food? Choose from reasonably priced sandwiches, decent burgers, and salads, plus entrées in the $12 to $20 range. The real treats remain the decadent desserts, consumed eagerly by hipsters—or by their parents. & (Downtown)

MAISON MARCONI
106 W. Saratoga St.
Baltimore
410/727-9522
$$$

Maison Marconi has accumulated its share of legend and lore since it opened in 1920. There's the one about how Rudolph Valentino once worked as a busboy and lived in a room on the building's second floor (not true). Or the one about how H. L. Mencken used to sit at the same table every time he ate here (true). Through it all, Marconi's has earned a reputation for consistency, barely changing its Old World (some might even say frumpy) decor nor its pre-health-movement menu. For 80 years lobster Cardinale has been on the menu, and Marconi's owner promises the dish for 80 years more. Don't stray too far from the traditional in your meal selection and you'll be pleased. The restaurant has no busboys and no bartenders; waiters mix your drinks right at the table. You can count on quirkiness at Marconi's, and that's why old-time Baltimoreans love it. Lunch, dinner Tue–Sat. (Downtown)

PISCES
Hyatt Regency Hotel
300 Light St.
Baltimore
410/605-2835
$$$$

Perched on the 14th floor of the Hyatt

Pisces offers an excellent view of the Inner Harbor.

Hotel, Pisces has the best view of any restaurant in the Inner Harbor. From one of its windowside tables, you get a front-row seat to the lights of the harbor, the neon Domino's Sugar sign, and the triangular crown of the National Aquarium. The restaurant's interior is nearly as impressive as its views: lots of rounded edges, cool gray and blue accents, and bright blue halogen lights that hang from the ceiling like illuminated icicles. The menu, of course, is mainly seafood, with regional treats such as crab cakes and rockfish leading the way. The whole package combines to make Pisces a very romantic roost. Reservations recommended. Dinner Tue–Sun, brunch Sun. & (Downtown)

THE PRIME RIB
1101 N. Calvert St.
Baltimore
410/539-1804
$$$$

Romance, not power, rules supreme at Baltimore's favorite steakhouse.

The masculine clichés of brass and dark wood have been traded for elegant ebony and gold, the walk-in cigar humidor for a baby grand piano, which is teamed up with a stand-up bass during dinner Thursday through Sunday. The mature and moneyed clientele swears by the namesake prime rib as well as the thick filet mignon, flavorful rack of lamb, and a delicate center-cut veal chop. Seafood gets equal billing and might include jumbo lump crabcakes, soft shell crabs, or stuffed rockfish. The veteran staff—the chef has been working the grill since 1970—knows how to please. Jackets and reservations required. Dinner. & (Downtown)

RUBY LOUNGE
802 N. Charles St.
Baltimore
410/539-8051
$$

The beautiful people come here for three-dollar Absolut martinis on Thursdays and to order from a trendy American/Mediterranean menu that roams from designer brick-oven pizzas to homey pecan-fried chicken to a daily risotto special. In the romantic dim light, you'll be hard-pressed to decide which looks better: the food or the clientele. Dinner Tue–Sun. (Downtown)

RUTH'S CHRIS STEAK HOUSE
600 Water St.
Baltimore
410/783-0033
www.ruthschris.com
$$$$

Ruth's Chris is a steakhouse chain, but each outpost has its own personality. The Baltimore branch has traditional wood and brass appointments, an expense-account crowd, and a wine cellar that would impress Dionysus—nearly 10,000 bottles. The custom-aged, corn-fed, USDA prime gets cooked to order. If you're not in the mood for red meat, try the tasty blackened tuna. Dinner. & (Downtown)

SHULA'S STEAK HOUSE
Omni Inner Harbor Hotel

Ruth's Chris Steak House boasts a great wine cellar.

Norbert Bertling

Top 10 Baltimore Classics, Old and New

by Cynthia Glover, food and wine editor and head restaurant reviewer for *Baltimore* magazine.

1. **Ambassador:** Indian cuisine at its subtle, aromatic best, served in genteel surroundings by tuxedoed waiters. A lovely garden for outdoor dining in summer.

2. **Atlantic:** Stylish seafood, from classic to inventive, served up with flair for a hip, well-heeled crowd. Do not miss the fabulous oyster stew.

3. **Charleston:** Gussy up for low-country Southern dining with panache. Superb service and an outstanding and intriguingly eccentric wine list.

4. **Corks:** Fine, classically styled, thoughtful cooking paired with a first-rate, well-priced list of artisanal California wines. What more could you want?

5. **Gabler's:** Open in summer only, this screened-in-porch restaurant on the Bush River in Aberdeen is what pickin' steamed blue crabs Maryland style is all about.

6. **Maison Marconi:** A handsome slice of old Baltimore—not much has changed at this Continental stalwart since it opened in 1920. And that's just fine by us.

7. **Morton's:** Beef the way it should be served: well-aged, thick-cut, buck-naked, perfectly cooked with proper tooth, and densely flavored.

8. **Polo Grill:** Cosmopolitan New American dining in a hunt clubby atmosphere—an all-around upscale crowd-pleaser.

9. **Prime Rib:** The epitome of swank, from the heady leopard carpet, the sleek black-lacquer walls, and the sexy Lucite-topped piano to the ravishing cuts of beef.

10. **Ruby Lounge:** Bold flavors on the plate, a hot scene at the bar, and a sophisticated sensibility in the air make this hipster a winner.

101 W. Fayette St.
Baltimore
410/385-6630
$$$$
Former Baltimore Colts and Miami Dolphins coach Don Shula seems to be as successful at the grill as he was on the gridiron. The beef is excellent and the football theme is carried out to the extreme: Menus are printed on regulation pigskins, and the golden picture frames hold not

fine art but black-and-white photographs of hulking men in pads and helmets. The wait staff is anxious to please and even goes so far as to shine a flashlight into your steak so you can check that it's done properly. If you can tackle the $60, 48-ounce porterhouse—former Ravens running back Ernst Byner did it—you get your name on a wall (and probably a bad case of indigestion). The adjacent sports bar, Steak 2, also serves up da beef in a rollicking, TV-saturated atmosphere, at more moderate prices. Lunch, dinner. & (Downtown)

SOTTO SOPRA
405 N. Charles St.
Baltimore
410/625-0534
$$$$
Sotto Sopra offers chic Italian cuisine in a dramatic space filled with sprawling murals and halogen chandeliers. The well-heeled clientele come for Chef Riccardo Bosio's flavorful risotto Milanese blended with osso bucco ragout or saffron fettuccine dressed in a shrimp-and-Pernod cream sauce. The food almost always tastes as good as it sounds; Sotto Sopra earned Best Italian Restaurant status from *Baltimore* magazine in 1999, beating out the stalwarts in Little Italy. Lunch, dinner. & (Downtown)

SPIKE & CHARLIE'S RESTAURANT AND WINE BAR
1225 Cathedral St.
Baltimore
410/752-8144
$$$
The first undertaking in the mini-empire of local restaurateurs Spike and Charlie Gjerde (they also own Joy America Cafe, Atlantic, jr., and a share of Vespa) is the place to go

before or after a night at the nearby Lyric Opera House or Meyerhoff Symphony Hall (see Chapter 11, Performing Arts). The simply prepared New American cuisine is fresh and colorful and changes by the season, from a spicy autumnal pumpkin soup to a summery gazpacho. At the wine bar, ask for a two-ounce pour of a wine you're curious about before ordering it. If only diners could pull a similar maneuver before indulging in a plateful of one of Spike & Charlie's decadent desserts. Dinner. & (Downtown)

THE STRAND
105 E. Lombard St.
Baltimore
410/625-8944
www.thestrandcafe.com
$
Boot up your internal hard drive at this cybercafe a block north of the Inner Harbor. Deli-style sandwiches, big salads, panini (Italian sandwiches), and printers, scanners, and eight PCs with fast, T-1 Internet connections are available for consumption. Espresso, beer, wine, and harder stuff are also served. Breakfast, lunch, dinner; weekend brunch. & (Downtown)

TIO PEPE
10 E. Franklin St.
Baltimore
410/539-4675
$$$$
Baltimoreans come here to celebrate special occasions with Spanish treats like suckling pig or paella made with rice, chicken, veal, lobster, chorizo, shrimp, clams, and mussels. The crowning glory is the sangria, available in red or white and served in earthen pitchers. Reservations are a must. Lunch, dinner. & (Downtown)

WAYNE'S BAR-B-QUE
Light Street Pavilion
Baltimore
410/539-3810
$$

Among the Inner Harbor's mega-chain restaurants, homegrown Wayne's continues to thrive in an atmosphere of red-and-white-check tablecloths and antlered animal heads. Wayne's ribs were voted Baltimore's best a few years back, but, honestly, they didn't have that much competition. Aside from the barbecued ribs, chicken, and pulled-pork sandwiches, Wayne's tasty crab soup was declared in 1997 by then-Mayor Kurt Schmoke to be the "city's official bicentennial soup." (We're still waiting for the city's official appetizer, condiment, apéritif . . . .) If you enjoy the barbecue sauce, take a bottle home for $4.95. Lunch, dinner. &. (Downtown)

WOMAN'S INDUSTRIAL EXCHANGE TEA ROOM
333 N. Charles St.
Baltimore
410/685-4388
$

Having the door held open by a kindly old gentleman as you enter might be reason enough to come to this historic landmark, a vestige of the Woman's Industrial Exchange Movement, which provided income to needy women in the aftermath of the Civil War. Once you pass the handicrafts up front (see Chapter 9, Shopping), you'll probably be seated by Phyllis Sanders, a fixture at the Exchange since 1950. Order the chicken-salad sandwich and a slice of cherry pie from the grandmotherly waitresses outfitted in matching baby-blue uniforms and white aprons. Just be sure to finish everything on your plate, hon. Breakfast, lunch Mon–Fri only. (Downtown)

ZODIAC
1726 N. Charles St.
Baltimore
410/727-8815
$$

The dramatically dressed come here to dine on astrologically themed dishes with names like "Chimera Pasta" and "Beef Gemini." The booths are turquoise vinyl, the murals on the walls depict Zeus and other mythological figures, and the food's better than it probably has to be. Zodiac is conveniently located across the street from the Charles Theater and next door to Club Charles (see Chapter 12, Nightlife), which serves the same menu. Dinner. (Downtown)

NORTH

AMBASSADOR DINING ROOM
3811 Canterbury Rd.
Baltimore
410/366-1484
$$

The first floor of the Ambassador apartment building serves as the unlikely home to this exceptional Indian restaurant. All the northern Indian standards—tandoori chicken, vegetable samosas, and biryani rice dishes—are prepared simply and well. Don't miss the silky chicken tikka masala—boneless chicken breast marinated, grilled, and sautéed in an aromatic curry sauce. During fair weather, dine alfresco by a picturesque garden fountain. (North)

CAFE HON
1002 W. 36th St.
Baltimore

NORTH BALTIMORE

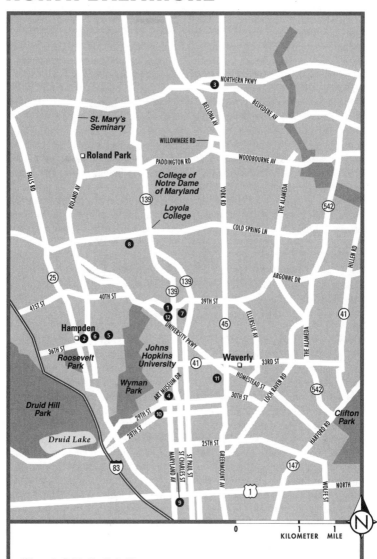

NORTHERN PKWY

BELVEDERE AV

St. Mary's Seminary

WILLOWMERE RD

Roland Park

PADDINGTON RD

WOODBOURNE AV

College of Notre Dame of Maryland

139

Loyola College

COLD SPRING LN

FALLS RD

ROLAND AV

YORK RD

THE ALAMEDA

542

25

40TH ST

139

139

39TH ST

ARGONNE DR

HILLER RD

41ST ST

41

Hampden

36TH ST

Roosevelt Park

Johns Hopkins University

Wyman Park

ART MUSEUM DR

UNIVERSITY PKWY

ELLERSLIE AV

45

Waverly

33RD ST

HOMESTEAD ST

LOCH RAVEN RD

THE ALAMEDA

542

Druid Hill Park

29TH ST

28TH ST

30TH ST

Clifton Park

Druid Lake

25TH ST

MARYLAND AV

ST CHARLES ST

ST PAUL ST

GREENMOUNT AV

HARFORD RD

147

83

1

WOLFE ST

NORTH

0   1 KILOMETER   1 MILE

N

Where to Eat in North Baltimore

1 Ambassador Dining Room
2 Cafe Hon
3 Cafe Zen
4 Gertrude's
5 Golden West Cafe
6 Holy Frijoles
7 Jeannier's
8 Loco Hombre
9 Nam Kang
10 Paper Moon Diner
11 Pete's Grille
12 Polo Grill

410/243-1230
$

Open only since 1992, Cafe Hon nevertheless goes a long way in trying to recapture the essence of a more innocent, more "hon" time in Baltimore's past. The chairs don't match, the tables look as if they were found at the Salvation Army down the block, and the chandeliers are made of tea cups. The menu ranges from gravy fries and "better-than-mom's meatloaf" to arugula salads topped with goat cheese. Pick up yer Bawlmer souvenirs at Hometown Girl (see Chapter 9, Shopping), located off the dining room. Breakfast, lunch, dinner; weekend brunch. (North)

CAFE ZEN
438 E. Belvedere Ave.
Baltimore
410/532-0022
www.CafeZen.cei.nu
$$

Although it calls itself a cafe, Chinese tea, not coffee, is the drink of choice at this pleasurably uncomplicated oriental restaurant. The mainly Chinese menu offers everything from the classics (marinated crispy duck) to the deliciously gourmet (tender spinach sautéed in garlic with shrimp, chicken, beef, or tofu). All dishes are prepared with Zen-like simplicity, and you can even order your meal with brown rice, a rarity at most Chinese restaurants. Best of all, the Senator Movie Theatre (see Chapter 12, Nightlife) shows first-run films just around the corner. Lunch, dinner. &
(North)

GERTRUDE'S
Baltimore Museum of Art
10 Art Museum Dr.
Baltimore
410/889-3399

$$$

Gertrude's is the domain of chef John Shields, celebrated cookbook author and host of Maryland Public Television's *Chesapeake Bay Cooking with John Shields*. The menu reads like a culinary what's what—and who's who—from the Bay's Eastern Shore: Miss Jean's Chesapeake crab soup, Mama Lan's black-bean clams, and two kinds of crab cakes. But Miss Jean probably should let her crab soup simmer a little longer to enhance the flavor, and the tasteless shrimp salad sandwich oozes oil. By the time you read this, perhaps the cuisine will have caught up with the handsome decor. Lunch, dinner; brunch Sun. & (North)

GOLDEN WEST CAFE
842 W. 36th St.
Baltimore
410-235-2326
$

Golden West serves southwestern huevos rancheros and green chili burritos in a North Baltimore row house. The results—especially brunch—are muy bueno. Lunches include more Tex-Mex fare, plus sandwiches stuffed with the likes of turkey, brie, and mango chutney. If you're hungry while browsing the shops on "The Avenue," Golden West is a good, quick stop. Don't leave without a trip to the restroom, fantastically wallpapered in vintage record albums. Breakfast, lunch, dinner; brunch Sun. (North)

HOLY FRIJOLES
908 W. 36th St.
Baltimore
410/235-BEAN
$

This hole-in-the-wall Mexican food joint may only have a dozen tables,

Hometown Specialties

Pit Beef: *A hunk of beef cooked long and slow in a barbecue pit, then sliced and customarily eaten on a kaiser roll with onions, horseradish, and/or barbecue sauce. Find it at any Baltimore street festival, Boog's BBQ at Camden Yards, and many down-home restaurants.*

Sno-Cones: *Shaved ice flavored with sweet syrup and served in a paper cone. Find them in any Baltimore neighborhood during the heat of summer.*

Coddies: *Silver-dollar-size fish cakes made from cod, mashed pota-toes, and eggs. Available at Broadway Market in Fells Point, Attman's Delicatessen, and Wayne's BBQ.*

Berger Cookies: *Vanilla cookies covered in sinfully rich chocolate fudge. Look for them at the Berger's Bakery outpost in Lexington Market, Eddie's Markets, local Royal Farms convenient stores, and area Giant supermarkets.*

but it still manages to serve up big food from south of the border. The na-chos are famous, loaded with fresh salsa, chopped serranos, black beans, and corn; the burritos and fiji-tas are big enough to make a Mexi-can mama weep. You can even order Jarritos Mexican sodas in flavors like guava and grapefruit. If you want something stronger, you'll have to bring your own. With so few tables, Holy Frijoles runs mainly take-out; call ahead to see if seating is available. Lunch, dinner Tue–Sat. (North)

JEANNIER'S
Broadview Apartments
105 W. 39th St.
Baltimore
410/889-3303
$$
Owner/chef Roland Jeannier serves reliable, traditional French cuisine in a restaurant hidden between the first and second floors of a 1950s apart-ment building. Sample from lamb chops jardiniere, seafood bisque with a dollop of cream, and, of course, a selection of rich custard desserts. Lunch, dinner Mon–Sat. ♿ (North)

LOCO HOMBRE
413 W. Cold Spring Lane
Baltimore
410/889-2233
www.locohombre.com
$$
For whatever reason, the locals go

Paper Moon Diner

loco for this bland East Coast interpretation of Tex-Mex cuisine, only a couple of steps better than Chi-Chi's. Avoid the lifeless enchiladas, tacos, and quesadillas and try one of the gourmet platos like salmon encrusted in serrano chilies and topped with a red-banana salsa. Lunch, dinner; brunch Sun. (North)

NAM KANG
2126 Maryland Ave.
Baltimore
410/685-6237
$$
You may feel like you're dinning in a basement at this Korean restaurant, because you are. The dining room has a drop ceiling, exposed brick, and wood trim that's been painted Pepto Bismol–pink. But Nam Kang tastes much better than it looks, with kimchi spicy enough to clear your nasal passages during the height of cold season, "colossal casseroles" of clams, mussels, and fish, and a host of Korean specialties like cuttlefish and raw jellyfish. The restaurant also serves a lineup of Japanese and Chinese dishes for diners with less adventurous palates. The combination lunch specials, which include entrée, relishes, and miso soup, are an excellent deal. Lunch, dinner. (North)

PAPER MOON DINER
227 W. 29th St.
Baltimore
410/889-4444
$
No, you haven't died and gone to Barbie heaven; it just looks that way. This bustling diner, open 24 hours a day, is decorated in a style that can only be described as 1970s Toy Chest. Here you'll find all the juvenile classics: Star Wars figures guarding the front windows, Tonka trucks parked above the grill, Pez dispensers lining door jambs, and Barbie dolls spinning from ceiling fans. Surprisingly, the food isn't an afterthought. Omelets—available anytime—are a sumptuous standout, as are the "Moon burgers" and homemade desserts like double-chocolate rum cake and chocolate-

> If you want to have a great Sunday brunch, try waking up at Regi's, Golden West Cafe, Hampton's, or Morning Edition Cafe.

chip peanut-butter pie. Just watch out for the mannequin in the restroom. Breakfast, lunch, dinner. ♿ (North)

PETE'S GRILLE
3130 Greenmount Ave.
Baltimore
410/467-7698
$
Huge breakfasts and even bigger $2.45 hamburgers have made Pete's Grille "the place to be," as its motto goes. Located on tumultuous Greenmount Avenue, Pete's is an oasis; its counter-top service, old-fashioned Coca-Cola glasses, affable waitstaff, and menu of five-dollar-or-less lunch specials harken back to a simpler, quieter time. Breakfast, lunch daily. (North)

POLO GRILL
Inn at the Colonnade
4 W. University Pkwy.
Baltimore
410/235-8200
$$$$
Walls painted in deep greens with dark wood trim and framed scenes from the racetrack convey a hunt-club atmosphere. The well-bred clientele dines on Chef Stephen Bohlman's exquisitely grilled grouper topped with a chipotle barbecue glaze or lamb chops smothered in a black-currant sauce. Is that Oprah Winfrey dining on the fried lobster

tail? Could be. It's reportedly her favorite. Lunch, dinner. ♿ (North)

NORTHEAST

ANGELINA'S
7135 Harford Rd.
Parkville
410/444-5545 or 800/CRABCAKE
www.crabcake.com
$$$
The phone number and Web address say it all. Angelina's makes crab cakes—big, fat, meaty crab cakes with little filler—and ships them year-round to tourists and displaced Baltimoreans all over the country. But Angelina's is first and foremost an Italian restaurant, opened by Joe and Angelina Tadduni in 1952. Several others have owned the restaurant over the years, but the homey decor and neighborhood feel remain. Skip all other desserts and order the cheesecake; it might be the city's richest. Lunch, dinner. ♿ (Northeast)

BEL-LOC DINER
1700 E. Joppa Rd.
Towson
410/668-2525
$
No ersatz diner here; the Bel-Loc is the real deal: cholesterol-laden breakfasts, messy turkey sandwiches swimming in gravy, and apple pie à la mode 24 hours a day. A Baltimore landmark since 1964, the Bel-Loc is

GREATER BALTIMORE

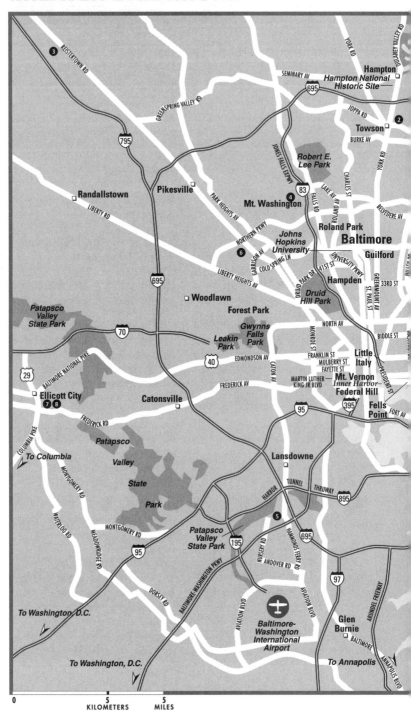

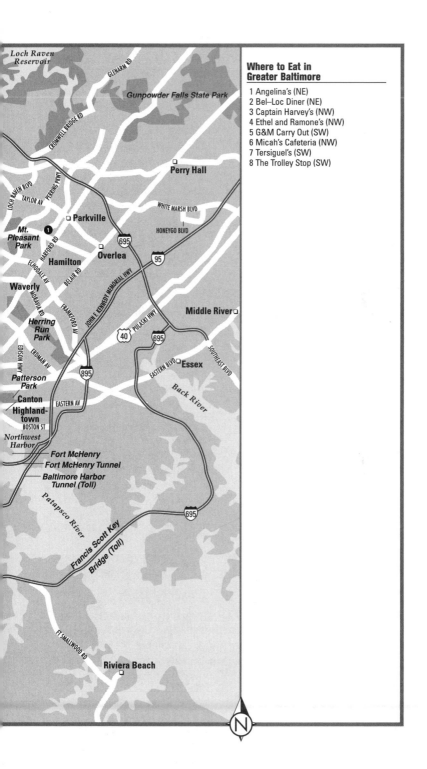

Loch Raven
Reservoir

Gunpowder Falls State Park

GLENARM RD

CROMWELL BRIDGE RD

PERRING PKWY

Perry Hall

**Where to Eat in
Greater Baltimore**

1 Angelina's (NE)
2 Bel–Loc Diner (NE)
3 Captain Harvey's (NW)
4 Ethel and Ramone's (NW)
5 G&M Carry Out (SW)
6 Micah's Cafeteria (NW)
7 Tersiguel's (SW)
8 The Trolley Stop (SW)

LOCH RAVEN BLVD

TAYLOR AV

PERRING PKWY

Parkville

WHITE MARSH BLVD

HONEYGO BLVD

Mt.
Pleasant
Park

HARFORD RD

695

ECHODALE AV

Hamilton

Overlea

95

BELAIR RD

Waverly

MORAVIA RD

FRANKFORD AV

JOHN F. KENNEDY MEMORIAL HWY

Middle River

Herring
Run
Park

40

PULASKI HWY

695

EDISON HWY

ERDMAN AV

895

SOUTHEAST BLVD

Patterson
Park

EASTERN BLVD

Essex

Canton

EASTERN AV

Back River

Highland-
town

BOSTON ST

Northwest
Harbor

Fort McHenry

Fort McHenry Tunnel

Baltimore Harbor
Tunnel (Toll)

Patapsco River

695

Francis Scott Key
Bridge (Toll)

FT SMALLWOOD RD

Riviera Beach

N

named for its location just inside the Baltimore Beltway (Exit 29) on the corner of East Joppa Road and Loch Raven Boulevard. & (Northeast)

NORTHWEST

CAPTAIN HARVEY'S
11510 Reisterstown Rd.
Reisterstown
410/356-7550
$$$
The original Captain Harvey was an old Chesapeake Bay waterman who first opened up a crab stall in Cross Street Market in 1935. His son runs the restaurant now, in Reisterstown, Maryland, about a 30-minute drive from downtown. These days, Captain Harvey's has a bit of a split personality: There's an attractive, upscale dining room with etched glass walls, rich wood trim, and attentive service; but there's also the adjacent crab shanty with hardshells served on trays, beer in plastic cups, and the Orioles on the tube. Pick and choose depending on your mood. Lunch, dinner. & (Northwest)

ETHEL AND RAMONE'S
1615 Sulgrave Ave.
Baltimore
410/664-2971
$
Ethel and Ramone's has its quirks

and its charms. First the quirks: It's usually understaffed, and if you complain about your meal the chef might jokingly pursue you with a meat cleaver. The charms: The first-floor interior is a cozy tea shop with floral wallpaper, antique photographs, and delicious Californian-Italian cuisine. Sample from fresh mesclun salads with goat cheese and smoked turkey, pasta topped with grilled portobello mushrooms and marinara sauce, and a choice of five unusual homemade soups. In other words, if you can put up with a few quirks, the charms are more than worth it. Take the light rail to the Mount Washington stop. Lunch, dinner Tue–Sun. (Northwest)

MICAH'S CAFETERIA
5401 Reisterstown Rd.
Baltimore
410/764-0606
$
Baltimore could use a few more quality soul-food restaurants. For now, Micah's is one of only a handful that does the Deep South proud with its delectable fried lake trout, candied yams, and brown gravy that's as comforting as a warm blanket on a cold winter's day. The setting is literally a cafeteria—you bus your own trays—and sectors of the place are often reserved for parties and family

---

TRIVIA

Every June, Cafe Hon sponsors a competition for Baltimore's Best Hon, a stereotypical old-time Baltimorean who talks funny, snaps her chewing gum, and uses lots of hair spray. Past contests have seen singers performing, "It's My Party and I'll Have Crabs If I Want To" and the love theme from *Titanic* sung in Baltimorese.

SOUTH BALTIMORE

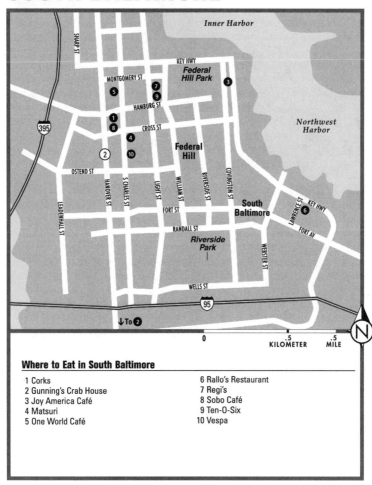

Where to Eat in South Baltimore

1 Corks
2 Gunning's Crab House
3 Joy America Café
4 Matsuri
5 One World Café

6 Rallo's Restaurant
7 Regi's
8 Sobo Café
9 Ten-O-Six
10 Vespa

reunions. Wear loose-fitting pants. Lunch, dinner. (Northwest)

SOUTH

CORKS
1026 S. Charles St.
Baltimore
410/752-3810

$$$

Corks's impressive wine list may span the globe, but its prices are decidedly closer to home. Unlike many restaurants that double wholesale prices for bottles of wine, Corks charges wholesale plus $11 for every bottle in the restaurant. The more expensive the wine, the more this deal works in your favor. Unlike the extensive wine

American Visionary Art Museum houses the Joy America Café.

list, Corks's menu is relatively short—just a couple of appetizers, a few soups, and about 10 entrées. Save room for dessert; the bread pudding is a winner. Reservations are advised. (South)

GUNNING'S CRABHOUSE
3901 S. Hanover St.
Baltimore
410/354-0085
$$
If Disney ever opened an "authentic Baltimore crab restaurant," it would probably pattern the place after Gunning's, an old-fashioned, blue-collar crab hall with brown-paper-covered tables, endless pitchers of beer, and waitresses who call you "hon." You don't just get Old Bay–seasoned crabs here, you get a taste of Old Baltimore, too. Opt for a seat in the outdoor crab garden, perfect for relaxing on those humid summer evenings. Call first to get directions; Gunning's can be hard to find for first-timers. Lunch, dinner. (South)

JOY AMERICA CAFÉ
800 Key Hwy.
Baltimore
410/244-6500
$$$$
It's only fitting that the offbeat American Visionary Art Museum should house an equally eclectic museum restaurant, full of artistic and playful culinary juxtapositions. Consider a salad of sweet potatoes and bitter arugula, spicy chunks of lobster tempered by a tomato and sweet potato ragout, or fresh tuna and shrimp ceviche that arrives in a martini glass. Even the menus themselves—decorated with twigs, bottle caps, and plastic jewelry—are works of art. Curiously, the room itself is decorated quite simply, but with a giant half-moon window that overlooks the harbor—and food this creative—who needs to look at the walls? Lunch, dinner. (South)

MATSURI
110 S. Charles St.
Baltimore

410/752-8561
www.matsurida.com
$

Federal Hill has nearly a school of sushi restaurant these days, but Matsuri's fresh salmon and yellowfin tuna consistently lead the class. Try the "rock 'n' roll," a mix of avocado, crab, tuna, salmon, and eel. Lunch, dinner. ﾋ (South)

ONE WORLD CAFE
904 S. Charles St.
Baltimore
410/234-0235
$

The vegan- and vegetarian-friendly food here runs the gamut from tofu barbecue to chili flavored with espresso beans. It's good, good for you, and cheap. Meanwhile, an ever-changing roster of desserts, "chubby" cookies, fresh-squeezed juices, and coffee brews du jour keep the regulars stimulated. The restaurant is a quick walk from the Inner Harbor. Breakfast, lunch, dinner; weekend brunch. ﾋ (South)

RALLO'S RESTAURANT
838 E. Fort Ave.
Baltimore
410/727-7067
$

This classic diner/coffee shop has been serving up comfort food to South Baltimoreans since the 1930s. The grill fires up at 5:30 a.m. and doesn't stop until the last of the dinner crowd have unbuckled their belts. The homey chicken stew tastes as if it's been made by a kind-hearted cook who truly cares about your individual well-being. Rallo's makes a good stopover for lunch before or after a visit to the nearby Baltimore Museum of Industry (see Chapter 6, Museums) or Fort Mc-

Henry (see Chapter 5, Sights and Attractions). Breakfast, lunch, dinner. (South)

REGI'S
1000 Light St.
Baltimore
410/539-7344
www.regisbistro.com
$$

Regi's, located about a block south of the Maryland Science Center in Federal Hill, makes a convenient escape from touristy Inner Harbor restaurants. The lunch menu includes reasonably priced—and reasonably tasty—quesadillas, burgers and sandwiches, salads, and pastas, but the less-than-stellar dinner entrées don't quite justify the prices charged. However, the Sunday brunches of custom-made omelets, breakfast burritos, and frittatas, washed down with spicy Bloody Marys or bubbly mimosas, are worth every penny. Lunch, dinner; Sunday brunch. (South)

SOBO CAFÉ
6 W. Cross St.
Baltimore
410/752-1518
$

This hip, eclectic neighborhood haunt has bright yellow walls, original art, and a chalkboard menu of good, fun, and inexpensive food. Dinner specials vary nightly and might include a guava curry coconut veggie stir fry or the aptly named "big ass" pork chop. Note the wines classified from the "Old World" (France) and the "New World" (California). Lunch, dinner. (South)

TEN-O-SIX
1006 Light St.
Baltimore

What Happened to Haussner's?

Beloved Haussner's Restaurant, famous for its homey German cuisine and sprawling art collection, finally said auf wiedersehen *to its adoring public in 1999 after serving Wiener schnitzel to Baltimoreans for 73 years. The restaurant's incredible artwork, which included a few Whistlers, Rembrandts, and Homers among the mostly obscure nineteenth-century German painters, fetched more than $12 million at a Sotheby's auction. Almost as remarkable as its artistic treasures was the restaurant's famous ball of string, an 825-pound giant, rolled over the years from string once used to tie 19,799,950 bundles of napkins. If you'd like to see what 825 pounds of napkin string looks like, visit the the Antique Man (1735 Fleet St.) antiques store in Fells Point, which purchased the ball at a local auction for $8,250—or $10 per pound.*

410/528-2146
$$
This exotic charmer in Federal Hill combines Thai and continental cuisine to produce some truly interesting dishes. Start your meal with an order of flavorful crab-and-shiitake spring rolls before moving onto the rack of lamb with zinfandel sauce or Thai pork loin. How hot do you want it? Order your food on a spice-rating scale from 1 to 10, with 10 being "native Thai." Reservations are a must. Dinner. (South)

VESPA
1117-21 S. Charles St.
Baltimore
410/385-0355
$$
Sleek, stylish, and Italian just like its motor-scooter namesake, Vespa opened in 1999 and has been zipping along ever since. Its menu features an inviting mix of Italian pastas, pizzas, and appetizers perfect for nibbling with a glass of wine. It's a popular destination for the attractive younger set of Federal Hill. Insider's secret: Wine by the glass is half-price Friday and Saturday nights from 11 p.m. to 1 a.m. Lunch, dinner; brunch Sun. ₤ (South)

SOUTHEAST

AMICCI'S
231 S. High St.
Baltimore
410/528-1096
$$
Get a taste of Little Italy without blowing a load of lire. Almost all of the pasta dishes here are under $10, and the seafood swims in below $15. The

SOUTHEAST BALTIMORE

T i P

Warning: A native Baltimorean's favorite condiment is mayonnaise. If you don't want it on your hamburger or steak sandwich (sacrilege to a Philadelphian), be sure to speak up.

setting is casual—almost too casual—with black-and-white-check vinyl table cloths and framed posters on the walls. Try the signature "shrimp and bread thing," a scooped-out loaf of Italian filled with shrimp in a scampi cream sauce. Lunch, dinner. (Southeast)

ATLANTIC
2400 Boston St.
Baltimore
410/675-4565
$$$
With its coolly lit dinning room, plasma projections dancing on the walls, and interior waterfall, Atlantic goes a long way in trying to convince its hip clientele they're dining under-water. The specialties of the house, not surprisingly, involve seafood: oysters on the half-shell garnished with tendrils of seaweed, a "filet mignon" of fresh tuna, shad stuffed with roe and wrapped in pancetta. Unfortunately, the entrées aren't always the best catch, but the appetizers or "small plates" are consistently good, as are the cooling Atlantic martinis made with Ketel One vodka, a touch of blue curaçao, and Lemoncello, a French lemon liquor. Lunch, dinner; brunch Sun. ﾐ (Southeast)

ATTMAN'S DELICATESSEN
1019 E. Lombard St.
Baltimore
410/563-2666
www.attmans.com
$
You wanna make your Jewish mother proud? Then order a corned-beef sandwich and a potato knish, and grab a seat in the "Kibitz Room." Attman's is an 85-year-old leftover of Baltimore's famed Corned Beef Row, the culinary stomping grounds for the neighborhood's once-substantial Jewish population. The corned-beef sandwiches, jumbo kosher hot dogs, and opinionated chatter from the white-aproned guys behind the counter make for the most authentic deli experience you'll find south of New York City. Free parking. Breakfast, lunch Mon–Sat. (Southeast)

BERTHA'S
734 S. Broadway
Baltimore
410/327-5795
$$
The ubiquitous bright-green bumper stickers that command all to "Eat Bertha's Mussels" are standard issue for misplaced Baltimoreans the world over. Manager Jack Walsh once saw one on the back of a taxi in Havana and says he's heard of Bertha's bumper stickers riding around on car backs as far away as Kenya. The black bivalves themselves are tasty enough—opt for them in garlic butter. Bertha's also has a rollicking jazz scene in its front pub (see Chapter 12, Nightlife) and a wide selection of mi-

crobrews and European ales. The paella—a mix of clams, mussels, shrimp, and fish over rice—won't fool too many Spaniards, but, then, they don't print "Eat Bertha's Paella" on the bumper stickers. Lunch, dinner; brunch Sun. (Southeast)

THE BLACK OLIVE
814 S. Bond St.
Baltimore
410/276-7141
www.theblackolive.com
$$$$

Could this be Baltimore's best restaurant? It's been declared just that by more than a few local publications. The Black Olive calls itself a Greek restaurant, but you won't find any gyros or moussaka on its menu. What you will find is the freshest seafood from around the world. Owner Stelios Spiliadis personally introduces diners to that evening's international catch: green mussels from New Zealand, lobster tails from Brazil, wild turbo from Spain, fresh sardines from Portugal. The fish is usually grilled whole and plated without sauce, allowing its natural flavors to come through. Black Olive also does lamb marinated in garlic, beef kabobs, and other meaty specials. Dinner only. ♿ (Southeast)

BO BROOKS
Lighthouse Point
Baltimore Marine Center
Baltimore
410/488-8144
$$$

After serving some of Baltimore's best crabs from an aged barnlike structure in northeast Baltimore, Bo Brooks went upscale with the opening of its new seafood house in Canton. The crabs are just as fat and flavorful, and now you can choose from a roster of weekly seafood specials. Some might miss the hose-it-down atmosphere of the old Bo Brooks, but at least this place has windows. ♿ (Southeast)

BOCCACCIO
925 Eastern Ave.
Baltimore
410/234-1322
$$$$

Boccaccio is where local and national celebrities wrap vermicelli around their forks. Some eat in the airy and elegant main dining room, but others eat hidden away at a table stowed in the dark and low-ceilinged wine closet. (Note: No matter how famous you are, opt for the dining room; the wine closet has all the personality of, well, a closet.) The menu? No stodgy eggplant parmesan here—just gourmet Italian delicacies like fresh halibut under shrimp, mussels, and clams, and veal chops stuffed with ham and fontina cheese. Reservations are a must, as are a jacket and tie. Lunch, dinner. ♿ (Southeast)

BOP
800 S. Broadway
Baltimore
410/563-1600
$

BOP was baking tomato pies the brick-oven way long before every big-chain Italian restaurant installed a brick oven and started plopping sun-dried tomatoes on their pizzas. Here you can choose from more than 50 toppings, ranging from cream cheese to hamburger to pineapples (certainly not the recommended combination). Even actor Kevin "Extra" Bacon has been known to eat here when he's in town. Lunch, dinner daily. (Southeast)

CAESAR'S DEN
223 S. High St.
Baltimore
410/547-0820
www.intl-mall.com/caesarsden
$$$

This 30-year veteran of Little Italy is known for its consistently pleasing, traditional Italian food. You'll find all the standards here: linguini with clam sauce, chicken caprese, veal marsala, and grilled seafood, all done simply and well. Lunch, dinner. & (Southeast)

CHARLESTON
Sylvan Building
1000 Lancaster St.
Baltimore
410/332-7373
www.charlestonrestaurant.com
$$$$

Celebrity chef Cindy Wolf puts a nouvelle twist on good ol' southern cooking. Consider heads-on Gulf shrimp with tasso ham and andouille sausage over creamy grits or a sweet potato flan with a dark rum sauce. Although you can't get Dixie beer here, the impressive wine book lists more than 400 bottles in addition to a fine selection of single-malt scotches, single-barrel bourbons, and cognac. Dinner. & (Southeast)

DALESIO'S
829 Eastern Ave.
Baltimore
410/539-1965
$$$

An elegant, intimate restaurant featuring northern Italian cuisine, a notable wine list, and an upstairs balcony that overlooks several formstone-covered row houses and a less-than-scenic Is That My Car? auto-detailing shop. Watch your Lexus being buffed while enjoying the house specialty, Seafood Dalesio's—lobster, shrimp, clams, and mussels swimming in an Italian vodka crème sauce. Lunch, dinner. & (Southeast)

DA MIMMO RISTORANTE
217 S. High St.
Baltimore
410/727- 6876
$$$$

If all the celebrities photographed with Chef Mimmo and his wife and mounted on his restaurant's walls could somehow spring to life, it would make for great dinner theater (or at least a vintage episode of "The Love Boat"). Tony Bennett would be a guest star, as would Cher, Bobby Vinton, William Shatner, and Maureen Stapleton. Pavorotti, who appears in several photographs, would sing and everybody would chow down on Mimmo's hefty veal chops, tender tenderloin, or portobello mushrooms stuffed with crabmeat. One big bonus: Da Mimmo's has its own parking lot. Call ahead and reserve a spot when you make your reservation. Lunch, dinner. (Southeast)

FUNK'S DEMOCRATIC COFFEE SPOT
1818 Eastern Ave.
Baltimore
410/276-3865
$

Funk's democratically welcomes all walks of life—both carnivore and vegetarian—to its laid-back environs, where it's hard to find any meal above five bucks. The vegan moussaka, made with potatoes, eggplant, onions, garlic, and fresh oregano from the owner's alley garden is a winner, as are the potato knishes. Funk's offers the usual coffee drinks—cappuccinos, espresso, and everything in between. The decor is predictably funky—metal coffee pots have been hot-wired with bulbs and shades and now serve as table lamps, and you're just as likely to hear Johnny Cash as you are Miles Davis on the sound system. Don't forget to browse the used bookstore upstairs. Breakfast, lunch, dinner. & (Southeast)

HAMILTON'S
888 S. Broadway
Baltimore
410/522-2195
www.AdmiralFell.com
$$$$

Attached to the Admiral Fell Inn, Hamilton's specializes in New American cuisine, meaning tired old tenderloin gets jazzed up with fava beans, spetzel, mustard greens, and sunburst squash, or sweetbreads meet oyster mushrooms, leeks, and a pancetta-shallot sauce. Wines from an ample cellar, as noted by *Wine Spectator,* quench your thirst. Complimentary valet parking is a big plus in parking-space-challenged Fells Point. Dinner. & (Southeast)

HELEN'S GARDEN RESTAURANT
2908 O'Donnell St.
Baltimore
410/276-2233
$$

Helen's might be the best dinner deal

in town. Come on a Wednesday evening and just about every entrée (regularly priced from $12 to $19) is just ten bucks. Choose from pecan-crusted brook trout, grilled salmon with a ginger-mango glaze, and other well-prepared New American cuisine. The charming restaurant also has an extensive and reasonably priced wine list, with happy hour tastings held in the first-floor bar. If you're exploring Canton Square during lunch Thursday through Saturday, stop by for the $3.95 burger special—perhaps the best lunch deal in town. Brunch served Sat and Sun. (Southeast)

HENNINGER'S TAVERN
1812 Bank St.
Baltimore
410/342-2172
$$$

First it was a tavern, then a VFW hall for World War I Polish vets, then a candy store, and in the 1970s it became a tavern again. If you look closely, you can find evidence of all its incarnations. Current owner Kenny Vieth has a thing for black-and-white disaster and 1940s Hollywood glamour girl photos, which he mounts in ancient frames on mismatched wall paper. The place oozes a certain Fells Point charm. The food? Entrées change every two weeks, so you know the almond-crusted halibut is

---

T I P

Like local color with your seafood? Then visit Faidley's, an institution at Lexington Market since 1886, for what might be the city's best crab cake. Or try Nick's, in Cross Street Market, for three stalls of oysters, shrimp, fried fish, and sushi. Both have wooden stools, cheap beer, and more characters than a John Waters movie.

Wine lovers should check out the wine lists at Spike & Charlie's, Corks, Charleston, Ruth's Chris Steak House, and Hamilton's.

fresh; the pan-fried breaded oysters and the mussels in white wine and garlic, thankfully, remain constants. Dinner. (Southeast)

IKAROS
4805 Eastern Ave.
Baltimore
410/633-3750
$$
A Greektown fixture since 1969, Ikaros serves up homey, even motherly Greek cuisine. This means that, like most motherly cooking, presentation comes second to sheer quantity, vegetables are usually overcooked and limp, and salads drown in dressing. But the home-baked bread is delicious, and the traditional lamb dishes and the moussaka are obviously baked with T.L.C., if not with gourmet flair. The preponderance of thick-accented Greeks who dine here adds to the Athenian authenticity. Lunch, dinner. & (Southeast)

JIMMY'S RESTAURANT
801 S. Broadway
Baltimore
410/327-3273
$
The grill's been sizzling since 1946 at Jimmy's, where the service is always friendly and the food is classic diner fare: breakfast all day, plus club sandwiches, burgers, fried seafood platters, steaks, and chops. More interesting than the food is the cast of neighborhood characters who talk current events at the counter and call each other "Goddamn liars" when reminiscing about the old days. Local politicos also lunch here, seeking the community pulse. There's beer on tap and plastic bottles of syrup on every table—a strange but somehow comforting combination. Open daily 5 a.m. to 10 p.m. (Southeast)

KALI'S COURT
1606 Thames St.
Baltimore
410/276-4700
$$$
A relaxed atmosphere of exposed brick trimmed in wood and a magnificent teak bar welcomes diners to this Fells Point charmer. Steaks and chops are on the menu, but the fish selections, fired in a wood-burning brick oven, are the stars of the show. Choose from several varieties each night; they are roasted whole, leaving them crispy on the outside and tender within. Lunch, dinner. & (Southeast)

KELLY'S
2108 Eastern Ave.
Baltimore
410/327-2312
$$
Some Baltimore restaurants are crab joints, plain and simple, while others disguise themselves as something else during most of the year and then reveal their crabby

halves come summer. Kelly's is just such a place: It's a friendly, neighborhood Irish pub for most of the year, but come crab season hammers start slamming and there's a premium on paper towels. The crustaceans in question are quite good—and very spicy, requiring prodigious amounts of beer to cool one's palate. But what else would you expect from an Irish pub? Reservations are recommended during crab season. Late-night karaoke Fri and Sat. Lunch, dinner Wed–Sun. (Southeast)

LA TAVOLA
248 Albemarle St.
Baltimore
410/685-1859
www.mbd.com/latavola.html
$$$
A light, airy decor of coral pinks and pastel-colored plates gives La Tavola a feeling more reminiscent of south Florida than southern Italy. The menu isn't traditional Italian either: Pasta gets topped with fresh spinach, raisins, pine nuts, ricotta, and nutmeg, while a ragout of lamb swims in a white wine sauce. Meanwhile, the light, tubular calamari might be the best you'll find anywhere in the city. La Tavola earned a reputation for its good value when it opened in 1996, but it has since increased its prices to a level more in line with its peers in Little Italy. Expect to pay up to $14 for a plate of pasta and $16 for eggplant parmesan—without a house salad included. Lunch, dinner. ৬ (Southeast)

LIQUID EARTH
1626 Aliceanna St.
Baltimore
410/276-6606
Potent juice concoctions like the "anti-ox detox," a blender-full of or-

ganic carrots, cabbage, and red beets might be just the thing to cure what ails you. The vegetarian-friendly cuisine includes the "Philly Cheese Phake"—portobello mushrooms, onions, and cheese on a baguette—and vegan vichyssoise, a creamy soup made from sautéed onions and potatoes. ৬ (Southeast)

MARGARET'S CAFE
909 Fell St.
Baltimore
410/276-5605
$
Duck into Margaret's, hidden off the main drag, for a healthy snack of fresh veggies, salad, grilled fish, or soup in a friendly, laid-back setting with exposed brick and an artistic vibe. Everything you order here seems to burst with color—as does the art on the walls at the Halcyon Gallery, housed on the second floor. Lunch, dinner; weekend brunch. (Southeast)

NACHO MAMA'S
2907 O'Donnell St.
Baltimore
410/675-0898
$
Chain restaurants have been into decorating with garage-sale bric-a-brac for a while now, but Nacho Mama's looks like a Bennigan's gone bad. Nearly every inch of wall, ceiling, and bar space is covered with portraits of Elvis, Baltimore Orioles memorabilia, and ads for National Bohemian Beer, a.k.a., "Natty Boh," a cheap favorite that used to be brewed locally. Regulars line up for the heavy burritos and nachos served in real metal hubcaps instead of plates. Lunch, dinner. (Southeast)

OBRYCKI'S
1727 E. Pratt St.

Baltimore
410/732-6399
www.obryckis.com
$$$

Ask a local where you should go for crabs near the Inner Harbor and chances are they'll mention Obrycki's, a Baltimore classic since 1944. The atmosphere—and the prices—are decidedly more upscale than the usual crab shack, but you'll still find brown paper on the tables, cold pitchers of beer, and some of the best crabs anywhere in town. Other crabby creations (crab cakes, crab soup) and assorted Chesapeake Bay bounty are also on the menu. Remember that Obrycki's closes each winter; call first to see if they're open and reserve a table well in advance. Lunch, dinner. &. (Southeast)

PETER'S INN
504 S. Ann St.
Baltimore
410/675-7313
$$

Peter's Inn may appear to be more of a funky neighborhood bar than a restaurant, but the entrées served by the pierced and tattooed wait staff are surprisingly gourmet. The menu, which changes weekly, might include pumpkin-encrusted tuna steak, chicken with a crab-spiked mustard crème sauce, or sautéed shrimp snuggled next to a spicy black-bean cake. If you can't snag one of the dozen or so tables, cool your heels at the bar or on the comfy couch in the intimate back room. No reservations or credit cards accepted. (Southeast)

PIER POINT
1822 Aliceanna St.
Baltimore
410/675-2080

Pier Point offers food from the Chesapeake Bay.

$$$

Chef Nancy Longo does some imaginative things with food from the Chesapeake Bay. She smokes crab cakes, fries oysters coated in corn meal, and stuffs quesadillas with bits of delicate smoked duck. The results are some of the most creative meals you'll find anywhere in town. Hometown director Barry Levinson agrees; he had Longo cook for his entire crew after filming one of his locally shot movies. Lunch, dinner; brunch Sun. (Southeast)

RESTAURANTE SAN LUIS
246 S. Broadway
Baltimore
410/327-0266
$

The tacos made with beef tongue should clue you in immediately that this isn't some Americanized Tex-Mex joint. San Luis cooks authentic Salvadoran cuisine—tamales, pollo guisado (chicken with vegetables over a bed of rice), and several kinds of papusas. It's good and inexpensive,

Pier Point

and nearly everyone in the restaurant speaks Spanish. Lunch, dinner. (Southeast)

SIP & BITE RESTAURNT
2200 Boston St.
Baltimore
410/675-7077
$

The Sip & Bite is a Baltimore classic, open 24 hours a day, seven days a week. The traditional diner atmosphere comes complete with counter service and booths, a grill that sizzles nonstop, and a thin layer of "diner grime" that seems to cover everything in the place. Things can get pretty crowded (and crazy) at 2 a.m. on a Saturday night. Daily specials, "fresh from Chef Mike's kitchen," range from chicken kabobs to Hungarian goulash, in addition to the typical greasy-spoon fare. (Southeast)

VACCARO'S
222 Albemarle St.
Baltimore
410/685-4905
$

Half the fun of eating dessert at this pasticceria is watching people's expressions as towers of gelati, brick-sized tiramisu, and overflowing cannolis are placed in front of them. The "Colosseos," Belgian waffles loaded with ice cream and other sinful ingredients, could feed the entire cast of the *Godfather*—*I, II,* and *III*. When dining in Little Italy, don't bother eating dessert anywhere else. There's an outpost of Vaccaro's in the Light Street Pavilion, but the food just seems to taste better at its home base. Dessert only, daily; weekends open to 1 a.m. ᕁ (Southeast)

ZE MEAN BEAN CAFÉ
1739 Fleet St.
Baltimore
410/675-5999
$

Eastern European comfort food meets cozy café at this Fells Point favorite. Pirogues, borscht, and chicken Kiev seem perfectly at home in a traditional coffeehouse setting of exposed brick and wooden beams, lighted candles, and live music every night of the week. (Accordion music on Thursdays!) Come on Sundays for the jazz brunch and a menu that features the "Polish Cowboy"—two cinnamon pancakes with spiced maple syrup, scrambled eggs, and grilled Polish sausage. Lunch, dinner; brunch Sun. ᕁ (Southeast)

SOUTHWEST

G&M CARRY OUT
804 N. Hammonds Ferry Rd.
Linthicum Heights
410/636-1777
$$

The crab cakes are legendary: eight ounces of pure lump crab meat rolled into a mound the size of a baseball and served on crackers with French fries and coleslaw, or as a sandwich between two halves of a kaiser roll with lettuce, tomato, and tartar sauce. G&M is conveniently located minutes from BWI Airport; make it either your first or last meal in town. Lunch, dinner. (Southwest)

TERSIGUEL'S
8293 Main St.
Ellicott City
410/465-4004
$$$$

Tersiguel's is Baltimore's closest thing to a romantic French countryside inn. The charming historic house was once the domain of a country dentist.

Now it's Chef Michel Tersiguel and his pastry-chef mother Odette who do the operating on the premises. Dining rooms are cozy and not overly fancy, with creaky floors and black-and-white vignettes of Parisian-looking faces on the foyer walls. Chateaubriand, steak au poivre, buttered escargots, and homemade pâtés round out the traditional menu. Reservations are a must. Lunch, dinner. (Southwest)

THE TROLLEY STOP
6 Oella Ave.
Ellicott City

410/465-8546
$

Around World War II, Ellicott City was so rough that military brass at Fort Mead barred the enlisted men from visiting. That was when the Trolley Stop was known as the "Bloody Bucket," for serving more knuckle sandwiches than turkey sandwiches. The atmosphere is friendlier at the historic restaurant nowadays, but it still attracts colorful locals who come for the inexpensive pit-beef sandwiches, burgers, and $9.95 lobster special on Tuesday nights. Lunch, dinner. (Southwest)

Baltimore Area CVA

5

SIGHTS AND ATTRACTIONS

At one time, "Baltimore sights and attractions" might have sounded oxymoronic. The truth is Baltimore has always had its points of interest—Fort McHenry, the Washington Monument, historic neighborhoods—but potential visitors were usually so busy trying to avoid Baltimore that they rarely took the time to explore. And, well, maybe Baltimoreans didn't really care. As former Sunpapers editor Philip Wagner told Holiday magazine in 1962, "It's true Baltimore's charms are so well-concealed that people drive through without stopping, but that saves us from a good many bores."

Back then, tourists could see Baltimore in about a day—if they stopped at all. These days, tourism brings in $3 billion annually, and hoteliers, restaurateurs, and tour operators will bend over backwards to make sure you—bore or not—see the entire city and spend a wad of money in the process.

The city's centerpiece attraction, of course, is the Inner Harbor and its world-class aquarium, museums, professional ballparks, and twin shopping plazas. The Harbor is where you'll find the city's glitz, commercialism, and 40-foot-high neon electric guitars. The scene is fun and tacky and beautiful all at the same time. But Baltimore's other neighborhoods and attractions—its still well-concealed charms—are where you'll find the city's unique character and culture, the stuff that makes people who were born here stay their entire lives.

For the most part, you can visit Baltimore's major sights and attractions without using a car. From the Inner Harbor, neighborhoods like Mount Vernon, Federal Hill, and Little Italy are within walking distance, and Fells Point, Canton, and Fort McHenry are a water-taxi ride away. If you would prefer to let others guide you, Baltimore has nearly a dozen walking, motor coach, and boat tours that will show you the city from land or water.

NOTABLE NEIGHBORHOODS

BOLTON HILL

During the 1920s Jazz Age, Bolton Hill earned a reputation as Baltimore's "Gin Belt" for its alcohol-soaked bashes attended by the neighborhood's literati and glitterati, such as classicist Edith Hamilton and Zelda and F. Scott Fitzgerald. Fitzgerald wrote *Tender Is the Night* from his row house in the 1300 block of Park Avenue and pronounced, "I belong here, where everything is civilized and gay and rotted and polite." Bolton Hill's architecture—Gothic churches, impressive brick row houses built after the Civil War (some inhabited by defeated Confederate higher-ups), and Renaissance Revival mansions—give the parlor neighborhood an atmosphere similar to Washington's Georgetown or Boston's Beacon Hill. Unlike those two districts, however, Bolton Hill remains quiet and primarily residential, an architecture buff's delight. (Downtown)

CANTON

Baltimore's latest revitalization success story traces it roots to 1785, when merchant John O'Donnell purchased a track of land on the water just east of Fells Point and named it Canton, after the Chinese port he had done business with so many times before. (Baltimoreans, as they're apt

Baltimore Area CVA

Historic row houses line the Federal Hill neighborhood.

to do, eschew the traditional pronunciation, Can-TON, and accent the first syllable, CAN-ton). The Canton Company established America's first industrial park here, opening up huge canning factories and building tidy row houses for its workers. Those same canning factories now hold shops, offices, and, at Tindeco Wharf, pricey waterfront apartments. As in Federal Hill, the row houses have skyrocketed in value as young professionals renovate and move in. Most activity revolves around the refurbished American Can Company and its Bibelot Bookstore (see Chapter 9, Shopping), Boston Street and its

TRIVIA

The 16-foot-tall marble statue of George Washington atop the Washington Monument is not empty handed. If you look closely, you'll note he's holding a rolled up document—his resignation as commander of the army, an event that occurred in 1783 in Annapolis, then the nation's capital.

Historic Ellicott City

Beneath its facade of meticulously restored early nineteenth-century buildings, cozy antiques stores, and crowded restaurants, Historic Ellicott City's heritage as a western fringe town endures. On any given afternoon, you'll find a congenial melting pot of aging hippies, bikers, antique-hunting yuppies, good ol' boys, and rebellious suburban youths hanging out on its quaint Main Street. Located about a half hour from downtown Baltimore, the town got its start in 1772, when the Ellicott brothers established a mill at the junction of the Patapsco River and Tiber Creek. Throughout the years, the town has boomed, gone bust, and been nearly wiped out by floods—a doozy in 1886 killed 1,000 people and destroyed every mill along the Patapsco River.

Today, the town's unique shops, restaurants, and interesting sights make for a perfect afternoon excursion. However, like all great historic structures, Ellicott City's nineteenth-century buildings are supposedly overrun by ghosts. The Howard County Tourism Office, located behind the post office at Hamilton and Main Streets (800/288-8747), gives spooky ghost tours and historical walks on weekends from April through November. Reservations are required. Tours cost $7 for adults and $5 for children.

popular dance clubs, and O'Donnell Square, a pretty, green swatch lined with shops, restaurants, and rollicking pubs between Linwood Avenue and Potomac Street. (Southeast)

FEDERAL HILL

Federal Hill—both the mound of earth just south of the harbor and the adjacent neighborhood—were named in the aftermath of a rowdy party celebrating the state's ratification of the U.S. Constitution, when 4,000 people ate and drank gluttonous quantities of venison, mutton, and beer and shouted "Huzzah to the Constitution!" During the Civil War, Union troops occupied the hill and trained their guns on the mostly pro-South city below. The neighborhood, which once accommodated dock workers at the steamship factories along its eastern base, has been undergoing steady gentrification for years and now houses many young professionals, who enjoy the convenient walk to work downtown. Stroll the neighborhood's cobblestoned streets—partic-

Now that's *Italian.*

ularly East Montgomery Street, one block south of the waterfront—to see wonderfully restored historic row houses from the Federal era. The hill itself, topped by a pleasant park with unequaled views of downtown, is described more thoroughly in Chapter 10, Parks and Gardens. (South)

FELLS POINT

The history of Fells Point reads like something from a Robert Louis Stevenson novel: ship captains and slave labor, whores and missionaries, brothels and bars. As Baltimore's original port, it attracted its share of characters. Englishman Edward Fell bought the land in 1726, and his son William gave the streets its English-sounding names: Lancaster, Bond, and Thames (pronounced to rhyme with "James" in Baltimorese). For nearly 200 years, the area filled with the sounds of hammers banging on anvils and the scent of pine tar as 18 shipyards cranked out swift-sailing Baltimore clipper ships. Frederick Douglas labored as a slave here and then returned a free man to purchase a row of houses that still stand. A young Billie Holliday sang at her uncle's lounge on Caroline Street. In the late 1960s, community activists, shouting "The British couldn't take Fells Point, the termites couldn't take Fells Point, and the State Roads Commission can't take Fells Point," preserved the character of the neighborhood from impending highway construction. One of its leaders, a fireplug named Barbara Milkulski, won a seat in the U.S. Senate in 1988.

Fells Point's gritty character endures, even if its brothels and missions haven't. You'll still see sailors and homeless folks, but mostly twenty- and thirty-somethings in search of dinner and drinks at one of its numerous clubs and bars. During the day, antiques stores, a public market, and retro boutiques make for interesting shopping. (Southeast)

HAMPDEN

Vintage fedoras and trendy women's clothing. Eisenhower-era end tables and $2,500 handcrafted bed frames. Meat-loaf sandwiches and soba noodles. Hampden's main drag, West 36th Street, sometimes seems like a mixed-up time machine, shifting from the '50s to the present day and back again, all within the span of about four blocks. Once a thriving mill town, the neighborhood retains its white, working-class population, even as its eclectic retail mix attracts an increasing number of urban hipsters and suburbanites in search of unique gifts and a good meal. Inspect the neighborhood's row houses, talk to a few Hampdenites, and you'll quickly find out why John Waters thought the local character authentic enough to use Hampden as the setting for his flick *Pecker*. It's old-time Bawlmer, with a modern twist.

HIGHLANDTOWN
Just northeast of Canton, Highlandtown remains an unblemished example of old-time Baltimore. Here you'll find row houses with white marble steps, screen doors painted with sylvan scenes, window shrines dedicated to religious figures, and plenty of formstone—gray stucco blocks, popular cover for redbrick row homes during the 1940s and '50s. The area's main thoroughfare, Eastern Avenue, might contain a few more pawnshops than Polish butchers these days, but several organizations, such as the Fells Point Creative Alliance, are trying to find new uses for abandoned

buildings. Drive the somewhat frowsy commercial strip and explore residential streets to see a side of Baltimore that hasn't changed much since the mid-twentieth century.

INNER HARBOR
Baltimore's showplace is filled year-round with sights, sounds, and nonstop activity. Water taxis buzz along the water's edge, bands blast music from Harborplace Amphitheater, and restaurants overflow onto outdoor patios during summer. The scene is the antithesis of early years along the waterfront, when work, not play, was the rule of the day. Read the yellow historical placards placed along the redbrick promenade, and you'll get an idea of what life used to be like. During the nineteenth-century, clipper ships carrying everything from Eastern Shore produce to South American guano deposited goods at the bustling warehouses that lined the harbor walls. In the early twentieth century, workers toiled on steamships, and the harbor filled with waste and sewage, giving off a scent "like a billion pole cats" wrote H. L. Mencken. But by World War II, the wharves lay vacant, abandoned for deeper water downriver.

The rumblings of rebirth began as early as 1959, with the nearby development of Charles Center. But it wasn't until 1980 that the Rouse Company completed Harborplace—twin, teal-roofed shopping pavilions.

TRIVIA

Designed by architect I. M. Pei and completed in 1977, Baltimore's 423-foot-tall World Trade Center is the tallest pentagonal building in the world.

In the following years, the National Aquarium and several hotels opened, and suddenly tourists had a reason to visit downtown. Now you'll find Oriole Park, PSINet Stadium, ESPNZone, the Hard Rock Café, Port Discovery, and more hotels along the water's edge. And while the city is indisputably better off because of the harbor's success, the area—with its proliferation of big, chain restaurants—has lost much of what once made it uniquely ours. So while you should certainly visit the Inner Harbor, don't miss the city's other neighborhoods, or you'll miss what makes Baltimore Baltimore.

LITTLE ITALY

Originally the stomping grounds of German, Irish, and then Jewish immigrants, tiny Little Italy didn't pick up its Neapolitan nature until the late nineteenth century, with the construction of St. Leo the Great Roman Catholic Church. Restaurants opened to serve the burgeoning population and have been spooning out spaghetti and meatballs ever since. Along with St. Gabriel's, St. Leo's remains the spiritual center of the neighborhood and the site of rollicking street festivals every summer and heated boccie tournaments every Friday night (see Chapter 10, Sports and Recreation). Shopping and sightseeing are limited,

but stroll around the garlic-scented neighborhood and chat with real live Italians, who keep a watchful eye on the neighborhood's comings and goings from their marble front stoops. (Southeast)

MOUNT VERNON

Robber barons, merchant princes, debutantes, and other members of Baltimore's nineteenth-century upper crust lived in Mount Vernon. They established elite social clubs—like the Maryland Club, still in existence—and threw terrific bashes that sometimes ended with soused party-goers wading in the square's fountains. But by the 1920s, the city's aristocracy had begun fleeing to the northern and northwestern suburbs as nearby boarding houses began to dilute real-estate values. They left behind their spectacular row houses, which were subsequently divided into apartments and offices. These buildings remain well preserved, much to the credit of the Mount Vernon Improvement Association and, more recently, the Mount Vernon Cultural District.

The area was once Baltimore's grandest tourist attraction before being overshadowed by the Inner Harbor. In 1896 *Harper's* magazine called Mount Vernon and its monument to George Washington (from whence the area gets its name) "the most impos-

DOWNTOWN BALTIMORE

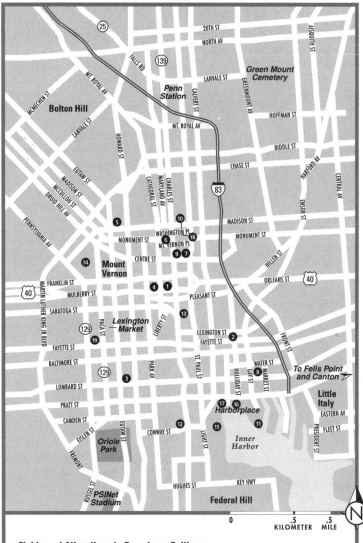

0   .5   .5
KILOMETER   MILE

Sights and Attractions in Downtown Baltimore

1 Basilica of the Assumption of the Blessed Virgin Mary
2 City Hall
3 Emerson Tower
4 Enoch Pratt Library
5 First and Franklin Street Presbyterian Church
6 Garrett-Jacobs Mansion
7 George L. Peabody Library
8 Holocaust Memorial
9 Mount Vernon and Washington Places
10 Mount Vernon Place United Methodist Church
11 National Aquarium in Baltimore
12 Old Otterbein Methodist Church
13 Old St. Paul's Episcopal Church
14 Orchard Street Church
15 *Pride of Baltimore II*
16 Top of the World
17 USS *Constellation*
18 Washington Monument
19 Westminster Hall and Burying Ground

Emerson Tower

ing site to be found in any American city." Walk along its four grassy squares, stroll its cobblestone streets, and peer into the windows and doorways of the once-opulent mansions—you might agree. (Downtown)

MOUNT WASHINGTON
One of Baltimore's first suburbs, now part of the city proper, makes a nice escape from downtown along the light-rail line. Several interesting shops (see Shopping, Chapter 9) and notable restaurants along Sulgrave Avenue warrant exploration.

ROLAND PARK
Parts of this fashionable neighborhood were designed by the Olmsted brothers, sons of great urban architect Frederick Law Olmsted. Drive along Roland Avenue and its leafy side streets to gawk at the grand Victorians occupied by many of Baltimore's old-money families. If you've read Anne Tyler's *The Accidental Tourist,* you might recognize Roland Park as the book's setting.

UNION SQUARE/ HOLLINS MARKET
When Hollywood went looking for a suitable place to recreate nineteenth-century New York for the movie *Washington Square*, they chose Baltimore's Union Square. The redbrick row houses that line a small park in the area remain as charming as ever, but recent attempts at neighborhood renewal have yielded mixed results. By the 1950s, the area's significant Lithuanian population had all but moved out, but Lithuanian Hall (851 Hollins Street) still hosts a regular schedule of traditional dance groups, choir practice, and the spastic Night of 100 Elvises in December. Hollins Market (see Chapter 9, Shopping), favored shopping destination of H. L. Mencken, retains the hose-it-down atmosphere it always had. Artists, attracted by low rents and houses with character, began moving in during the 1960s and dubbed the 'hood SoWeBo (Southwest Baltimore). The artistic side is celebrated every summer, with the anything-goes SoWe-Bohemian Festival. (Southwest)

DOWNTOWN

BASILICA OF THE ASSUMPTION OF THE BLESSED VIRGIN MARY
Cathedral and Mulberry Sts.
Baltimore
410/727-3565
www.baltimorebasilica.org
With its twin Byzantine spires and neoclassical design, America's first Roman Catholic Cathedral was hailed as an "architectural original" upon its completion in 1821. (It's slated for a renovation in hopes of returning it to its past luster.) Architect Benjamin Henry Latrobe designed the cathedral for free as he was completing work

on the U.S. Capitol in Washington, D.C. Both structures are similar in their "new world" designs and great domes. Baltimorean John Carroll, the first archbishop in the United States and founder of Georgetown University, lies buried in the cathedral's crypt. Pope John Paul II visited in 1995, and Mother Teresa graced the basilica in 1996. Open daily 7–5. Guided tours Sun at noon. Free. ♿ (Downtown)

CITY HALL
E. Fayette and Holliday Sts.
Baltimore
410/396-3100

In 1865, 22-year-old architect George A. Frederick submitted the winning design for City Hall, an award that netted him a $400 prize and a very promising future. Frederick's Second Empire design included a mansard roof capped by a 227-foot-high white marble dome, projecting pavilions, and exterior brick walls from 2.5 to 7 feet thick. The hulking structure was completed in 1875 at a cost to taxpayers of nearly $2.3 million—$200,000 under budget (probably the last city project to accomplish that feat). You can tour the building and see city government in action (or inaction) by making an appointment through the Women's Civic League, 410/837-5424. (Downtown)

George L. Peabody library, p. 92

Baltimore Area CVA

EMERSON TOWER (BROMO SELTZER TOWER)
Eutaw and Lombard Sts.
Baltimore

Chemist Isaac Emerson, the discoverer of the headache and hangover remedy Bromo Seltzer, modeled his company's headquarters after Florence's Palazzo Vecchio. However, unlike the architect of the thirteenth-century stone watch tower, Emerson, always the savvy promoter, topped the building with a 51-foot, 17-ton revolving replica of the blue Bromo Seltzer bottle. Lit by 596 lights, the bottle was visible to seamen 20 miles out. The monstrosity was removed in 1936, but the building's distinctive gravity clock, with B-R-O-M-O-S-E-L-T-Z-E-R around its 24-foot face, remains one of the city's most recognizable landmarks. Closed to the public. (Downtown)

ENOCH PRATT LIBRARY
400 Cathedral St.
Baltimore
410/396-5500
www.pratt.lib.md.us

When the new central branch of Baltimore's public library system opened in 1933, people flocked to view its spacious central hall, a 100-foot-long room with marble columns, a terrazzo floor, and a hand-painted frieze depicting 17 Early American and British painters. (The interior is slated for a much-needed renovation.) The design was revolutionary in its inviting department-store look—with street-level window displays for books and posters—that encouraged citizens to enter and browse. Special collections include the letters and manuscripts of H. L. Mencken as well as Edgar Allan Poe memorabilia, including a lock of his hair. Open by appointment only. A gift shop offers literary knickknacks and a dry audio tour only a librarian could love. Mon–Wed 10–8, Thu and Sat 10–5, closed Fri, Sun. ♿ (Downtown)

FIRST AND FRANKLIN STREET PRESBYTERIAN CHURCH
210 W. Madison St.
Baltimore
410/728-5545.
This impressive Gothic Revival building has the tallest steeple in town and stained-glass windows by John Lafarge and Tiffany. Open by appointment, or stop by the church office next door. Sun service at 11 a.m. (Downtown)

GARRETT-JACOBS MANSION
11 W. Mount Vernon Pl.

Baltimore
410/539-6914
In 1872, the most lavish house on Mount Vernon Place was bought by B&O Railroad president John W. Garrett as a wedding gift for his son and daughter-in-law. The Engineering Society of Baltimore owns the property these days, but they will let you tour the magnificently restored 40-room interior, a favorite of Hollywood productions, including *Diner, 12 Monkeys,* and *Her Alibi.* Tour daily at 11 a.m. and 1 p.m. $5 adults, $4 seniors, students. (Downtown)

GEORGE L. PEABODY LIBRARY
17 E. Mount Vernon Pl.
Baltimore
410/659-8179
When the Peabody opened in 1878, it was the third-largest library in the country. Only the U.S. Library of Congress and Harvard University's library held more books. Although its 250,000 volumes remain an impressive collection, the library's stack room—five tiers of ornamental cast-iron balconies encircling a dramatic sky-

Aquarium Tips

During the summer, the best times to visit the National Aquarium are right when it opens, at 9 a.m., or later in the day, between 5 and 8 p.m. Keep in mind that you can tour the aquarium for an hour and a half after the building closes. Visitors must purchase timed tickets for admission, which often sell out by midday. For guaranteed entry, call Ticketmaster (410/481-7328 or 800/551-7328) by 3 p.m. the day before you visit to purchase a timed admission ticket. If you're staying at a hotel, check with the concierge about purchasing tickets.

lighted court and a black-and-white marble floor—is the real draw. On weekends, the library crowds not with bookworms but with private wedding receptions. Mon–Fri 9–3. ♿ (Downtown)

HOLOCAUST MEMORIAL
S. Gay and E. Lombard Sts.
Baltimore

Baltimore's memorial to the tragedy of the Holocaust spans a city block, several streets north of the National Aquarium. The memorial's center-piece, a haunting metal sculpture by artist Joseph Sheppard depicting emaciated bodies being consumed in a cone-shaped flame, lies within a plaza meant to resemble a railyard. "Those Who Cannot Remember the Past are Condemned to Repeat It," reads the sculpture's pedestal. It's an impression that's hard to forget. (Downtown)

MOUNT VERON AND
WASHINGTON PLACES
Charles St. and Mount Vernon Pl.
Baltimore

Four grassy squares in the form of a Greek cross surround the Washington Monument and constitute one of America's first urban parks. Statuary

© Bill McAllen

Pride of Baltimore *replica, p. 95*

in the east and north squares includes local luminaries such as George Peabody, the merchant who left a chunk of his fortune to the institute that bears his name; Severn Teackle Wallis, a nineteenth-century political reformer and uncle of Wallis Warfield, the Baltimore divorcée who married an English king; Roger Brooke Taney, Chief Justice of the U.S. Supreme Court from 1835 to 1864; and a horse-bound John Eager Howard, the original landowner and the only Baltimorean to get three streets named after him (one for each of his names).

In the south square, the city dedicated a statue of Lafayette in 1924 to the memory of fallen French and American comrades of World War I. The west square contains several bronze sculptures by Antoine-Louis Barye, a favorite sculptor of local art collector William Walters. (Downtown)

MOUNT VERNON PLACE UNITED METHODIST CHURCH
10 E. Mount Vernon Place
Baltimore
410/685-5290
Known to many as "that green church near the Washington Monument," the United Methodist Church was completed in 1872. It was built out of green serpentine marble mined from Baltimore County. The Gothic church's fantastic exterior overshadows its comparably plain interior, but the building is open for weekday tours and services on Wednesday and Sunday. A plaque on the side of the church facing Mount Vernon Place notes that "Star-Spangled Banner" composer Francis Scott Key died in 1843 on the site, formerly the house of his daughter Elizabeth and her husband, Charles Howard. (Downtown)

NATIONAL AQUARIUM IN BALTIMORE
Pier 3, 501 E. Pratt St.
Baltimore
410/576-3800
www.aqua.org
Generally regarded as one of the best collections of aquatic species in the world, the National Aquarium in Baltimore does for fish what the Louvre does for art. You'll find all sorts of undersea and amphibian creatures here: stingrays, electric eels, giant octopi, seals, and a half-dozen different species of sharks. A simulated tropical rainforest occupies the building's distinctive triangular crown, and a marine mammal pavilion holds entertaining live dolphin shows daily. Not surprisingly, the aquarium can get very crowded; refer to the "Aquarium Tips" sidebar for a few suggestions on making your visit hassle-free. Allow two and a half hours for a complete tour. $14 adults, $10.50 seniors, $7.50 ages 3–11. & (Downtown)

OLD OTTERBEIN UNITED METHODIST CHURCH
112 W. Conway St.
Baltimore
410/685-4703.
Up until World War I, all services were delivered in German in Baltimore's oldest church, built in 1785 of brick imported from England. The

church, as well as the surrounding neighborhood, was named for Philip Wilhelm Otterbein, a hell-fire pastor whose memorial marker outside the building contains one of the oldest chiseled errors in the city: Otterbein was born on June 3, 1726, not June 4. Sun service at 11 a.m.; tours afterward. (Downtown)

OLD ST. PAUL'S EPISCOPAL CHURCH
N. Charles and Saratoga Sts.
Baltimore
410/685-3404
The congregation traces its roots back to 1692, but the Romanesque basilica itself, the fourth church building on this site, was built in 1856. Tours by appointment; Sun services at 8 and 10:30 a.m. (Downtown)

ORCHARD STREET CHURCH
512 Orchard St.
Baltimore
410/523-8150

Legend has it that this church was an important stop on the Underground Railroad. Former-slave Truman Pratt and other free blacks built the site's first American Methodist Episcopal Church in 1837. The current church, built in 1887, houses the Baltimore Urban League. Tours by appointment. (Downtown)

PRIDE OF BALTIMORE II
Inner Harbor
Baltimore
410/539-1151
www.pride2.org
Baltimore's goodwill sailing vessel tours the world for nearly half the year, bringing a touch of Charm City to ports abroad. The ship is a replica of the *Pride of Baltimore*, the city's first ambassador ship, which sank in the Atlantic in 1984 and was modeled after the *Chasseur,* nicknamed the Pride of Baltimore after confounding the British Navy during the War of 1812. When the ship is at its home-

---

Flag Facts

- *The 30-by-42-foot flag that Mary Pickersgill stitched to fly above Fort McHenry cost $405 in 1814. The flag's 1999 restoration (including display case and endowment) by the Museum of American History in Washington, D.C., cost approximately $18 million.*

- *By presidential decree, an American flag has flown above Fort McHenry since the Truman administration—but it's not always the giant replica of Pickersgill's original. According to park officials, that behemoth can't be flown in winds more than 12 miles per hour for fear of it ripping out its support. A smaller (17-by-25-foot) flag is flown on other days, and a smaller-still (5-by-9-foot) 50-star flag is flown at night or in the rain.*

GREATER BALTIMORE

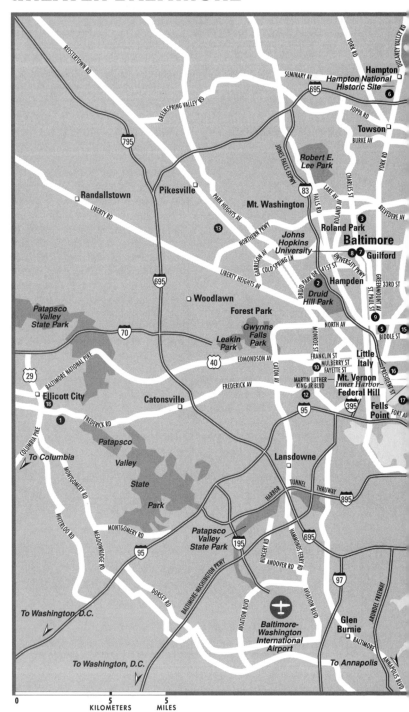

REISTERTOWN RD

SEMINARY AV

695

Hampton
Hampton National
Historic Site
6

YORK RD

DULANEY VALLEY RD

GREEN-SPRING VALLEY RD

JOPPA RD

Towson

795

BURKE AV

YORK RD

Randallstown

Pikesville

JONES FALLS EXPWY

Robert E.
Lee Park

83

LAKE AV

CHARLES ST

BELVEDERE AV

LIBERTY RD

PARK HEIGHTS AV

Mt. Washington

FALLS RD

ROLAND AV

3
Roland Park

Baltimore

13

NORTHERN PKWY

Johns
Hopkins
University

UNIVERSITY PKWY

8 7
Guilford

GARRISON AV

COLD SPRING LN

41ST ST

GREENMOUNT AV

33RD ST

LIBERTY HEIGHTS AV

2

DRUID PARK DR

Hampden

ST. PAUL ST

Patapsco
Valley
State Park

Woodlawn

Forest Park

Druid
Hill Park

9

70

Gwynns
Falls
Park

Leakin
Park

NORTH AV

MONROE ST

5   15

BIDDLE ST

40

EDMONDSON AV

CATON AV

FRANKLIN ST
MULBERRY ST
FAYETTE ST

Little
Italy

16

BALTIMORE NATIONAL PIKE

29

Ellicott City
18

FREDERICK AV

10

MARTIN LUTHER
KING JR BLVD

12

Mt. Vernon
Inner Harbor–
Federal Hill

PRESIDENT ST

COLUMBIA PIKE

To Columbia

FREDERICK RD

1

Catonsville

95

395

Fells
Point

17

FORT AV

Patapsco

Valley

State

Park

Lansdowne

MONTGOMERY RD

WATERLOO RD

MEADOWRIDGE RD

MONTGOMERY RD

95

Patapsco
Valley
State Park

195

HARBOR

TUNNEL

THRUWAY

895

695

DORSEY RD

BALTIMORE-WASHINGTON PKWY

AVIATION BLVD

NURSERY RD

ANDOVER RD

HAMMONDS FERRY RD

97

AVIATION BLVD

ARUNDEL FREEWAY

To Washington, D.C.

Baltimore-
Washington
International
Airport

Glen
Burnie

BALTIMORE

ANNAPOLIS BLVD

To Washington, D.C.

To Annapolis

ANNAPOLIS BLVD

0   5   5
KILOMETERS   MILES

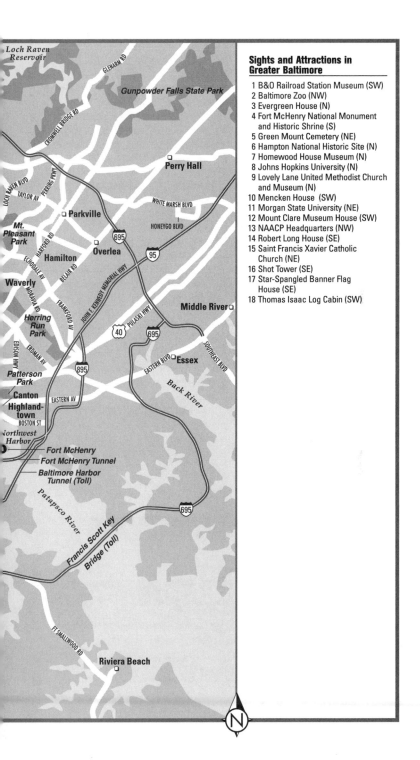

Sights and Attractions in Greater Baltimore

1 B&O Railroad Station Museum (SW)
2 Baltimore Zoo (NW)
3 Evergreen House (N)
4 Fort McHenry National Monument and Historic Shrine (S)
5 Green Mount Cemetery (NE)
6 Hampton National Historic Site (N)
7 Homewood House Museum (N)
8 Johns Hopkins University (N)
9 Lovely Lane United Methodist Church and Museum (N)
10 Mencken House (SW)
11 Morgan State University (NE)
12 Mount Clare Museum House (SW)
13 NAACP Headquarters (NW)
14 Robert Long House (SE)
15 Saint Francis Xavier Catholic Church (NE)
16 Shot Tower (SE)
17 Star-Spangled Banner Flag House (SE)
18 Thomas Isaac Log Cabin (SW)

town berth, visitors are free to tour its deck and hull. Call the *Pride* office for a schedule. (Downtown)

TOP OF THE WORLD
World Trade Center
401 E. Pratt St.
Baltimore
410/837-VIEW
When President Ronald Reagan visited this 27th-floor observation deck, he peered through a telescope and quipped to then-mayor William Donald Schaefer, "The Russians are coming!" Even on the clearest of days you won't be able to see the former Soviet Union, but you do get a sweeping panorama of Baltimore from five sides. Look over the harbor to the southeast at traffic on I-95 appearing to drop suddenly into the Patapsco River. (Cars are actually disappearing into the Fort McHenry Tunnel.) A gift shop offers Charm City souvenirs. Well worth the price of admission. July–Aug Mon–Sat 10–8, Sun 11–8. Rest of the year Mon–Sat 10–5:30, Sun 12–5:30. $3 adults, $2 seniors and children. ⅖ (Downtown)

USS CONSTELLATION
Pier 1, Inner Harbor
Baltimore
410/539-1797
www.constellation.org
The last Civil War vessel still afloat made a triumphant return to the Inner Harbor in 1999 after a $7.3 million renovation. The three-masted sloop-of-war was first launched in 1854 and served on anti-slaver patrols off the coast of Africa before protecting U.S. merchant ships from Confederate raiders during the Civil War. Today, visitors can walk her historic decks and hull and learn more of her history at the Constellation Visitors Center. Daily 10–6. $6 adults, $4.75 seniors, $3.50 children 6–14, children under 5 free. ⅖ (Downtown)

WASHINGTON MONUMENT
N. Charles St. and Monument Ave.
Baltimore
410/396-0929
A $100,000 public lottery helped finance America's first monument to its first president. Original plans to build the memorial downtown were rejected by citizens, who were fearful that the 178-foot column would fall and crush their homes or attract lightning. The monument's base contains a small but interesting museum, including proposed designs that didn't pass muster. Architect Robert Mills, who later designed D.C.'s Washington Monument, eventually won out, and the structure was completed in 1829. Take the 228-quadriceps-straining steps to the top for expansive views of downtown. $1 donation requested. Wed–Sun 10–4. (Downtown)

WESTMINSTER HALL AND BURYING GROUND
Fayette and Greene Sts.

TRIVIA

Why *Johns* Hopkins? Because his first name was the last name of his great-grandmother, Margaret Johns, who married Gerald Hopkins in 1700.

Eschewing the tobacco business of his father, H. L. Mencken pestered the editors at the *Baltimore Morning Herald* until, in 1899, they finally published his first story, all of five lines: "A horse, a buggy and several sets of harness, valued in all at about $250, were stolen last night from the stable of Howard Quinlan, near Kingsville. The county police are at work on the case, but so far no trace of either thieves or booty has been found."

Baltimore
410/706-2072

Four of Baltimore's earliest mayors and a slew of generals and veterans from the American Revolution and the War of 1812 rest in peace here, but, not surprisingly, it's the gravesite of Edgar Allan Poe that gets most of the attention. Poe, who was found semi-conscious in a doorway on Lombard Street on October 2, 1849, died five days later of uncertain causes; he was buried at this historic cemetery next to his wife (and first cousin), Virginia, and his aunt, Maria Poe Clemm. You can pay your respects for free daily from 8 a.m. until dusk or tour the church's catacombs from April through November on the first and third Friday and Saturday of the month. Reservations required. Tours $4 adults, $2 seniors and children. (Downtown)

NORTH

EVERGREEN HOUSE
4544 N. Charles St.
Baltimore
410/516-0341

This magnificent Italianate mansion was owned by Baltimore's railroading Garrett family from 1878 to 1942. The building was a modest Classical Re-

vival house when it was built in 1858, but two generations of free-spending Garretts proceeded to add a bowling alley, a billiard room, a private theater, and other such necessities, until eventually the structure grew to its current 48-room stature. The tour covers 23 rooms, many decorated with post-Impressionist paintings, Tiffany glass, rare books, and Japanese netsuke. Mon–Fri 10–4, Sat and Sun 1–4. Tours begin on the hour; last tour leaves at 3 p.m. $6 adults, $5 seniors, $3 students. (North)

HAMPTON NATIONAL
HISTORIC SITE
535 Hampton Lane
Towson
410/823-1309
www.nps.gov/hamp

The history of the Hampton estate and its Ridgely family caretakers reads like an epic novel or a made-for-TV miniseries. It spans six generations, beginning with Captain Charles Ridgely (1733-1790), who built the expansive Georgian mansion and then threw a wild stag party while his erstwhile wife, Rebecca, led a Methodist prayer meeting upstairs. Five successive generations of Ridgelys made improvements to the estate and its spectacular gardens. At its peak, Ridgley property equaled half the area of

Most Baltimoreans know that every Halloween an unidentified visitor places three roses and half a bottle of cognac on the gravesite of Edgar Allan Poe. Fewer people know that a mysterious person visits the burial shrine of another literary icon and permanent resident, satirist Dorothy Parker, on the anniversary of her birthday and leaves a single rose and a dry martini.

present-day Baltimore. Tours depart daily on the hour from 9 a.m. to 4 p.m. $5 ages 17 and up. (North)

HOMEWOOD HOUSE MUSEUM
Johns Hopkins University
3400 N. Charles St.
Baltimore
410/516-5589

Charles Carroll Jr. built this exquisite house in 1801 with monies given to him for his wedding by his father Charles Carroll of Carrollton, one of Baltimore's leading citizens and a signer of the Declaration of Independence. Charles Jr., not the type to look a gift horse in the mouth, spared no expense in its classic Federal design and furnishings. The house has been restored to its early nineteenth-century grandeur and retains many of its original furnishings. Tours Tue–Sat 11–4, Sun 12–4; last tour departs at 3 p.m. $6 adults, $5 seniors, $3 students. (North)

JOHNS HOPKINS UNIVERSITY
3400 N. Charles St.
Baltimore
410/516-8000
www.jhu.edu

When B&O railroad magnate and one-time whiskey-maker Johns Hopkins left $7 million to establish a university and hospital in 1876, it was the largest philanthropic bequest ever made. (By comparison, Hopkins alum Michael Bloomberg, of Bloomberg Financials, has given a total of $100 million and all he's gotten is a physics building named after him.) More than 3,400 undergraduates and 1,300 graduate students in liberal arts and engineering attend the Homewood campus, the university headquarters having moved from downtown in 1915. The prestigious medical school and hospital are located in an iffy East Baltimore neighborhood. Free tours of the Homewood campus depart from Garland Hall Mon–Fri at 10 a.m., noon, and 3 p.m. ♿ (North)

LOVELY LANE UNITED METHODIST CHURCH AND MUSEUM
2200 St. Paul St.
Baltimore
410/889-1512

The mother church of Methodism in the United States was built in 1887, complete with individually regulated steam heaters in the floor and hatracks under the seats. A museum showcases changing exhibits about Methodism in America as well as a permanent collection of manuscripts by Francis Asbury, the first American Methodist bishop. Sun services at 10 a.m. during summer, 11 a.m. rest of

Green Mount Cemetery

the year; tours after services or by appointment Mon–Fri. (North)

NORTHEAST

GREEN MOUNT CEMETERY
Greenmount Ave. at Oliver St.
Baltimore
410/539-0641
Anybody who was anybody in Baltimore rests in peace at this fashionable Victorian graveyard. Visit the gate office to pick up a list of the 73 most-visited grave sites and a map. Among the notables: Lincoln assassin John Wilkes Booth; 16 Civil War generals (6 Confederates); Baltimore philanthropists Enoch Pratt, William and Henry Walters, Johns Hopkins, and Moses Sheppard; Betsy Patterson Bonaparte (the local belle who married Napoleon Bonaparte's younger brother Jerome); and Central Intelligence Agency chief mole Allen W. Dulles. Mon–Sat 9–3:45. Gate office closes at 11:45 on Sat. Free. (Northeast)

MORGAN STATE UNIVERSITY
1700 E. Coldspring Lane
Baltimore
443/885-3333
www.morgan.edu
Founded in 1867 as the Centenary Biblical Institute, Morgan State University produces the highest number of African American undergraduates in the state. Pick up a campus map at the admissions office in Montebello Hall (2300 Argonne Drive, 443/885-3000) or reserve a spot on a guided tour by calling ahead. Don't miss the campus's James E. Lewis Museum of Art (Murphy Fine Arts Building, 443/885-3030) and its collection of African American, African, and European art. Mon–Fri 9:30–4:30, Sat and Sun 11–4. Call for summer hours. Free. & (Northeast)

SAINT FRANCIS XAVIER CATHOLIC CHURCH
Caroline and E. Oliver Sts.
Baltimore
410/727-3103
Founded in 1864, this is the oldest

African American Catholic church in the United States. Open by appointment. Sun services at 7:30 a.m., 10 a.m., and 12:15 p.m. (Northeast)

NORTHWEST

BALTIMORE ZOO
Druid Hill Park
Baltimore
410/396-7102 or 410/366-LION
www.baltimorezoo.org
Chartered in 1876, the Baltimore Zoo had accumulated an inventory of 215 deer, one alligator, two black bear, and one three-legged dog by 1880. These days, the 180-acre zoo's exhibits are for more diverse and include a simulated African watering hole with hippos, gazelles, and zebras; a leopard lair; a reptile house; and a nationally recognized children's zoo. The park is about 10 minutes north of the Inner Harbor off I-83. MTA sponsors a zoo shuttle from the Inner Harbor during summer months. Mon–Fri 10–4, Sat 10–8, Sun 10–5:30.

Baltimore Zoo

Baltimore Area CVA

$9 adults, $5.50 ages 62 and up and ages 2–15. ૐ (Northwest)

NAACP HEADQUARTERS
4805 Mount Hope Dr.
Baltimore
410/358-8900
The National Association for the Advancement of Colored People was founded in New York City in 1909 and moved its headquarters to this former Trappist monastery in 1986. You can tour the facility's conference room and thumb through old issues of the group's ground-breaking publication, *Crisis,* in its library. By appointment only. ૐ (Northwest)

SOUTH

FORT McHENRY NATIONAL MONUMENT AND HISTORIC SHRINE
End of E. Fort Ave.
Baltimore
410/962-4290
www.nps.gov/fomc
On September 13-14, 1814, the star-shaped garrison withstood 1,500 rounds of bombs over a 25-hour period, successfully protecting Baltimore from an invading British armada and Cockney accents for years to come. Bobbing aboard a British truce ship about a mile from the embattlement, a poet-lawyer named Francis Scott Key jotted down the first few lines of a poem he called "The Defense of Fort McHenry," later renamed "The Star-Spangled Banner" and made America's national anthem in 1931. The fort never saw action again, but it did serve as an active military post on and off for the next 100 years.

Begin your tour at the visitors center with the 16-minute film that cli-

Fort McHenry protected Baltimore from a British armada.

maxes with curtains opening to reveal the soul-stirring sight of the American flag flying high above the fort. The fort's barracks, restored to their early nineteenth-century appearance, contain artifacts—including a couple of unexploded British bombs—and descriptions of the Battle of Baltimore. Open daily, June–July 8–8, Aug 8–7, rest of the year 8–5. Fort admission $5 adults, under age 16 free; grounds and film are free. (South)

SOUTHEAST

ROBERT LONG HOUSE
812 S. Ann St.
Baltimore
410/675-6750
Baltimore's oldest urban residence has been restored to its 1765 appearance. It has also been furnished authentically to reflect the area's nautical past. Drop into the visitors center next door for the historical displays and information about Fells Point. The historic home is open by appointment. (Southeast)

SHOT TOWER
Front and Fayette Sts.
Baltimore
Built in 1828 with 1.1 million bricks, this simple hollow column was used to produce 500,000 25-pound bags of lead shot until it closed in 1892. Molten lead was poured through sieves at the top of the tower and cooled into round balls when it hit the water 234 feet below. Closed to the public. (Southeast)

STAR-SPANGLED BANNER FLAG HOUSE
844 E. Pratt St.
Baltimore
410/837-1793
With the threat of British invasion imminent, Fort McHenry's commanding officer, George Armistead, informed local seamstress Mary Pickersgill, "It is my desire to have a flag so large that the British will have no difficulty in seeing it." Pickersgill responded

The USS *Constellation* was the first tourist attraction at the Inner Harbor when it docked at Pier 1 in 1969.

accordingly and stitched a monstrous 30-by-42-foot flag, so cumbersome that she had to sew parts of it at a nearby brewery. Guided tours lead visitors through Pickersgill's circa-1793 house, filled with period objects, and the adjacent 1812 Museum, which displays battle artifacts. Tue–Sat 10–4. $4 adults, $3 seniors, $2 children. & (Southeast)

SOUTHWEST

B&O RAILROAD STATION MUSEUM
Maryland Ave. and Main St.
Ellicott City
410/461-1944
In 1831, the first train station in the nation linked downtown Baltimore with bustling Ellicott City. The stretch of track gained fame as the site of the famous race between Peter Cooper's steam-powered locomotive, Tom Thumb, and a railcar drawn by a horse. As the story goes, after an

early lead, the Tom Thumb blew a band on its boiler and never recovered. Read about the event, climb on an old caboose, watch model trains huff and puff, and mingle with costumed interpreters. Hours vary. $4 adults, $3 students, $2 children. (Southwest)

MENCKEN HOUSE
1524 W. Hollins St.
Baltimore
The "Sage of Baltimore" occupied this modest three-story row house overlooking Union Square for the majority of his 75 years. In his memoirs he writes of the house's leaky roof, inefficient Latrobe stove, and oft-flooded cellar. From his second-floor study, he coined phrases like "booboisie" to describe the ignorant upper class and defined Puritanism as "the haunting fear that someone, somewhere, may be happy." A plaque distinguishes the house, currently closed to visitors. (Southwest)

MOUNT CLARE MUSEUM HOUSE
Carroll Park
1500 Washington Blvd.
Baltimore
410/837-3262
www.erols.com/
mountclaremuseumhouse
Maryland's only existing pre–Revolutionary War mansion was built in 1760. Detailed tours describe the lives of its former occupants, Charles Carroll and his wife Margaret Tilghman, from his commode chair to her beauty secrets. Tue–Fri 11–4, Sat and Sun 1–4; last tour departs at 3:30. $5 adults, $3 seniors and students, $1 ages 5–12. (Southwest)

THOMAS ISAAC LOG CABIN
Mill Dr. and Main St.
Ellicott City
410/750-7881
Ellicott City's Main Street comprises part of the historic National Road that linked the Atlantic seaboard with the developing Ohio River Valley. This circa-1780 cabin serves as a sort of Colonial way station, offering eighteenth-century rest-stop trinkets like tavern pipes, handmade soap, and weather pots guaranteed to be more accurate than modern weather-bureau predictions. Weekends only. (Southwest)

CITY TOURS

AFRICAN AMERICAN RENAISSANCE TOURS
410/728-43837 or 410/727-0755
Baltimore's black history comes alive during these motor-coach tours covering major Afrocentric sites such as the Great Blacks in Wax Museum (see Chapter 6, Museums and Galleries), NAACP headquarters, and the Orchard Street Church, which was a stop on the Underground Railroad.

Here Lies Dorothy Parker

While visiting NAACP headquarters, notice the small shrine in a grove of white pines near the building. Beneath the brass plate lie the cremated remains of writer and satirist Dorothy Parker. How did a famous New Yorker's ashes end up in northwest Baltimore at NAACP HQ? Parker, well known for her witty one-liners—her epitaph reads "Excuse my dust"—was also a champion of equality. In her will she stipulated that her estate should go to Dr. Martin Luther King Jr., but King was assassinated less than a year later, and Parker's estate as well as her ashes were passed on to the NAACP. Her ashes were interred here in 1988, after sitting in storage at a New York law office for 20 years.

Good writing runs in the family: Francis Scott Key's great-great-nephew was none other than author F. (Frances) Scott Fitzgerald.

Tours can accommodate groups or individuals; box lunches are provided. During Black History Month (February), costumed interpreters at various stops add an authentic touch.

BALLPARK TOURS
ORIOLE PARK AT CAMDEN YARDS
333 W. Camden St.
Baltimore
410/547-6234
Take a gander at the Orioles dugout, press box, scoreboard control room, and the club-level suites, where the bigwigs sit. Tours last an hour and 15 minutes and take place daily except on days of afternoon home games. Tickets are available from the Orioles box office at the north end of the ballpark warehouse on a first-come, first-serve basis. Mon–Fri 11 a.m., noon, 1 p.m., 2 p.m.; Sat 10:30–2 on the half-hour; Sun 12:30, 1 p.m., 2 p.m., 3 p.m. Call to check tour times during the off-season. $5 adults, $4 seniors and ages 12 and under. & (Downtown)

CONCIERGE PLUS, INC.
410/580-0430
See Meg Ryan's Fells Point apartment from *Sleepless in Seattle* or the bar owned by *Homicide*'s Munch, Bayliss, and Lewis characters as well as other Charm City sites made famous (or infamous) by Tinseltown on the "Hollywood on the Harbor" tour. Or, if you'd prefer less gazing and more grazing, look into "A Taste of Little Italy," a walking tour of the historic neighborhood that includes

samples from three area restaurants. Costs range from $30 to $35 per person.

HARBOR CITY TOURS
410/254-TOUR
www.tourbaltimore.com
The wonderfully animated Frances Zeller narrates most of these tours from the helm of her distinctive blue-and-white tour bus. Daily tours last 90 minutes and cover most of the city's major sights and historically significant neighborhoods. Pickup available from major downtown hotels and outside the Light Street Pavilion. $10 per person.

STADIUM TOURS
PSINet Stadium
Baltimore
410/261-RAVE
See where sweaty football players shower, where TV journalists pontificate, and where corporate honchos entertain guests at the home of Baltimore's NFL team, the Ravens. Tickets for public tours of the Ravens' locker rooms, press box, and luxury suites are available at the main box office on the west side of the stadium. One-hour tours daily (except on game days) at 10 a.m., 11 a.m., noon, 1 p.m., and 2 p.m. $5 adults, $4 seniors and ages 12 and under. & (Southwest)

SUNRISE EXPEDITIONS
410/534-9500
www.sunrise-exp.com/kayak
See Baltimore from a different per-

spective—from a kayak. Guided tours take paddlers from Canton to the Inner Harbor and around Fort McHenry. The three-hour tours cost $45. Longer trips cover the northeast Gunpowder River delta.

ZIPPY LARSON'S SHOE LEATHER SAFARIS
410/817-4141
Baltimore's tour-guide maven offers 36 different, highly personalized tours of behind-the-scenes Baltimore, mainly for groups. Specialty excursions include themes like Baltimore row houses, ethnic neighborhoods, secret gardens, or Wallis Warfield Simpson, the Baltimore divorcée who married an English king. Meals at off-the-beaten-path restaurants are included with the variable fee.

CRUISES

CLIPPER CITY
Light Street Promenade
Baltimore
410/539-6277
www.sailingship.com
This lovely tall-ship replica is available for cruises and Inner Harbor tours. Two-hour sailing excursions Mon–Sat at noon and 3 p.m., Sun at 3 p.m. and 6 p.m. $12 adults, $2 children. Three-hour champagne brunches Sun at 11 a.m. $30 adults. Very entertaining calypso and reggae sails, with live Caribbean bands, Fri and Sat at 8 p.m. $20 adults. No sailing during winter.

HARBOR CRUISES
Light Street Promenade
Baltimore
410/727-3113 or 800/695-BOAT

www.harborcruises.com
The *Bay Lady* and *Lady Baltimore*, two modern "mini-cruise ships" with climate-controlled and open-air decks, host lunch, dinner, and moonlight cruises year-round, with meals typical of dinner-theater fare. The Friday night crab feast, held from June through September, is a popular option. Prices range from $21.95 per person for moonlight cruises to $52 per person for Saturday dinner excursions. Special kids' cruises are held Fridays May through August. &

MINNIE V
Harborplace Amphitheater
Baltimore
410/685-3750, ext. 372
www.mdhs.org
The *Minnie V* was used for dredging oysters as recently as 1995. Now this sturdy skipjack, built in 1906, hosts summertime lecture cruises on topics that range from the Battle of Baltimore to the steamboating history of the Chesapeake. Two-hour tours June–Sept Tue and Thu 6 p.m. $20 adults, $19 seniors, $18 members of Maryland Historical Society. Light refreshments are included. Not recommended for toddlers.

SCHOONER NIGHTHAWK CRUISES
1715 Thames St.
Baltimore
410/327-SAIL
This restored schooner built in 1880 takes passengers on several kinds of cruises: a buffet moonlight sail with music, a murder-mystery cruise, and a crab-feast sail. Prices range from $32.50 to $45 per person, depending on the cruise. Call for a schedule and to make reservations.

6

MUSEUMS AND GALLERIES

Baltimoreans are pack rats by nature. Perhaps it's our allegiance to the past, or maybe our well-reported fear of change, that makes us such expert gatherers. Whatever the underlying cause, all this hoarding makes for some fine and funky museums.

In the early twentieth century, local art collectors Henry Walters and his father, William, as well as spinster sisters Etta and Claribel Cone, amassed fantastic holdings of art; when they died, they left Baltimore with the foundations for two of today's most-respected art museums in the country, the Walters Art Gallery and the Baltimore Museum of Art. Other local collectors haven't had such grandiose goals in mind. Consequently, Baltimore also has museums devoted to incandescent light bulbs, World War II electronics, Star Wars memorabilia, and tattoos.

On the gallery front, blue-collar Baltimore is transforming into—gasp!—a bit of an art town. While it may not resemble New York's SoHo just yet, a critical artistic mass is building. Artists have discovered cheap housing in several of Baltimore's traditionally working-class neighborhoods—Hampden and Highlandtown—and several of the city's abandoned mills and warehouses have been converted into affordable studio space. Nonprofit arts organizations such as the Fells Point Creative Alliance promote exhibits in local galleries and coffee shops, nurturing the ever-expanding art scene.

ART MUSEUMS

AMERICAN VISIONARY ART MUSEUM
800 Key Hwy.
Baltimore

410/244-1900
www.avam.org
The only art museum in the country dedicated entirely to "outsider art" (works created by untrained artists), AVAM's rotating exhibits showcase

what overly creative people can do with too much time on their hands. Recent exhibits have included a bust of Isaac Stern done completely in match sticks and a 1965 Thunderbird covered entirely in jewels. Perhaps even more fascinating than the art itself—which often varies in quality—is the detailed descriptions of the artists' often tragic lives. Appropriately, the museum's eclectic restaurant, Joy America Café, serves up some of the most visionary cooking in Baltimore (see Chapter 4, Where to Eat). Tue–Sun 10–6. $6 adults, $4 seniors and students. ♿ (South)

BALTIMORE MUSEUM OF ART
Art Museum Dr. at N. Charles St.
Baltimore
410/396-7100
www.bma.org

Quite honestly, the BMA should get even more national attention than it currently receives. It displays some incredible pieces of modern and contemporary art: the country's largest collection of paintings by Matisse, 17 canvases by Andy Warhol, and walls of work by Paul Cézanne, Pablo Picasso, and Vincent van Gogh. The museum also has a fine store, a lovely outdoor sculpture garden, and the handsome Gertrude's (see Chapter 4, Where to Eat). Wed–Fri 11–5, Sat and Sun 11–6. $6 adults, $4 seniors and students, under age 18 free; Thu free to all. ♿ (North)

CONTEMPORARY MUSEUM
100 W. Centre St.
Baltimore
410/783-5720
www.contemporary.org

After setting up temporary exhibits in spaces such as Greyhound bus stations and office-building lobbies, the Contemporary Museum now occupies a permanent home, a block west of the Walters Art Gallery. The museum shows eclectic modern art in an industrial space of stark white walls, exposed water pipes, and a concrete floor. Exhibits change every six months or so and feature a provocative mix of regional, national, and international artists in diverse media. Tues-Fri 10-5, Sat-Sun 11-5. Free, suggested donation. ♿ (Downtown)

WALTERS ART GALLERY
600 N. Charles St.
Baltimore
410/547-9000
www.thewalters.org

Examples from 50 centuries of human creativity are crammed into this hulking marble building in Mount Vernon. Bequeathed to the city "for the benefit of the people" by railroad magnate Henry Walters, the elegant collections of Asian art, illuminated manuscripts, arms and armor, and eighteenth- and nineteenth-century paintings by European masters are displayed in fittingly opulent surroundings. Abbreviated exhibits (and reduced admission) are in effect as the museum undergoes an $18.5 million renovation, to be completed by spring 2001. Tue–Fri 10–4, Sat and Sun 11–5, first Thu 10–8. $5 adults, $3 seniors and ages 18–25, $1 ages 6–17; free Sat 11–1. ♿ (Downtown)

SCIENCE AND HISTORY MUSEUMS

B&O RAILROAD MUSEUM
901 W. Pratt St.
Baltimore
410/752-2490
www.borail.org

Ground-zero for railroading buffs, this

DOWNTOWN MUSEUMS

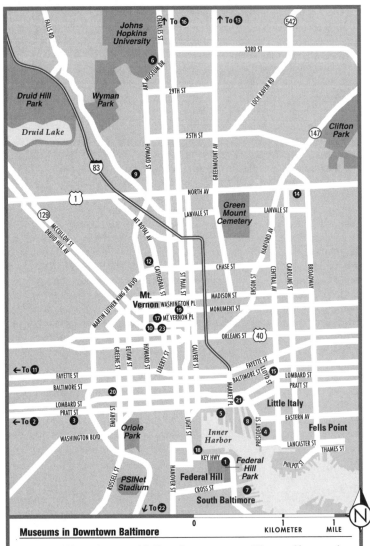

Museums in Downtown Baltimore

1 American Visionary Art Museum
2 B&O Railroad Museum
3 Babe Ruth Museum and Birthplace
4 Baltimore Civil War Museum
5 Baltimore Maritime Museums
6 Baltimore Museum of Art
7 Baltimore Museum of Industry
8 Baltimore Museum of Public Works

9 Baltimore Streetcar Museum
10 Contemporary Art Museum
11 Edgar Allan Poe House and Museum
12 Eubie Blake Cultural Center
13 Fire Museum of Maryland
14 Great Blacks in Wax Museum
15 Jewish Museum of Maryland

16 Lacrosse Museum and National Hall of Fame
17 Maryland Historical Society
18 Maryland Science Center
19 Mount Vernon Museum of Incandescent Lighting
20 National Musem of Dentisy
21 Port Discovery Children's Museum
22 Star Toys Museum
23 Walters Art Gallery

When Jack Dunn signed George Herman Ruth to a $600 contract to pitch for the Baltimore Orioles of the International League, he also became the 19-year-old's legal guardian. The Baltimore newspapers then dubbed Ruth "Jack Dunn's Baby," which was shortened to his famous nickname, Babe.

museum is a fantastic 22-sided round-house that once served as the B&O line's first station and principal maintenance facility. Located a mile west of the Inner Harbor (don't walk it), the museum displays nearly 200 pieces of equipment, including a 320-ton, 7,500-horsepower Allegheny—the strongest and heaviest locomotive ever built. Open daily 10–5. $6.50 adults, $5.50 seniors, $4 children. & (Southwest)

BALTIMORE CIVIL WAR MUSEUM
601 S. President St.
Baltimore
410/385-5188
The first casualties of the Civil War occurred in Baltimore—the first of many stories related in this museum located in the renovated head house of historic President Street Depot. There's not much to touch or do here (read: the kids will be bored), but the extensive text panels provide a fascinating account of Baltimore during the Civil War, including the roles of African American soldiers and the historic train station itself. Open daily 10–5; winter hours vary. $2 adults, $1 children. & (Southeast)

BALTIMORE MARITIME MUSEUMS
E. Pratt St. (Ticket booth at Pier 3)
Baltimore
410/396-3453
This is really four museums in one:

the submarine U.S.S. *Torsk,* which sank the last two enemy warships in World War II; the coast guard cutter *Taney,* the last surviving ship that fired on Japanese warplanes at Pearl Harbor; the lightship *Chesapeake,* a historic bay patrol boat; and the bright red Seven-Foot Knoll Lighthouse, which marked the entrance to Baltimore Harbor for 135 years, until it was moved to dry land in 1986. Open daily 10–6. $5.50 adults, $3 seniors and children. (Downtown)

BALTIMORE MUSEUM OF INDUSTRY
1415 Key Hwy.
Baltimore
410/727-4808
www.thebmi.org
Did you know that Baltimore was home to the country's first umbrella factory? You will after visiting this fascinating museum, preserved in an ancient oyster-packing plant. Much of the antiquated equipment here still works, and friendly tour guides are happy to demonstrate the rickety printing presses, die-cutters, and oyster-canning machines for you. On the way to Fort McHenry and accessible via water taxi. Memorial Day–Labor Day Tue–Fri and Sun noon–5, Sat 10–5; rest of the year Wed 7–9, Thu–Fri and Sun noon–5, Sat 10–5. $3.50 adults, $2.50 seniors and students. & (South)

Baltimore's Finest Fine Arts Events

- **Artscape:** *One of the country's largest celebrations of fine, performing, literary, and culinary arts. The weekend festival features loads of live music and tentfuls of artists and artisans selling their works. Held every July.*
- **FreeStyle:** *A chance for art enthusiasts to mix and mingle, eat some finger foods, sip a little vino, and check out what's on the walls at the Baltimore Museum of Art for free. There's often live music and kids' activities. First Thursday of every month from 5 to 9 p.m.*
- **Out of Order:** *Maryland Art Place sponsors this offbeat exhibition during which anyone can hang their art and price it as they please. Yes, you'll see some real ugly stuff but some real bargains, too. Held in May.*
- **Open Studio Tour:** *Every May, participating Baltimore artists open their studios to the public for two days, with most displayed works for sale. Sponsored by School 33 Art Center, where you can pick up a tour map to the studios.*

BALTIMORE MUSEUM OF PUBLIC WORKS
751 Eastern Ave.
Baltimore
410/396-5565
When half of this sewage pumping station was converted into a museum in 1982, it was the first of its kind to showcase the often-ignored world of city infrastructure. The somewhat dated-looking exhibits depict "Baltimore Before Indoor Plumbing," "Tunneling Beneath Baltimore," and an interesting historical film, *Public Works and You.* Unfortunately, the most fascinating section—the massive pumping station itself—is off-limits to visitors. Make sure to read the rest room walls sprinkled with trivia about Baltimore's public works: Did you know there are 16,000 manhole covers in Baltimore? Tue–Sat 10–4. $4 adults, $2 children. ♿ (Downtown)

BALTIMORE STREETCAR MUSEUM
1905 Falls Rd.
Baltimore
410/547-0264
www.baltimoremd.com/streetcar
Like train tracks and tin cans, streetcars are an important part of Baltimore's past. These elegant beauties,

Great Blacks in Wax Museum

first pulled by horse and then powered by electricity, were the mainstays of public transportation up to 1963. You can go for a ride in a vintage car or check out a dozen of them in various stages of renovation at the museum's carhouse. June–Oct Sat and Sun noon–5, Nov–Jan Sat noon–5. $5 adults, $2.50 seniors and children 4–11; $15 maximum family charge. (North)

FIRE MUSEUM OF MARYLAND
1301 York Rd.
Lutherville
410/321-7500
www.firemuseummd.org
Seventy blocks of Baltimore City burned to the ground in 1904; as a result, Marylanders tend to take their fires—and fire engines—seriously. At this suburban museum, you'll see plenty of snappy red hand-drawn, horse-drawn, and self-powered firefighting equipment dating back to colonial times. May, Sept–Nov Sat 11–4; June–Aug Tue–Sat 11–4. $5 adults, $4 seniors and firefighters, $3

children. (North)

GREAT BLACKS IN WAX MUSEUM
1601-03 E. North Ave.
Baltimore
410/563-3404
www.gbiw.org
The name of this unique museum succinctly describes what's on display: 120 wax recreations of important men and women from ancient Africa to contemporary times. Most interesting are the stories behind the black leaders you didn't learn about in school, such as Henry "Box" Brown, a slave who shipped himself to the North—and freedom—in a wooden box. Tue–Sat 9–6, Sun 12–6. $5.75 adults, $5.25 seniors and college students, $3.75 ages 12–17, $3.25 ages 2–11. (Northeast)

JEWISH MUSEUM OF MARYLAND
15 Lloyd St.
Baltimore
410/732-6451
www.jhsm.org
Tours of two historic synagogues are

Top 10 Works of Art and Architecture in Baltimore

By John Dorsey, former art critic for the *Baltimore Sun.*

ART

1. **Buddha**, China, c. A.D. 690, 41.5 inches high, painted lacquer over wood. This is the oldest Chinese Buddha of painted lacquer over wood known to have survived; but it is compelling less for its uniqueness than for its combination of austere grandeur and transfixing serenity. The Walters Art Gallery, 600 N. Charles St., 410/547-9000.

2. **The Blue Nude (Souvenir de Biskra)**, Henri Matisse, 1907, 36 1/4 by 55 1/4 inches. An icon of modernism and one of Matisse's greatest works, this monumental figure rules the Cone Collection's Matisse gallery with a presence at once majestic, exotic, voluptuous, and challenging. The Baltimore Museum of Art, 10 Art Museum Dr., 410/396-7100.

3. **Head of a Man from a Funerary Relief**, Greece, c. 325–317 B.C., 12 11/16 inches high, marble. With furrowed brow, mouth open as if about to speak, and face framed by swirling hair and beard, this dynamic, expressive head from the very beginning of the Hellenistic period is a fine example of the glory that was Greek art. The Walters Art Gallery.

4. **Lady's Cabinet Dressing Table**, attributed to William Camp (flourished 1801–1822), Baltimore, 1800–1810. A work of the highest style, based on a design by the renowned English cabinetmaker Thomas Sheraton, this is probably the greatest piece of furniture ever made in Maryland; and with its urn, eagle swag, painted glass, and inlaid wood decoration, it is a virtual catalog of the Baltimore Federal period furniture-maker's art. The Maryland Historical Society, 201 W. Monument St., 410/685-3750.

5. **Rinaldo and Armida**, Anthony van Dyck, 1629. Based on a popular epic of its time, this superbly colorful and dramatic Baroque painting has been called van Dyck's finest allegorical work; it also has a distinguished history—it was commissioned for King Charles I of England and after his death spent 250 years in the collection of the Dukes of Newcastle before emigrating to America. The Baltimore Museum of Art.

ARCHITECTURE

6. **Basilica of the Assumption** (former Roman Catholic Cathedral of Baltimore), Benjamin H. Latrobe, 1805–1821. The first Roman Catholic cathedral in the United States, massive and monumental outside, all fluid floating space inside, this is Baltimore's greatest work of architecture, the extant masterpiece of one of the foremost architects to work in America, and one of the world's great neoclassical buildings; eminent British architectural historian Nikolaus Pevsner called it "North America's most beautiful church." Cathedral and Mulberry Sts.

7. **Homewood**, Charles Carroll of Homewood, 1801 and after. In the early nineteenth century the city was ringed by beautiful Federal period country houses, of which this is the great survivor; its lyrical facade leads to an interior rich with architectural decoration, lovingly restored and open to the public. Charles and 34th Sts., 410/516-5589.

8. **Mount Vernon Place**, various architects, nineteenth century. A century ago Henry James called this the "parlour" of Baltimore, and it still is; the cruciform park around Robert Mills's Washington Monument remains one of the finest urban spaces in the nation, the four parks flanked by major cultural institutions and much fine architecture (including the spectacular interior of the Peabody Library, open to the public). But above all it is the human scale that makes Mount Vernon Place so satisfying and that reflects so well the comfortable spirit of its provincial city. Charles and Monument Sts.

9. **Mercantile Safe Deposit and Trust Company Building**, Wyatt and Sperry, 1886. This fine Richardsonian Romanesque building has fortresslike walls, dramatic arched windows, excellent brickwork and much carved-stone detail; in its time it was hailed in a national architectural magazine as "the most admirable of the commercial buildings in Baltimore" and much the same could be said today. Calvert and Redwood Sts.

10. **Highfield House Condominium**, Ludwig Mies van der Rohe, 1964. One of Baltimore's two buildings by the great German architect (the other one is One Charles Center), the Highfield is distinguished by the typically Miesian overall simplicity of its tower set on a platform, by a horizontality that reflects consciousness of its residential neighborhood, and by aesthetically satisfying details such as the beautiful proportions of its windows. 4000 N. Charles St.

the highlights of this museum, located in what used to be the heart of the city's Jewish population. The Lloyd Street Synagogue—the third-oldest temple in the country—was built in 1845 and looks more like a bank or courthouse than a place of worship. The B'nai Israel Synagogue was built in 1876 and still operates as Baltimore's oldest. Be sure to explore the remains of neighboring Corned Beef Row (see Attman's Deli in Chapter 4, Where to Eat) after your visit. Tue–Thu, Sun noon–4. $4 adults, $2 children. (Southeast)

MARYLAND HISTORICAL SOCIETY
201 W. Monument St.
Baltimore
410/685-3750
www.mdhs.org
Here's a sampling of things you'll find in "Maryland's attic": a Revolutionary War general's tattered uniform, Cal Ripken's baseball bat, and Francis Scott Key's handwritten, rough draft of "The Star-Spangled Banner," complete with original gaffes like *"through* the dawn's early light." If you're looking to get a grip on what makes Maryland Maryland, spend some time here. Tue–Fri 10–5, Sat 9–5, Sun 11–5. $4 adults, $3 seniors and students, under 12 free; Sun free to all. (Downtown)

MARYLAND SCIENCE CENTER
601 Light St.
Baltimore
410/685-5225
www.mdsci.org
Recall all those long-forgotten scientific concepts at this museum containing a planetarium and three-floors of hands-on exhibits covering space, health, energy, and the Chesapeake Bay. The real draw is the five-story IMAX movie theater and its huge

films that stimulate your mind while unnerving your stomach. Summer Mon–Thu 9:30–5, Fri–Sun 9:30–8; rest of the year Mon–Fri 10–5, Sat and Sun 10–6. $10.50 adults, $9 seniors and ages 13-18, $7.50 ages 4-12. &. (Downtown)

OTHER MUSEUMS

BABE RUTH MUSEUM AND BIRTHPLACE
216 Emory St.
Baltimore
410/727-1539
George Herman "Babe" Ruth was born in this redbrick row house, the home of his maternal grandparents, on February 6, 1895. The museum preserves memorabilia from Ruth's early days, when he pitched for the Baltimore Orioles, to the slugger's glory days with the Yankees. The museum also contains artifacts of Oriole greats Cal Ripken Jr., Eddie Murray, Frank Robinson, and others. Allow an hour to view the collection. Open Apr–Oct daily 10–5 (10–7 during Ori-

Babe Ruth

TIP

If you're interested in seeing more of Baltimore's maritime sights, buy a National Historic Seaport pass, one ticket that gets you into 15 of Baltimore's maritime-related sights, including the Museum of Industry, Fort McHenry, USS *Constellation,* and all the Baltimore Maritime Museum vessels, as well as providing free transportation via the Harbor Shuttle. Tickets are valid for an entire year and can be purchased at the Baltimore Maritime Museum's ticket booth at Pier 3, at the Historic Seaport ticket kiosk along the Light Street promenade, or by calling 410/396-3453. $15.75 adults, $10.50 ages 6–12, $2 age 5 and under.

oles home games), rest of year 10–4. $6 adults, $4 seniors, $3 ages 5–16. (Downtown)

BALTIMORE TATTOO MUSEUM
1534 Eastern Ave.
Baltimore
410/522-5800
www.baltimoretattoomuseum.com
Anyone who has a tattoo or ever thought about getting one will be intrigued by this small Fells Point museum. Its walls are covered with the framed designs of well-known tattoo artists such as Charles Wagner and Norman Keith Collins, a.k.a. "Sailor Jerry," who attained legendary status from his Honolulu tattoo parlor during the 1960s and '70s. Tattoo memorabilia and early patents for tattoo machines, including two submitted by Thomas Edison, are also on display. If you'd like to go home with a souvenir, pick out a design and step into one of the four tattoo studios. Daily noon to 9, $1. ♿ (Southeast)

EDGAR ALLAN POE HOUSE AND MUSEUM
203 N. Amity St.
Baltimore
410/396-7932
Poe occupied this tiny three-story brick home—the "little house on the lovely street with the lovely name," as he called it—from 1832 to 1835 with his grandmother, aunt, and cousin Virginia, whom he later married. Among the sparse exhibits are the author's writing desk, a creepy por-

TIP

If you want to check out an IMAX movie without fiddling with the hands-on exhibits at the Maryland Science Center, go to the NightMax program, a twin bill—or even triple bill—of larger-than-life movies held every Friday and Saturday evening.

trait of his wife (painted after she had died), and, of course, a stuffed raven. The house, which was considered to be in the country when Poe lived there, is now engulfed by the Poe Homes, a public housing project. Apr–July and Oct–Dec Wed–Sat noon–3:45; Aug and Sept Sat only noon–3:45. $3. (Southwest)

EUBIE BLAKE CULTURAL CENTER
847 N. Howard St.
Baltimore
410/625-3113
The great entertainer, famous for catchy Jazz Age hits like "I'm Just Wild About Harry," was born in east Baltimore in 1883. Memorabilia, including posters, playbills, and Blake's personal artifacts, fill this museum along Antique Row (See Chapter 9, Shopping). Additional items on display highlight the careers of more jazz artists with Baltimore roots: Billie Holiday, Cab Calloway, Chick Webb, and others. The center also hosts jazz workshops for professional musicians and aspiring students wishing to hone their chops. Call for hours and admission prices. (Downtown)

LACROSSE MUSEUM AND
NATIONAL HALL OF FAME
113 W. University Pkwy.
Baltimore
410/235-6882
www.lacrosse.org

Holy ground for lacrosse fans, this museum chronicles 360 years of the sport's history through videos, photographs, art, and trophies. It's located next to Hopkins's Homewood Field—site of some significant lacrosse history in its own right. Mon–Sat 10–3. $3 adults, $2 ages 6–16. & (North)

MOUNT VERNON MUSEUM OF
INCANDESCENT LIGHTING
717 Washington Place
Baltimore
410/752-8586
Seventy years ago, museum curator Hugh Francis Hicks had the bright idea to start saving lightbulbs. Now choice samples of his 60,000 bulbs are displayed in the two-room, one-corridor museum. Interesting specimens include a Betty Boop bulb, a model boat in a 10-inch bulb, and the world's largest and smallest incandescent lights. Open first Thu of every month 4–8 and by appointment. Donations accepted. (Downtown)

NATIONAL MUSEUM OF
DENTISTRY
31 S. Greene St
Baltimore
410/706-0600
www.dentalmuseum.
umaryland.edu
Honestly, a trip to the dental museum is far more fun than a trip to the den-

tist's office. Here you can match celebrities with their smiles and watch classic commercials for toothpaste and mouthwash on the "Tooth Jukebox." The museum's "teeth de résistance" are several sets of George Washington's false choppers. (FYI: They're not made of wood.) Wed–Sat 10–4, Sun 1–4. $4.50 adults, $2.50 seniors, students, and children. ♿ (Downtown)

PORT DISCOVERY CHILDREN'S MUSEUM
35 Market Pl.
Baltimore
410/727-8120

Designed with help from the playful folks at Walt Disney, Port Discovery contains three floors of exhibits with an apocalyptic-looking jungle gym made from corrugated steel, chain-link fence, ropes, and wood as its centerpiece. The kids will love it, and you'll spend the after-noon trying to track them down on the enormous structure. Other exhibits include a simulated trip back to ancient Egypt, Miss Perception's Mystery House, and a creative play area for kids under 5. Tue-Sun 10–5:30. $10 adults, $7.50 ages 3–12. ♿ (Downtown)

STAR TOYS MUSEUM
811 Camp Meade Rd.
Linthicum
410/859-1261
www.meerkatmeade.com

Holy Yoda! Inside this nondescript two-story home located near BWI Airport lies a treasure trove of *Star Wars* memorabilia: "Feel the Force" boxer shorts, *Star Wars* bed sheets, a Chewbacca Frisbee, a Luke Skywalker toothbrush, and 5,000 more pieces of *Star Wars* bric-a-brac. And you think *you're* a *Star Wars* fan. Open by appointment only. Free. (Southwest)

The Collecting Cones

Baltimoreans Claribel and Etta Cone were two spinster sisters who palled around with early twentieth-century intellectuals like one-time Baltimore resident Gertrude Stein and regularly purchased works by emerging painters with names like Picasso, van Gogh, and Matisse. Before the elder sister, Claribel, died in 1929, she stipulated to her sister Etta that, "in the event the spirit for modern art in Baltimore becomes improved," the collection should be donated to the Baltimore Museum of Art. In 1949, despite objections from New York's Museum of Modern Art that the collection was "too good for Baltimore," Etta bequeathed the sisters' gallery to their hometown museum. Today, the "Cone Collection" remains the most memorable part of a visit to the BMA.

GALLERIES

C. GRIMALDIS GALLERY
1716 N. Charles St.
Baltimore
410/539-1080
One of Baltimore's best-known galleries for abstract art showcases work primarily by contemporary American artists. You'll find work here in all media. Artists are shown separately, and exhibitions change every month. Tue–Sun. (Downtown)

GOMEZ GALLERY
3600 Clipper Mill Rd.
Baltimore
410/662-9510
www.gomezgallery.com
Walter Gomez says he likes art that "pushes the boundaries," and most of the gallery's shows do just that. Gomez specializes in bringing the best of "midlevel" international artists to Baltimore, as well as exposing up-and-coming artists from the city's artistic community. He was the first to exhibit the work of renowned local photographer Con-

nie Imboden. The gallery is located in the refurbished Meadow Mill complex, adjacent to the Woodberry light-rail stop. Duck into the adjacent Gallery Café, and taste its "global cuisine." ♿ (Northwest)

MARYLAND ART PLACE
218 W. Saratoga St.
Baltimore
410/962-8565
www.MDartplace.org
A valuable resource for Baltimore's artists, MAP doesn't just show the work of emerging Baltimore artists, it also showcases performance art, most notably its "14 Karat Cabaret," a bimonthly series sure to expand your own ideas regarding the definition of art. Tue–Sat 11–5. Gallery admission free; event prices vary. (Downtown)

MEYERHOFF GALLERY AT MICA
Fox Building
1301 Mount Royal Ave.
Baltimore
410/225-2280
The exhibition center of the Maryland Institute College of Art—the oldest

School 33 Art Center

© Jon Goell

TRIVIA

The first passenger train in the United States departed from Mount Clare (current site of the B&O Railroad Museum) on Jauary 7, 1830, a one-and-a-quarter-mile jaunt to the Carrollton Viaduct. The first telegraph message was sent on wires along the B&O right-of-way from Mount Clare to Washington in 1844. The missive: "What hath God wrought?" The *Sunpapers* buried the historic event on page 2 under "Local Matters."

four-year art college in the country—features ever-changing exhibits mainly by student, faculty, and alumni artists. Think of it as an opportunity to see what the artists of tomorrow are creating today. Mon–Wed and Sat 10–5, Thu–Fri 10–9, Sun 12–5. ♿ (Downtown)

SCHOOL 33 ART CENTER
1427 Light St.

Baltimore
410/396-4641
This gallery, housed in an old Baltimore City public school, showcases 18 exhibitions per year by mainly local and regional artists. The school is also a great place to take classes in photography, ceramics, drawing, and painting, and it hosts several community arts events yearly. (South)

Six Flags America

7

KIDS' STUFF

The kids won't be bored in Baltimore. With several museums geared especially for youngsters, a first-rate aquarium, and an excellent zoo, Baltimore is very much a kid-pleasing town. Most of the city's family-friendly activities cluster around the Inner Harbor and are accessible via the brick promenade or by taking the Water Taxi or Harbor Shuttle—fun treats in themselves.

ANIMALS, ANIMALS

BALTIMORE ZOO
Druid Hill Park
Baltimore
410/366-LION
As if a trip to the zoo weren't kid-friendly enough, the Baltimore Zoo goes one step further by designing a special area just for the little ones. Kids get to climb inside turtle shells, help groom goats, explore a spooky bat cave, and walk underneath a glass-bottomed river otters' den. Between Thanksgiving and early January, ZooLights illuminates the night with thousands of holiday lights and glowing animal sculptures. And during the last two weeks in October, ZooBoo! introduces youngsters to snakes, spiders,

toads, and other scary critters. Open daily 10–4, with extended hours in the summer after Memorial Day. $9.00 adults, $5.50 seniors, $5.50 ages 2-15. &. (Northwest)

NATIONAL AQUARIUM IN BALTIMORE
Pier 3, 501 E. Pratt St.
Baltimore
410/576-3800
www.aqua.org
Five levels of fish and a dolphin show that rivals anything at Sea World: What more could a kid want? There's also a Children's Cove exhibit with horseshoe crabs, sea stars, and a variety of other animals that young marine biologists can investigate and, in some cases, touch. Be sure to check out feeding time at

the simulated Atlantic coral reef on Level 4. July, Aug daily 9–8; Sept, Oct, Mar, June Sat–Tue 9–5, Fri 9–8; Nov–Feb Sat–Thu 10–5, Fri 10–8. $14 adults, $10.50 seniors, $7.50 ages 3–11, $5 after 5 on Fri Nov–Mar. & (Downtown)

MUSEUMS AND LIBRARIES

B&O RAILROAD MUSEUM
901 W. Pratt St.
Baltimore
410/752-2490
www.borail.org
Little engineers and train-conductor wannabes will love climbing aboard several of the huge engines and coaches at this expansive museum. They'll probably be equally fascinated by the tiny trains, houses, and streetscapes of a vintage model-train set that stretches 40 feet. On weekends, the Mount Clare Express transports visitors a mile or so to the spot where the first stone was laid for the B&O line. Open daily 10–5.

$6.50 adults, $5.50 seniors, $4 children. & (Southwest)

BALTIMORE MARITIME MUSEUMS
E. Pratt St. (Ticket booth at Pier 3)
Baltimore
410/396-3453
Give the kids a taste of the seafaring life on one of three historic vessels. A visit to the shark-faced World War II submarine USS *Torsk* might inspire junior to enlist right away. The coast guard cutter *Taney,* the last ship still afloat that saw action in Pearl Harbor, has several decks worth exploring. The lightship *Chesapeake* gives kids a look at life on a bay patrol boat. Open daily 10–6. $5.50 adults, $3 seniors and children. (Downtown)

BALTIMORE MUSEUM OF INDUSTRY
1415 Key Hwy.
Baltimore
410/727-4808
www.thebmi.org
Baltimore magazine justly named this

National Aquarium in Baltimore, p. 122

Baltimore Area CVA

At the National Aquarium's ray exhibit, say hello to the giant hawksbill sea turtle nicknamed PITA, which aquarium staff will tell you stands for Pain in the Anatomy—or something like that.

place "best hands-on kids museum" a few years back. There may be no other museum in the country where a kid can get a feel for old-time industry by shucking oysters, putting together a cardboard truck on an assembly line, or cranking out a few handbills on a job press from 1880. Best of all, it's fun for adults, too. Memorial Day–Labor Day Tue–Fri and Sun noon–5, Sat 10–5; rest of the year Wed 7–9, Thu–Fri and Sun noon–5, Sat 10–5. $3.50 adults, $2.50 seniors and students. & (South)

BWI AIRPORT OBSERVATION GALLERY
BWI Airport
Linthicum
410/859-7033

Watch planes land and take off, pretend to control a jet from a mock cockpit, and check out a trail of airplane parts from various Boeing jets—landing gear, a nose section, an engine, and other scraps. Then browse the Smithsonian Museum Shop, a satellite store of the National Air and Space Museum in Washington. Open daily 8–9. Free. & (Southwest)

ENOCH PRATT FREE LIBRARY
Kids' Room
400 Cathedral St.
Baltimore
410/396-5402
www.pratt.md.lib.us

Enoch Pratt Library's kids' room has thousands of books, naturally, but also a couple of stuffed dinosaurs and a beautiful ceramic goldfish pond that's been a favorite of local kids for generations. Call to find out about weekly readings and special programs. Free. & (Downtown)

FIRE MUSEUM OF MARYLAND
1301 York Rd.
Lutherville
410/321-7500
www.firemuseummd.org

Kids are allowed to climb aboard only one of the many well-preserved vintage fire engines at this suburban museum, but they can try on an entire pint-sized wardrobe of fire-fighting uniforms. Thursdays and Saturdays around noon kids practice escaping from the "fire safety house." May, Sept–Nov Sat 11–4, June–Aug Tue–Sat 11–4. $5 adults, $4 seniors and firefighters, $3 children. & (North)

FORT McHENRY
East End of Fort Ave.
Baltimore
410/962-4290

Plenty of hidden nooks and musty ammunition shelters will keep the kids entertained—and the cannons look pretty cool, too. The grounds outside the fort make for good picnicking and kite-flying. June–July daily 8–8, Aug daily 8–7, rest of the year daily 8–5. Fort admission $5 adults, under age 16 free; touring grounds and visitors center free. & (South)

MARYLAND SCIENCE CENTER
601 Light St.
Baltimore
410/685-5225
www.mdsci.org

Sure, the kids will think they're having fun, but actually they'll be learning about ecology, astrophysics, and paleontology. That's the idea behind this hands-on science museum. It also has a planetarium to interest budding astronomers, an IMAX theater, and the K.I.D.S. Room, specially designed for youngsters ages three to seven. A Friendly's Express within the museum serves up kid-friendly burgers, chicken tenders, and ice cream. Summer Mon–Thu 9:30–5, Fri–Sun 9:30–8; rest of the year Mon–Fri 10–5, Sat and Sun 10–6. $10.50 adults, $9 seniors and ages 13-18, $7.50 ages 4–12. ﹩ (Downtown)

PORT DISCOVERY
35 Market Pl.
Baltimore
410/727-8120

Let them loose for a while in this children's museum and they'll never want to leave. Besides the three-story, post-industrial jungle gym that serves as the museum's center-piece, kids can explore sarcophagi and mummies in the Indiana Jones–like ancient Egypt exhibit, solve a whodunit—and crawl through a 22-foot kitchen drain pipe—in Miss Perception's Mystery House, and get crafty with safe power and hand tools at the R&D Dream Lab. Although the museum has play space designed for children under five, kids between 6 and 12 will get the most out of the Port Discovery experience. Open daily 10–5. $10 adults, $7.50 ages 3–12. ﹩ (Downtown)

Jungle gym at Port Discovery

WASHINGTON MONUMENT
Mount Vernon Pl. and
Washington Pl.
N. Charles St.
Baltimore
410/396-0929

For whatever reason, kids seem to enjoy climbing winding staircases that lead to a pinnacle of some sort. They'll get that challenge here on the Washington Monument's 228 steps leading to expansive views of Baltimore's downtown. Make sure the kids are up to the climb—piggyback rides or babes in arms would be a struggle for adults. $1 donation requested. Wed–Sun 10–4, first Thu of each month 10–8. (Downtown)

STORES KIDS LOVE

ALL WOUND UP
Light Street Pavilion
Baltimore
410/783-7842

Oinking pigs, barking dogs, flying birds: Wind them up and watch

Looking for a unique and educational toy or gift? Try one of the Inner Harbor's museum gift shops, such as the Imagination Factory: The World's Best Kids' Store in the Port Discovery Children's Museum, the Science Store in the Maryland Science Center, or the Aqua Shop in the National Aquarium. You can browse any of them without paying museum admission.

them go nuts at this appropriately named store. Kids can try just about every windup gizmo in this store, before they—or you—buy. (Downtown)

DAPY
Pratt Street Pavilion
Baltimore
410/539-6771
At this wonderland of pop culture, you can amuse yourself with Etch-a-Sketch on a key chain, Magic 8-Balls, inflatable pink flamingoes, and merchandise from the latest Hollywood blockbuster. Lots of Elvis, James Dean, and Marilyn Monroe tchotchkes for the more mature "kids," too. (Downtown)

DISCOVERY CHANNEL STORE
Light Street Pavilion
Baltimore
410/576-0909
It's the popular educational television network come to life—and everything's for sale! Real fossils from 65 million years ago, telescopes, African artifacts, plastic bugs, model airplanes, and cool rocks. More-adult selections include everything from World War II leather bomber jackets to scented candles to books on feng shui. (Downtown)

FORGET-ME-NOT FACTORY
8044 Main St.
Ellicott City
410/465-7355
You'll be able to identify this shop by the proprietor's husband and Ellicott City denizen Barry Gibson, who usually stands outside, dressed in whatever costume is appropriate for the season, blowing giant bubbles and passing out "fairy dust" to kids. During the December holidays, he might be Father Winter; near Valentine's Day, he's Cupid. (No need to tell the kids that during the rest of the week he runs a dental laboratory.) Inside the store, you'll find three levels of dolls, games, and fairyland paraphernalia straight from a C. S. Lewis book. (Southwest)

THE FUDGERY
Light Street Pavilion
Baltimore
410/539-5260
It's not enough that they have delicious fudge in flavors ranging from chocolate-caramel-nut to heavenly hash; the talented teenagers who work here also put on a very entertaining show as they bake the stuff. You haven't experienced proper fudge-making until you've seen it blended to a Stevie Wonder–

inspired chorus of "Isn't Fudge Lovely?" Shows occur spontaneously each day, after which the audience gets to sample the goods. (Downtown)

GRRREAT BEARS AND CHILDHOOD DELIGHTS
1643 Thames St.
Baltimore
410/276-4429
If this store contained real animals instead of stuffed, the Humane Society would have a field day. The living conditions are deplorable: shelf after shelf of animals stacked on top of one another. Dogs cohabit with cats, bears next to sheep, mice on top of elephants, and Beanie Babies everywhere. Elsewhere in the beastly chaos are books (not all about animals) and other "childhood delights." Bring the kids to this fantastic menagerie and you won't have to take them to the zoo. (Southeast)

KEN-ZO'S YOGI MAGIC MART
1025 S. Charles St.
Baltimore
410/727-5811
A 15-minute walk from the Inner Harbor, Ken-Zo's is an old-fashioned magic shop full of marked playing cards and magic wands, as well as a hoard of classic novelty items: fake blood, snapping chewing gum, rubber snakes, crazy wigs, and the obligatory rubber chickens. Professional clowns Ken and Bernie Horsman own the place, and their son Spencer, a ventriloquist prodigy, has been featured on *The Late Show* with David Letterman and in numerous national magazines. Don't leave without seeing a trick. Closed Sun. (South)

MUMBLES AND SQUEAKS TOY GALLERY
8133 Main St.
Ellicott City
410/750-2803
Crammed to its wooden beams with handmade and educational toys, this Ellicott City shop is a trip back in time to when all toy stores didn't have fluorescent lights and silly giraffe mascots. Heck, it even has a cozy fireplace. The store is set in an ancient stone building that reportedly once belonged to members of the Ellicott family, founders of the town. (Southwest)

NEXT STOP SOUTH POLE
Light Street Pavilion
Baltimore

T I P

The Light Street Pavilion's second-level food court satisfies finicky taste buds. Choose from cheese steaks, pizza, gyros, chow mien, burritos, and dozens of other quick-service options. Instead of fighting for table space in the crowded market, take your food outside and dine on the amphitheater steps. A steady stream of jugglers, magicians, and musicians will entertain you on the weekends. Dinner theater was never this good—or so cheap.

TIP

Even if no game is in town, you can still check out Oriole Park at Camden Yards or PSINET Stadium, where the Ravens play. See the "City Tours" section in Chapter 5, Sights and Attractions, for details on behind-the-scenes stadium tours.

410/659-0860
If you've got a thing for penguins, don't miss this tiny boutique located on the second floor of the Light Street Pavilion. Here you'll find stuffed penguins, windup penguins, penguin pens, penguin magnets, books about penguins, penguin boxer shorts, penguin—well, you get the idea. (Downtown)

RESTAURANTS KIDS LOVE

CAFE HON
1002 W. 36th St.
Baltimore
410/243-1230
www.cafehon.com
Burgers, gravy fries, mac 'n' cheese, and a little taste of old Baltimore are the house specialties at this Hampden hot spot. The kids' menu includes grilled cheese, meatloaf, tuna sandwiches, pasta, and more. Don't forget a slice of pie for dessert. See also Chapter 4, Where to Eat. ⟨ (Northwest)

ESPN ZONE
Power Plant
601 E. Pratt St.
Baltimore
410/685-3776
www.espn.sportzone.com
Kids love the loud music, the flashing lights, and the hundreds of video screens—and that's just the atmosphere in the dining room. The second-floor arcade contains dozens of way-cool interactive and virtual-reality games, all with a sports theme. You can throw footballs to wooden Ravens receivers—who might be more proficient at catching passes than the real players—fire slap shots at a goalie, and take a few swings against Orioles pitching ace Mike Mussina. Visit on a weekday if you want to avoid excessive lines. ⟨ (Downtown)

FUDDRUCKERS
125 Market Pl.
Baltimore
410/625-0995
A kid's meal consisting of a burger, hotdog, or chicken fingers with fries, cookies, and a drink costs a paltry 99 cents with the purchase of an adult meal. Even McDonald's can't beat that. Fuddruckers is conveniently located between the National Aquarium and Port Discovery. ⟨ (Downtown)

HARD ROCK CAFE
Power Plant
601 E. Pratt St.
Baltimore
410/347-7625
Your kids may not have ever heard of Jimmy Page, much less care about

seeing his Gibson Les Paul guitar, but they'll probably want to come here anyway. The Hard Rock mystique captures young people at an early age. The collection of gold record albums (be sure to explain to them what a record is) and the '57 Chevy suspended above the bar are nothing compared with the incredible 40-foot neon guitar on the roof. The guitar has become the revitalized Power Plant's trademark. & (Downtown)

PHILLIPS HARBORPLACE
Light Street Pavilion
Baltimore
410/685-6600
Kids can color on the place mats and snack on a $4.95 fried-fish sandwich with fries and a soda while you sample the $16.95 Maryland crab-cake platter. A better deal at this tourist mecca might be the always-packed buffet trough, offering an all-you-can-eat dinner special that's only $8.95 for kids and free for guppies under five. & (Downtown)

PLANET HOLLYWOOD
201 E. Pratt St.
Baltimore
410/685-7827
The somewhat weak collection of Hollywood hand-me-downs—Hey! Erik Estrada's sunglasses from his days on *CHiPs!*—might be less than thrilling for adults, but kids seem to go for the over-the-top leopard-skin carpeting, flashing lights, and TVs playing an endless stream of movie clips. & (Downtown)

SORRENTO'S MAIN STREET STATION
8167 Main St.
Ellicott City
410/465-1001
Historic Ellicott City's kid-friendly restaurant has miniature trains whizzing around, 26 flavors of milkshakes, and large cheese pizzas for less than five bucks. The rest of the reasonably priced menu features burgers, subs, and sandwiches perfect for a quick bite. Lunch, dinner. & (Southwest)

Baltimore's First Elephant

In 1923, schoolchildren saved their pennies to help the Baltimore Zoo acquire an elephant, but not all adults were as enthusiastic about having such a large animal lumbering around Druid Hill Park. The Park Board, under Republican Mayor William Broening, was against the "undesirable alien from Calcutta" for fear it would trample keepers and children. But Howard Jackson, a Democrat, pushed for the pachyderm and won the election on the "get-an-elephant" plank. The elephant, Mary Ann, was a citywide favorite until her untimely death in 1942, when she tragically tripped while sleeping and broke her back.

VACCARO'S ITALIAN PASTRY SHOP
222 Albemarle St.
Baltimore
410/685-4905
What kid wouldn't be entranced by one of Vaccaro's bathtub-size portions of gelati (Italian ice cream) or a stack of Belgium waffles loaded with ice cream, chocolate sauce, and cherries? Vaccaro's has an outpost on the first level of the Light Street Pavilion at Harborplace, but the headquarters are worth the walk to Little Italy. (Southeast)

PLACES TO PLAY

CHECKERED FLAG GO-KART RACING
10907 Pulaski Hwy.
White Marsh
410/335-6393
Get your motor running and head out on the highway to Checkered Flag, about 25 minutes from downtown. Here you'll find a kiddie track, a fast track, and a "slick" track that's treated with special chemicals to allow cars to fish tail around corners. Keewl! Cars average about 18 to 20 miles per hour and cost $4 per four-minute ride. A snack bar refuels hungry racers. Summer 10 a.m.–11 p.m.; the facility is usually closed during winter. (Northeast)

INNER HARBOR PADDLE BOATS AND TRIDENT BOATS
On the waterfront by the World Trade Center
Baltimore
410/539-1837
Paddle around the harbor on a colorful boat, or if it's too hot—or you're too lazy—cruise in the electric-powered Trident boats. (Downtown)

MODEL TRAIN RIDES
Leakin Park
Edmondson Ave. at Hilton Pkwy.
Baltimore
410/396-7931
Weather cooperating, on the second Saturday of every month visitors to Leakin Park can ride a model train around a half-mile, seven-inch-wide track. The engines, which are only about four feet long and run on diesel, gas, wood, or electric power, pull a line of cars (benches really) that can accommodate up to 60 people. The activity is free, but the club of model-train enthusiasts who sponsor the activity accepts donations. (Northwest)

NORTHWEST FAMILY SPORTS CENTER ICE RINK
5600 Cottonworth Ave.
Baltimore
410/433-2307
This family-friendly ice rink is open nearly year-round and offers a regular roster of speed- and figure-

For a unique fright during Halloween weekend, check out the Baltimore Museum of Industry's Haunted Factory Tour, during which actors re-create gruesome industrial accidents from Baltimore's past. You'll never look at a conveyor belt the same way. Not recommended for kids under six.

Hurtle through the air at Six Flags.

skating lessons. Times for open skating sessions vary through winter and summer but usually occur for at least several hours every day. Call first. $5.25 per person; $1.50 skate rental. (Northwest)

SIX FLAGS AMERICA
Largo
301/249-1500
www.sixflags.com/america
A $40 million makeover in 1999 transformed the Adventure World Theme Park in Largo into Six Flags America.

Gotham City, a Batman-themed playground, includes several nauseatingly wicked roller coasters (the Joker's Jinx hurls riders at 60 mph through 65 vertical and horizontal curves, four upside-down loops, and a corkscrew in all of 90 seconds), plus the Batman Thrill Spectacular show, complete with motorcycle stunts and plenty of pyrotechnics. Bring your bathing suit for the Paradise Island Water Park. May–Labor Day daily, Sept–Oct weekends. $31.99 adults, $21.99 seniors, $15.99 children

Dinner Theater For Kids

Every Saturday and daily during the summer months, F. Scott Black's Young People's Players present traditional fairy tales and children's stories, featuring a local crop of young actors. The cost for lunch and a show is $10 per person. 100 E. Chesapeake Ave., Towson, 410/321-6595.

If you happen to detect a whiff of seafood while visiting the Port Discovery museum, it might not be your imagination. For nearly 80 years the building served as the city's primary seafood market. Plans called for the building to be converted into a women's prison in the 1960s and for it to be razed in the 1970s. In the 1980s several nightclubs opened but quickly went belly up. However, the children's museum has been one of the city's most popular attractions since it opened in 1998.

under 48 inches tall. $7 parking. Take I-695 to I-97 to Exit 7 (Rt. 3/301 S.) to Rt. 214 W. (South)

SOUTHWAY BOWLING CENTER
S. Charles and W. Hamburg Sts.
Baltimore
410/727-9263
This classic bowling alley specializes in a Baltimore original: duckpin bowling, which kids like because the bowling balls are about the size of softballs and fit easily in small hands. The pins are pint-sized, too. (South)

SPORTS
10 Halesworth Rd.
Cockeysville
410/666-2227
Come here for 40,000 square feet of softball and hardball batting cages, an 18-hole indoor miniature-golf course, a climbing wall, and a huge arcade of video games, air-hockey tables, and skeeball. Adults and the very young may quickly become overstimulated, but Sports' target market might never want to leave. Located about 20 minutes north of the city, off I-83, Exit 17. ৬ (North)

Joe Sugarman

8

PARKS, GARDENS, AND RECREATION AREAS

Let's be honest: You probably didn't come to Baltimore to visit its parks. The city lacks nationally recognized, sprawling urban playgrounds like New York's Central Park, Philadelphia's Fairmount, or Washington's Rock Creek. Instead, residents get by on a few pockets of unexpected wilderness and several grand old public spaces that, unfortunately, have seen better days.

Beyond the city limits, several excellent state parks, notably Gunpowder Falls and Patapsco Valley, keep heavy-duty hikers and bikers occupied through much of the year. In Baltimore County, Loch Raven and Prettyboy reservoirs supply the city not only with fresh drinking water but also prime areas for boating and fishing. And Ladew Topiary Gardens, with its shrubs meticulously sculpted into leaping dogs and other lifelike animals, is a favorite warm-weather escape.

No, you probably didn't come to Baltimore to play in its parks, but wilderness experiences can be had here nonetheless. You just have to know where to look.

Unless otherwise noted, the parks included in this chapter do not charge admission; most are open from dawn until dusk.

CARROLL PARK
1500 Washington Blvd.
Baltimore
410/396-7931
Carroll Park, set in an urban-industrial section of town, has the chutzpah to call itself the "Pride of Parks." And, well, it's actually not too shabby.

In addition to a couple of baseball diamonds and six tennis courts, highlights include a unique 12-hole golf course (see Chapter 10, Sports and Recreation) and Mount Clare Mansion, the pre–Revolutionary War home of Charles Carroll, signer of the Declaration of Independence and the original proprietor of the land (see Chapter 5, Sights and Attractions). (Southwest)

CLIFTON PARK
Harford Rd. and Saint Lo Dr.
Baltimore
410/396-7931
More than a golf course (see Chapter 10, Sports and Recreation), Clifton Park also has a shaded playground and well-maintained tennis courts. The Italianate mansion within the park once served as the country home of Johns Hopkins, benefactor of the university. Nowadays, the area isn't country, and the building holds the offices of a community youth organization, Civic Works. (Northeast)

THE CONSERVATORY AT DRUID HILL PARK
Swan Dr. and Gwynns Falls Pkwy.
Baltimore
410/396-0180
Druid Hill Park's peaceful conservatory is one of those well-concealed charms of Baltimore City. The garden's Palm House, an ornate, 90-foot-tall greenhouse lush with towering palm trees, was once a staple on early-twentieth-century postcards. The circa-1888 building and four adjacent greenhouses will display those huge palms once again, as well as other vegetation from different climates, when a $1.2 million redevelopment is completed. Stop by on your way to the Baltimore Zoo. Thu–Sun 10–4. Free. (Northwest)

CROMWELL VALLEY PARK
2002 Cromwell Bridge Rd.
Towson
410/887-2503
Eastern bluebirds, bobolink, meadowlark, great blue heron—and dozens of bird-watchers—flock to Cromwell Valley Park. The 365-acre grounds, acquired in 1993 by Baltimore County as part of Maryland's Program Open Space, was originally three separate farms; the old stone houses, weathered barns, and white horse-fencing remain in use by the county. Besides watching for birds, you can roam the circuit of trails that wind across the farms, through wide-open meadows, and into thick woods. The park also hosts a full schedule of educational events that range from birding walks to classes on edible plants. You'll hardly realize you're minutes from the Baltimore Beltway. (North)

CYLBURN ARBORETUM
4815 Greenspring Ave.
Baltimore
410/367-2217
Cylburn Arboretum is a pleasant surprise that attracts myriad school

TRIVIA

Cylburn mansion was originally owned by Jesse Tyson, a Baltimore industrialist and bachelor until his 60s, when he married 19-year-old Edyth Johns. Upon completion of his manse in 1888, he reportedly exclaimed: "I have the fairest wife, the fastest horses and the finest house in Maryland." He died 16 years later, and his wife remarried—a younger man.

groups for a touch of outdoor splendor in northwest Baltimore. Its 176 acres contain several cedar-covered loop trails as well as herb, rose, vegetable, and wildflower gardens. Don't bring a football, however; athletics and picnics are prohibited in the arboretum in order to preserve the naturalness of the grounds. Cylburn Mansion, completed in 1888 and listed on the National Register of Historic Places, houses the park's offices and a tiny third-floor museum. Museum open Tue and Thu only. Grounds open daily 6 a.m. to 9 p.m. (Northwest)

DRUID HILL PARK
2700 Madison Ave.
Baltimore
410/396-7931
Despite the unfortunate decline of the surrounding neighborhood, Druid Hill Park retains an air of Old World allure. The grand dame dates to 1860, when the city purchased the Druid Hill estate belonging to Colonel Nicholas Rodgers, whose rehabbed 1801 mansion now holds the headquarters of the Baltimore Zoo (see Chapter 5, Sights and Attractions). The layout of the park followed the

nineteenth-century style of English gardens, with its miles of looping carriage and bridle paths (now mainly roads) and picnic groves shaded by oaks and maple trees—many with carved names and initials dating to the 1800s. Druid Hill is still a picnickers paradise, and families book its pavilions for reunions long before the summer begins. The park's renovated pool and excellent tennis courts provide summer fun for thousands of area residents. (Northwest)

FEDERAL HILL PARK
Light St and Riverside Ave.
Baltimore
You'll get the best view of the city's skyline from atop this 80-foot mound of earth, clay, and thousands of crushed oyster shells. Grab a bench and watch the boats sail in and out of the harbor while the kids play at the popular hilltop playground. Statuary of several hometown heroes marks the hill, including Colonel George Armistead, defender of Fort McHenry during its 1814 bombardment; and General Samuel Smith, who in his 87 years fought in two wars for America's independence and served as a member of Congress, president of the

U.S. Senate, secretary of the navy, and mayor of Baltimore. The land itself became a park in 1879, 14 years after Union troops abandoned their hilltop garrison; several quiet cannons still point toward the city, perhaps a subtle reminder to townsfolk that we had better stay in line. (South)

GUNPOWDER FALLS STATE PARK
410/592-2897

Gunpowder Falls sprawls across Baltimore and Harford counties in four distinct sections, the most popular being the Hammerman Area, with its swatch of sand along the Gunpowder Falls River. It's a fine getaway if you don't feel like schlep-

ping to the Atlantic beaches. Windsurfers and sea kayakers play here too, and you can take lessons on or rent both kinds of watercraft from a concession within the park (410/666-WIND). The Central Area's Sweet Air section, accessible on the Dalton-Bevard Road in Baldwin, is popular with equestrians (bring your own horse), and the historic Jerusalem Mill houses a small museum, blacksmith shop, and Revolutionary War–era gun factory (open only on weekends). The scenic, 21-mile North Central Railroad Trail (see Chapter 10, Sports and Recreation) runs through the park, paralleling the Gunpowder River and its tribu-

Gunpowder Falls State Park

Susan O'Brien/Dept. of Natural Resources

taries. $2 per person for Hammerman Area. (North and Northeast)

GWYNNS FALLS/LEAKIN PARK
Edmondson Ave. at Hilton Pkwy.
Baltimore
410/396-7931

Despite the fact that these Siamese parks are often the answer to the question, "Where should we dump the body?" Gwynns Falls/Leakin Park, a lush expanse of wilderness in the middle of west Baltimore, warrants daytime exploration. The Gwynns Falls Trail, a recently completed 4.5-mile hiker-biker trail of pavement and choppy dirt, runs from the western end of Franklintown Road near Winans Way to Leon Day Park, in the community of Rosemont. It's a surprisingly scenic hike through thick woodland and lush undergrowth overlooking Gwynns Falls. When fully completed, the greenway will run along the stream for 14 miles to Carroll Park and then to the Inner Harbor and beyond. Besides peddling or romping about the woods, you can also shoot hoops, climb a jungle gym, or, best of all, ride scale models of ancient steam-powered trains (see Chapter 7, Kids' Stuff). (Northwest)

LAKE MONTEBELLO
Lake Montebello Dr. at Hillen Rd.
and W. 33rd St.
Baltimore

It's exactly a mile and a half around Lake Montebello, part of Baltimore City's reservoir system. Along the paved roadway, you'll meet all kinds of people doing their own thing: biking, walking, in-line skating—one guy even sets out a lawn chair and plays the trumpet. Red-winged blackbirds flock here in summer, too. (Northeast)

LADEW TOPIARY GARDENS
3535 Jarrettsville Pk.
Monkton
410/557-9570

Rich by inheritance, Harvey Ladew never held a job. To fill his days, he traveled around the world, played a mean game of polo, and, most importantly, toiled in his garden. When he died in 1976, he left this 22-acre work of art: 15 flower gardens, each with a different theme, and a house filled with English antiques, paintings, photographs, and fox-hunting paraphernalia. Most spectacular, however, is a topiary of shrubs cut to look like leaping dogs chasing a fox, swimming swans, a giraffe, and other animals come to life. April 15–Oct Mon–Fri 10–4, Sat and Sun 10:30–5; Memorial Day–Labor Day Thu to 8 p.m. Last tour leaves one hour before closing. House and gardens, $12 adults, $11 seniors and students, $4 children. Gardens only, $8 adults, $7 seniors and students, $2 children. (North)

LOCH RAVEN RESERVOIR
Loch Raven Dr. at Cromwell
Valley Rd.
Dulaney Valley
410/887-7692

Anglers come here to cast for trout

---

and smallmouth bass from rowboats and canoes, which can be rented from the Loch Raven Fishing Center. Hikers and mountain bikers hit the miles of off-road trails. Others just bring a picnic lunch and camp out on the spit of land that juts into the reservoir off Loch Raven Drive. With the sun setting across the water, it's truly one of the prettiest waterscapes in the metropolitan area. On weekends, a portion of Loch Raven Drive closes to traffic, and in-line skaters, families with baby strollers, and bikers rule the road. The 2,400-acre reservoir, which feeds Baltimore City and much of Baltimore and Anne Arundel Counties, also holds Pine Ridge Golf Club (see Chapter 10, Sports and Recreation) and the Loch Raven Trap and Skeet Club, where they've been clobbering clay pigeons five days a week since 1956. (North)

OREGON RIDGE PARK AND NATURE CENTER
I-83 N. to Exit 20, Shawan Rd. W. Hunt Valley
410/887-1815

During the mid-1800s, miners dug here for iron ore and for the limestone used in constructing some of Baltimore's most impressive buildings. The mines lie quiet now, except for the iron-ore cavity that's been filled by a natural spring and draws swimmers to its beaches every summer. On dry land, several miles of hiking trails lead trekkers through the thick wood and across a couple of trout streams (sorry, no fishing). On summer weekends, the Baltimore Symphony Orchestra performs alfresco in a grassy amphitheater (see Chapter 11, Performing Arts); in winter, provided there's snow, skiers navigate a tiny slope. School groups visit the nature center during the week to see the opossum, chipmunks, turtles, and snakes. Park open daily 8–6; nature center Tue–Sun 9–5. (North)

PATAPSCO VALLEY STATE PARK
410/461-5005

This park intersects suburban developments in Baltimore and Howard Counties, but its heavily wooded hiking and biking trails make suburbia seem a world away. The Avalon/Glen Artney/Orange Grove area is the park's busiest and contains some of the best mountain-biking trails in the state. The Grist Mill Trail, a 1.5-mile handicapped-accessible paved surface, takes visitors along the scenic Patapsco River; kids enjoy the area's swinging bridge. Fishing is permitted along the river, and camping is allowed at the Hollofield Area (see Chapter 3, Where to Stay).

Avalon/Glen Artney area entrance via South St. at U.S. 1 in Elkridge; Hilton Area entrance at Hilton Ave. in Cantonsville; Hollofield Area at U.S. Rt. 40 near Ellicott City; Pickall Area at Johnnycake Rd.; McKeldin Area off Marriottsville Rd. (Southwest)

PATTERSON PARK
200 S. Linwood Ave.
Baltimore
410/396-7931

In September 1814, a rag-tag Baltimore militia awaited the invasion of 16,000 British troops from the summit of Hampstead Hill, today the northwest corner of Patterson Park. The Americans defended the rise and marked the spot with several cannons and 60-foot-tall Oriental observation tower, built in 1891 and dubbed the Pagoda by locals. (Until the rundown structure is repaired, it remains closed to visitors.) Genteel ladies and well-dressed men used to stroll Patterson Park, probably commenting on the humidity. Softball players, ice skaters, and swimmers in an Olympic-size pool occupy the park these days. (Southeast)

PRETTYBOY RESERVOIR
Spook Hill Rd.
Hereford
410/795-6151

Prettyboy Reservoir traces its name to a nineteenth-century mare who, as legend has it, stopped to drink in a nearby stream, got stuck in the mud and drowned. The stream was named for the horse, and when the reservoir opened in 1933, it was named for the stream. The reservoir is peaceful and huge—it holds 20 billion gallons—and supplies Baltimore City and parts of the county with much of its drinking water. The area offers a couple of scenic hiking trails, but casting for white perch, smallmouth and largemouth bass, and 30 other species is the primary pastime. There's a boat launch but no rental concessions anywhere along the shoreline. The drive from downtown takes about 45 minutes. Just watch out for the mud. (North)

RIVERSIDE PARK
1800 Covington St.
Baltimore
410/396-7931

The antidote to many a hot summer in south Baltimore is Riverside Park and its huge outdoor swimming pool. Kids splash and scream during the day, but the post-21 crowd rules during evening adults-only swims. The park also contains a small playground, a shady gazebo, and a ball field for the athletically inclined. Pool open July and Aug daily. $1 per person. (South)

ROBERT E. LEE PARK
Falls Rd. and Lakeside Dr.
Baltimore

This dog-walker's paradise gives canines—as well as their owners—a chance to mix and mingle. Located

TRIVIA

In 1937, a small plane crash-landed in Patterson Park at 45 miles per hour after its motor died 2,500 feet over City Hall. Although several park-goers were shaken, no one was injured.

just north of the Baltimore City line, the park surrounds a former reservoir, Lake Roland, in old-growth oaks and maples and thick underbrush. In addition to dozens of different species of dogs, you might just spot an occasional great blue heron or beaver around dusk. The vast majority of the park lies beyond the light-rail tracks via a dirt path on the northwestern side of the park's main dog-walking area. Here you can lose yourself for hours along the winding trails lined with willow, cattails, and Virginia pine. (North)

Robert E. Lee Park

Joe Sugarman

ROCKY POINT PARK
801 Back River Neck Rd.
Essex
410/887-0217

You'll find this popular park where the Back and Middle Rivers meet, at the end of Back River Neck Road in Baltimore County. A small beach with a bathing area keeps residents cool in summer. Anglers get a fishing pier, boaters get a ramp, and picnickers have five reserved areas with tables and water views. Bathing area open Memorial Day–Labor Day daily 10–6. (Southeast)

SHERWOOD GARDENS
Stratford Rd. and Green Way
Baltimore

It's hard to believe that the spectacle of 80,000 tulips and dozens of flowering dogwoods and cherry trees has remained for the most part an "insider's secret." Usually by late April or early May the tulips are abloom in a symphony of reds, pinks, purples, yellows, and oranges. Neighborhood residents come out in formal attire and snap pictures in front of the flower beds, artists set up easels and paint the seven-acre scene, and dozens of picnickers lie blankets next to the radiant beds. If you're in Baltimore during tulip season, don't miss it. (North)

SOLDIERS DELIGHT NATURAL ENVIRONMENT AREA
Deer Park Rd.
Baltimore
410/461-5005

If you're not a botanist, you may not be familiar with this under-visited natural preserve. Soldiers Delight harbors an incredible variety of rare and endangered plants, unusual for this part of the country. Its secret lies in the area's underlying rock, metal-rich serpentine, which prohibits the growth of all but the hardiest of plants. Walk the white-blazed hiking trail, accessible near the visitor's center, and try to identify the fringed gentian, sandplain gerardia, and serpentine aster that call this unique area home. (Northwest)

WYMAN PARK
N. Charles and W. 29th Sts.
Baltimore

Glue sniffers and teenage drunks ruled Wyman Park up until the 1980s, when community groups got tough and cleaned up the grassy expanse. The park still sees the occasional miscreant, but more common are dog walkers out for a stroll with their pets.

A colossal statue honoring Robert E. Lee and Stonewall Jackson is one of two Baltimore monuments that recognize the Confederacy. Another, along Eutaw Street near Bolton Hill, memorializes the Confederate dead. (North)

9

SHOPPING

Baltimore may not be the ideal place to buy the what the current Vogue *cover girl is wearing, but it's a very good place for finding the vintage, the "previously enjoyed," and the handmade. The city's antique stores run the gamut from high-priced specialty shops, where you need an appointment to view the merchandise, to tiny treasure troves that are more like permanent garage sales. Almost uniformly, the prices are fair, and dealers tell stories of visiting New Yorkers who snatch up merchandise and sell the goods for twice the price to unsuspecting Manhattanites. The city's antiques stores congregate along Howard Street's "Antique Row" and in Fells Point, Federal Hill, Historic Ellicott City, and Hampden, as well as along the 10800 block of York Road in suburban Cockeysville.*

But Baltimore also has some interesting boutiques that carry new items: funky home accessories, handcrafted furniture, and jewelry produced by local and international artisans. Try Hampden's West 36th Street, a.k.a. The Avenue, for an eclectic selection of shops that sell everything from designer handbags to rhinestone-studded drawer pulls. Charming Mount Washington Village also has some interesting finds, as does North Charles Street in the heart of Mount Vernon.

When it comes right down to it, shopping in Baltimore is like attending a giant flea market: You never know what treasures you may find.

SHOPPING DISTRICTS

Antique Row

Baltimore's legendary line of antiques stores remains a living link to the heyday of North Howard Street, once a mecca for city shoppers. In the 1960s and '70s, most of the department stores moved to the suburbs, following the flight of the middle class, but many of Antique Row's *stubborn shopkeepers stuck it out and today survive off the tourist trade and sales to other dealers. The wares are high-end, with an emphasis on European furniture and decorative art. From the harbor, take the light rail to the row, which begins on the 800 block of North Howard Street.*

AMOS JUDD AND SONS
843 N. Howard St.
Baltimore
410/462-2000
The death or bankruptcy of rich people works to your advantage at this antiques store that gets much of its inventory through estate sales in Roland Park. The venerable shop, a family business for three generations, is a somewhat dark and musty affair—but an appropriate atmosphere for viewing ancient European treasures. Note the bust of founder Amos Earl Judd, who still welcomes visitors symbolically from a perch at the front of the store. Need some brass polished? This is the place to go. (Downtown)

ANTIQUE TREASURY
809-811 N. Howard St.
Baltimore
410/728-6363

The three floors of antique and collectible treasures run the gamut from old coins and costume jewelry to ancient glassware and Alice Marks's colorful Staffordshire-transferware china. A good shop for varied budgets and tastes. (Downtown)

CROSSKEYS ANTIQUES
801 N. Howard St.
Baltimore
410/728-0101
The amazing array of dangling European chandeliers looks purloined from some French chateau. For more than 20 years, the family-owned business has specialized in European and Early American furniture and accessories. Say hello to the old family dog, Royal. (Downtown)

REGENCY ANTIQUES
893-895 N. Howard St.
Baltimore
410/225-3455
If King Louis XIV were around today, this is where he'd shop (or have his servants shop). And he wouldn't have to pay beaucoup des francs to get bulbous, ornate furniture typical of his day, since Regency sells only reproductions. Among the très chic wares, you'll also find a few Chippendale

originals and a nice selection of antique chandeliers. (Downtown)

Federal Hill

The neighborhood's ongoing gentrification means you'll find custom kitchen tiles as well as secondhand curling irons. Several antiques warehouses border the neighborhood, and Cross Street Market—a shining star of the city's municipal market system—attracts all kinds for fresh vegetables, meats, and cheap lunches.

A COOK'S TABLE
717 Light St.
Baltimore
410/539-8600
Located just south of where Light Street meets Key Highway, A Cook's Table is set with a smorgasbord of equipment for the gourmet or gourmand: copper pots, a wall of pepper grinders, spatulas in umpteen different sizes—even food-fashions like colorful oven mitts and ties. The shop also offers weeknight cooking classes. (South)

THE ANTIQUE CENTER AT FEDERAL HILL
1220 Key Hwy.
Baltimore
410/625-0182
The latest Federal Hill warehouse to morph into an antiques center contains roughly 10,000 feet of dealers offering fine art, sturdy old furniture, and rare collectibles. Recent finds include a child's Velo bike from France ($149), an eight-foot-tall grandfather clock from the eighteenth century ($2,500), and a miniature suit of armor (not for sale). Located across from Harborview Marina and adjacent to the Antique Warehouse at 1300 (see below listing). Closed Mon. (South)

ANTIQUE WAREHOUSE AT 1300
1300 Jackson St.
Baltimore
410/659-0663
Thirty-five dealers sell silver, furniture, art, and jewelry in a vast warehouse that used to produce mechanical rollers. Many periods and styles are represented here, from eighteenth-century paintings to deco dressers. (South)

DAN BROS. SHOES
1032 S. Charles St.
Baltimore
410/752-8175
Most guidebooks don't recommend visiting shoe stores, but Dan Bros. isn't your everyday cobbler. In business since 1939, it's where visiting professional athletes like Roger Clemens, Larry Johnson, and Muhammad Ali pick up $1,000 Dazanzati lizard-skin boots in a low-end, homey atmosphere. But Dan Bros. also caters to people without million-dollar endorsement deals by stocking reasonably priced Rockports and Dexters. This is also the place to go for expert shoe repairs, done fast and cheap. (South)

GAINES McHALE ANTIQUES AND HOME
836 Leadenhall St.
Baltimore
410/625-1900
Generally acknowledged as *the* place in the city to go for high-end eighteenth- and nineteenth-century European antiques, Gaines McHale is a little hard to find but worth the effort for the serious collector. The shop, set in an old lumber warehouse, has 32,000 square feet of display space crammed with furniture and decorative pieces, as well as a terrier named Bailey. (South)

Gaines McHale Antiques and Home

MORSTEIN'S JEWELERS
1114 Light St.
Baltimore
410/727-3232

Another South Baltimore institution, Morstein's has been selling fine jewelry since 1898. Go for the expert repair work, appraisals, friendly service, and 100 years of experience. (South)

Fells Point

Fells Point may be best known for its raucous pubs (see Chapter 12, Nightlife), but during the day shoppers flock to the neighborhood's funky boutiques, vintage clothing stores, and Broadway Market for fresh meats and produce. Several dozen antiques stores offer heirlooms with decidedly more kitsch than class, but the prices are reasonable, and you just might be reunited with that avocado-green blender you gave away in 1979.

ANOTHER PERIOD IN TIME
1708 Fleet St.

Baltimore
410/675-4776

More than a dozen dealers under one roof sell everything from eighteenth-century furniture to Orioles World Series programs from 1966. You could lose yourself for hours looking through the bric-a-brac. (Southwest)

FLASHBACK
728 S. Broadway
Baltimore
410/276-5086

This emporium of old record albums and tacky tchtotckes is a required stop for fans of director John Waters: It formerly belonged to Edith Massey, a.k.a. the Egg Lady of Waters's *Pink Flamingoes* fame, and now is co-owned by Bob Adams, another semi-regular in Waters's nascent films. The director has been known to stop by and chat on occasion. (Southwest)

KILLER TRASH
1929 Eastern Ave.
Baltimore
410/675-2449

In the 1970s, owner Elaine Ferrare sold Nehru jackets to Sonny and Cher and sequined clothing to Elvis from her boutique in Las Vegas. Today, Ferrare sells the same goods, now considered "vintage," from her "nice 'n' sleazy boutique." Rows of leopard skin pants, polyester disco shirts, and *Brady Bunch*–era bellbottoms literally take up every inch of the store. Best of all, the prices are firmly rooted in the '70s as well. (Southwest)

STICKY FINGERS
802 S. Broadway
Baltimore
410/675-7588

Looking for a pair of thigh-high black leather boots? How about a bright blue bustier? Sticky Fingers and its pierced and tattooed staff can help. In fact, if you'd like your own navel pierced, they can help with that, too. (Southwest)

TEN THOUSAND VILLAGES
1621 Thames St.
Baltimore
410/342-5568
International middleman Ten Thousand Villages bolsters the pocketbooks of craftspeople in developing nations by buying their goods at fair prices and then selling them at equally fair prices from their nonprofit shops in the United States. The stores are operated by the Mennonite Church and carry handcrafted goods from more than 30 countries. (Southwest)

Charles Street Corridor

During the nineteenth century, Charles Street rivaled New York's Fifth Avenue as the fashion epicenter

Top 10 Unusual Stores in Baltimore
by Merrill Witty, local reporter of shopping and style trends

1. **Nouveau Contemporary Goods**—Fantastic furniture in unusual shapes. 519 N. Charles St., Downtown

2. **La Terra**—Wonderful accessories made from recycled goods. 4001 Falls Rd., Hampden

3. **Mud and Metal**—Artistic and functional home accessories. 813 W. 36th St., Hampden

4. **Pieces of Olde**—Ancient quilts given new life as beautiful pillows, stuffed animals, and handbags. 1717 Aliceanna St., Fells Point; 824 W. 36th St., Hampden

5. **Sticky Fingers**—Satisfies all your rubber-clothing needs. 802 S. Broadway, Fells Point

6. **Bill's Music House**—Where serious pickers go to buy a guitar. 743 Frederick Rd., Cantonsville

7. **Rugs to Riches**—Rugs, yes, and rich home furnishings too. 8307 Main St., Historic Ellicott City

8. **Dreamland**—Great retro clothing for fashion queens and drag queens. 1005 N. Charles St., Downtown

9. **Grreat Bears and Childhood Delights**—A peerless menagerie of stuffed animals. 1643 Thames St., Fells Point

10. **Next Stop South Pole**—A penguin lover's paradise. Light St., Pavilion

TRIVIA

Before lacing up his own shoes in the NBA, local hoops star Tyrone "Muggsy" Bogues worked at Dan Bros. shoe store after his senior year at Dunbar High School.

of the fledgling United States. Mount Vernon's grand dames, debutantes, and even first ladies from that backwater Washington would browse the merchandise. These days, Charles Street is less about fashion and more about fine art and home furnishings, but the unique finds remain.

A PEOPLE UNITED
516 N. Charles St.
Baltimore
410/727-4471
Ilam tea from Nepal, saris from India, sculpture from West Africa, and jewelry from Thailand fill the shelves and racks of this colorful shop. Almost all of the items have been made by women from poor countries, and proceeds from sales help support women's health care and education programs throughout the world. (Downtown)

CRAIG FLINNER GALLERY
505 N. Charles St.
Baltimore
410/727-1863
Antique prints, period maps, and vintage posters are Craig Flinner's specialty. The batch of 1920s-era French posters in vibrant colors, advertising everything from tobacco to tea leaves, are worth a gander alone. Wonderfully preserved vegetable-crate labels—Sweet Lou Yams, Frisco-brand vegetables—sell for just five bucks. (Downtown)

NOUVEAU CONTEMPORARY GOODS
519 N. Charles St.
Baltimore
410/962-8248
Charm City's funkiest home furnishings store is a psychedelic dream of oddly shaped dressers, purple sofas, deco dinning sets, and enough bubbling lava lamps to give you a buzz. There's also a variety of kitschy magnets, retro windup toys, and clothing you wouldn't wear to a job interview. (Downtown)

WOMAN'S INDUSTRIAL EXCHANGE
333 N. Charles St.
Baltimore
410/685-4388
The Woman's Industrial Exchange Movement of the late nineteenth century allowed destitute women a chance to earn money by consigning goods at stores like this one. Only a handful are left, and Baltimore's is the country's oldest. Consignors continue to sell embroidered wall-hangings, knitted scarves, and lots of lacey stuff. A tea room in the back (see Chapter 4, Where to Eat) sells famous chicken-salad sandwiches and home-baked pies. (Downtown)

Inner Harbor

The teal-roofed Pratt and Light Street Pavilions comprise what is known as Harborplace, the one-two punch of the Inner Harbor renaissance. Developed by the Rouse Company and opened in 1980, Harborplace was filled with a festive mix of local merchants and restaurants meant to imitate Baltimore's beloved municipal markets. The effort netted company founder James Rouse the cover of Time magazine and the city a place to shop downtown again. Today, Harborplace draws more than 15 million people annually, making it the most popular tourist attraction in the state.

THE GALLERY AT HARBORPLACE
E. Pratt and S. Calvert Sts.
Baltimore
410/332-0060 or 800/HARBOR1
www.harborplace.com
Downtown's shopping mall features the usual assortment of mall-stores—The Gap, Banana Republic, Lechter's, J. Crew—plus a few unique offerings, such as Black Market, an upscale women's clothing store that sells only black garments and is the perfect foil

to the White House (see Pratt Street Pavilion listing). The mall is light and airy, with fountains and a food court; reflecting its touristy customer base, it offers a "mall concierge" instead of the more common customer-service center. (Downtown)

LIGHT STREET PAVILION
301 Light St.
Baltimore
410/332-0060 (concierge), 410/332-4191 (info), or 800/HARBOR1 (events)
www.harborplace.com
An ever-changing array of vendors sells sunglasses, handmade jewelry, toys, and gifts from carts on the pavilion's second level; permanent offerings include a Discovery Channel Store. But mostly you'll find food here—and lots of it. The second-floor food court has Thai, Mexican, Greek, Italian, Chinese, and many other options, while sit-down places include Phillips Seafood, City Lights, Capitol City Brewing Company, Paulo's, and J. Paul's. (Downtown)

Woman's Industrial Exchange, p. 147

The Woman's Industrial Exchange

Must-Have Baltimore Souvenirs

- *"Eat Bertha's Mussels" bumper sticker, Bertha's*
- *Foam crab hat, Hometown Girl*
- *Can of Old Bay seasonings, any supermarket or Crabby Dick's*
- *Berger Cookies, Eddie's Markets, Royal Farms convenience stores, or Berger's Bakery at Lexington Market*
- *Zoo Doo, in 1- or 15-pound tins produced by the herbivores at the Baltimore Zoo*

PRATT STREET PAVILION
201 E. Pratt St.
Baltimore
410/332-0060 (concierge)
410/332-4191 (info)
800/HARBOR1 (events)
www.harborplace.com
Big chain restaurants dominate the Pratt Street Pavilion these days: Cheesecake Factory, Planet Hollywood, California Pizza Kitchen, Pizzeria Uno. But you'll also find homegrown Wayne's Bar-B-Que, one of the few restaurants remaining from the pavilion's earliest days. On the shopping side, you'll find the frenetic Dapy, purveyors of pop culture; the sweet-smelling Perfumes of the World; Hats in the Belfry; American Sports Classics; and the White House, a sophisticated women's clothing store that sells garments in any color you want as long as it's white. (Downtown)

Hampden

Ah, strange, wonderful Hampden. Once a struggling mill town, the neighborhood now boasts a revived main street of artsy boutiques, funky galleries, and kitschy antiques stores among the old discount shops and five-and-dimes that still serve the area's blue-collar base. Only in Hampden will you find 50-cent table settings at a Salvation Army on the same block as original sculpture fetching five grand. The mix is truly eccentric and absolutely worth a look.

FAT ELVIS
833 W. 36th St.
Baltimore
410/467-6030
How can you resist checking out a store named after the king of rock 'n' roll's obese period? Recent sightings have included a John F. Kennedy throw rug, a sing-a-long with Mitch-Miller LP, and a chrome hair dryer from the 1950s. No Elvises or Elvis paraphernalia have been spotted, however. (North)

GALVANIZE
927 W. 36th St.
Baltimore
410/889-5237
Come here for bowling shirts, platform shoes, and more polyester than a 1970s disco. The goods include an impressive selection of tacky an-

For one of the best deals in town on parking, pull up to the valet parking area on East Pratt Street behind the Pratt Street Pavilion after 5 p.m. or on weekends. Parking costs just seven dollars, or five dollars with validation from one of Harborplace's merchants or restaurants. Just make sure you give the car keys to someone who actually works at the shopping pavilion.

---

tiques and old blue jeans too, all at very un–New York prices. (North)

GUSTAFSON'S
1006 W. 36th St.
Baltimore
410/235-4244
Could that be a Dukes of Hazard serving tray next to a miniature Pillsbury Doughboy in the window? Why, yes, it is. (North)

HOMETOWN GIRL
1002 W. 36th St.
Baltimore
410/662-4438
A required stop after a meal at the adjoining Cafe Hon (see Chapter 4, Where to Eat), Hometown Girl sells authentic Bawlmer souvenirs: books about Charm City, greeting cards, and foam crab hats, perhaps the perfect gift for landlocked Aunt Tillie back in Oklahoma. (North)

IN WATERMELON SUGAR
3555 Chestnut Ave.
Baltimore
410/662-9090
Named after a Richard Brautigan novel, Leslie Waskins's smart home-accessories store sells handcrafted furniture, towering candles, original color photographs, and picture frames made from old tin ceilings—rust included. (North)

MUD AND METAL
813 W. 36th St.
Baltimore
410/467-8698
The shop's tagline, "Art you can live with," explains the clocks made from cans of Spam and the coffee tables constructed from old railroad ties. The store also sells beautiful ceramic and metal sculptures, jewelry made from recycled scraps, and a fantastic collection of drawer pulls in playful shapes like lips and ears. (North)

OH SAID ROSE
840 W. 36th St.
Baltimore
410/235-5170
The name of the store is cribbed from a Gertrude Stein story, but the sensuous and artistic clothing comes from designers such as Kusnadi, Trnka, and Faith by Celia Forrester. Some customers have been known to purchase their entire season's wardrobe in one visit. In addition to women's clothing and accessories, the store offers an interesting assortment of gifts, jewelry, and candles. (North)

PAPER-ROCK-SCISSORS
1111 W. 36th St.
Baltimore
410/235-4420

The self-described gallery of "art and cool stuff" showcases a changing array of one-of-kind art, paintings, and sculpture that ranges from painted rock heads (just what they sound like) to stunning human-form statues by Australian artist Phyllis Koshland. (North)

WILD YAM POTTERY
1013 W. 36th St.
Baltimore
410/662-1123

Three potters, one potter's wheel. Kathy Schuetz, Nancy Brady, and Cathy Hart produce pinch pots, coffee mugs, and exquisite clay tableware from the back of their shop. The artists' studio is wide-open to the browsing public, so you can see your vase take shape. (North)

Historic Ellicott City

Strict zoning laws have kept out the chain stores, so what you'll find here is truly one-of-a-kind. More than 15 antiques shops and unusual boutiques set in nineteenth-century stone buildings line charming Main Street and its adjoining avenues. Oella Mill, just up the hill from Ellicott City, houses additional antiques dealers in an old textile mill.

I LOVE THEATRE
8147 Main St.
Ellicott City
410/461-4230

Lovers of theater and film can peruse *Les Miserable* T-shirts, *Star Wars* neckties, and original-cast recordings from *Chicago.* The King is represented with a healthy mix of Elvis paraphernalia—cookbooks, beach towels, and hip-shaking Elvis clocks—and you can also pick up Maryland souvenirs like crab magnets and *Homicide* coffee mugs. (Southwest)

SHOPS AT ELLICOTT MILLS
8307 Main St.
Ellicott City

Oh Said Rose

Joe Sugarman

410/461-8700

More than 60 antiques dealers sprawl among two floors. Specialties include eighteenth-century English furniture, radios, old watches, dried flowers, linens, and a wonderful assortment of old maps and historic prints. (Southwest)

SUNFLOWER TRADING COMPANY
8202 Main St.
Ellicott City
410/465-5240

Authentic clothes straight from the Australian Outback fill what in 1850 was the lobby of the Howard House hotel. The owner travels Down Under several times per year and stocks up on Australian saddle jackets, hats, and other traditional and contemporary Aussie clothing for men and women. (Southwest)

TAYLOR'S ANTIQUE MALL
8179 Main St.
Ellicott City
410/465-4444

On four floors more than 100 dealers exhibit a little bit of everything. A recent visit yielded an autographed print of Douglas Fairbanks, a set of Davy Crockett trading cards from the 1950s, vintage manual typewriters, and a lovely armoire from nineteenth-century France. (Southwest)

WAGON WHEEL ANTIQUES
8061 Tiber Alley
Ellicott City
410/465-7910

The merchandise is typical garage-sale flotsam and jetsam, but the nineteenth-century horse-drawn hearse permanently at rest on the shop's jam-packed second floor is worth a gander, as is the sign by the first-floor ceiling that marks the high-water level during the flood of June 1972. (Southwest)

Mount Washington

If you need your hair styled, your fingernails polished, or your legs waxed, you should know that the tiny village of Mount Washington has a half dozen salons. But it also has several unique shops and restaurants to wile away the hours while your perm sets. Accessible via light rail.

Farmers Markets

You can find the freshest vegetables at area farmer's markets, including the Downtown Farmers Market, held every Sunday morning from June through Thanksgiving, under the I-83 overpass at Holiday and Saratoga Streets, and the Waverly Farmers Market, held every Saturday morning throughout the year (except during inclement winter weather) at East 32nd and Barclay Streets. In suburbia, head to the Towson Farmers Market, held every Thursday between 11 a.m. and 3 p.m. from June through October, along Allegheny Avenue between York Road and Washington Avenue.

CLAYWORKS
5706 Smith Ave.
Baltimore
410/578-1919
This community potters' paradise sells what members create. Potters with national reputations also exhibit here, and the prices are usually good—especially during its sales in June and around the December holidays. (Northwest)

OXOXO GALLERY
1617 Sulgrave Ave.
Baltimore
410/466-9696
Judy Donald holds up to 10 exhibitions per year in this little gallery with the unusual name, a play on how she used to sign letters as a child. The emphasis is on high quality, one-of-a-kind handcrafted jewelry by accomplished national and international artists. Tue–Sat. (Northwest)

SECOND TIME AROUND
5708 Newbury St.
Baltimore
410/542-4450
Regular customers hunt for designer consignments in a coffee-klatch-like environment. Owner Estee Klein receives haute couture clothing from as far away as Florida and California and sells them at good prices: Armani pantsuits for $240 ($1,500 retail), Todd Oldham jeans for $10, and Prada backpacks for $94, plus plenty of shoes, handbags, and accessories. (Northwest)

BOOKSTORES OF NOTE

ATOMIC BOOKS
1806 Maryland Ave.
Baltimore
410/625-7955
"Literary finds for mutated minds": Bettie Page comics, underground 'zines, lowbrow art, and other items you wouldn't show to Mom. John Waters shops here, as do Penn & Teller when they're in Baltimore. (Downtown)

BARNES AND NOBLE BOOKSELLERS
Power Plant
601 E. Pratt St.
Baltimore
410/385-1709
See those big, black smokestacks protruding from the top of the Power Plant facility? The interior of those stacks pass right through the center of this bookstore, making for a very dramatic setting in which to browse the store's 175,000 books and 1,500 magazines. (Downtown)

BIBELOT
American Can Company Complex
2400 Boston St.
Baltimore
410/276-9700
Maryland's largest independent bookstore chain might look like another national book-selling behemoth from the outside, but inside it's very much a homegrown retailer. Each outlet actively supports the community literary scene and hosts a comprehensive lineup of readings by local and national authors. Another hometown favorite—Donna's Coffee Bar and Cafe—serves up coffee drinks and desserts in each location (see Chapter 4, Where to Eat). Also at 1819 Reisterstown Rd., Pikesville, 410/653-6933; 2080 York Rd., Timonium, 410/308-1888; and 5100 Falls Rd. in Cross Keys Village, 410/532-8500. (Southeast)

To (Municipal) Market

Like row houses, Orioles baseball, and pre-snowstorm hysteria, Baltimore's municipal markets give the city its distinctive personality. Every market sells whole fish on piles of ice, fresh produce, meats of every cut, and inexpensive counter lunches. The markets are smelly, somewhat dirty, and a heck of a lot more fun than Safeway.

The biggest and most famous is Lexington Market, established in 1782 on land donated by Revolutionary War hero John Eager Howard and named for the Battle of Lexington. During the nineteenth century, more than 1,000 stalls covered three city blocks. Oliver Wendell Holmes was so taken with the scene he proclaimed Baltimore the "gastronomic metropolis of the union" and then blathered something about replacing the statue of Washington atop the monument with a canvasback duck. The market burned to the ground in 1949, and, with the collapse of downtown's shopping district in later years, the new Lexington Market is still trying to recapture generations raised on supermarkets. Don't miss the crab cakes at Faidley's, a Lexington Market tradition since 1886.

Other notable municipal markets (most close on Sundays):

- ***The Avenue Market**, 1700 Pennsylvania Ave. Located in what used to be the heart of the African American entertainment district. Outdoor jazz concerts on Friday nights pack the house.*
- ***Broadway Market**, 600–700 block of S. Broadway. Two brick sheds in the heart of Fells Point. You'll find everything from gourmet cheeses to homemade pirogies.*
- ***Cross Street Market**, E. Cross St. between Light and S. Charles. The closest market to the Inner Harbor. A mix of stalls cater to the gentrifying neighborhood: $12 cigars and tripe. Don't miss the oysters at Nick's.*
- ***Hollins Market**, Hollins and S. Carrollton Sts. The Italianate building dates to 1865, making it the oldest market structure in the city. Mencken used to do his shopping here.*

Cross Street Market

DRUSILLA'S BOOKS
817 N. Howard St.
Baltimore
410/225-0277
An afternoon spent here is a trip back to your childhood. Drusilla Jones specializes in antique children's books and illustrated classics that date from the nineteenth century to the 1980s. Ancient editions of *Raggedy Ann and Andy, The Wizard of Oz, Alice in Wonderland*, and thousands of other classics line the stacks in the airy Antique Row shop. (Downtown)

MAJOR SHOPPING MALLS

MONDAWMIN MALL
1200 Mondawmin Concourse
Baltimore
410/523-1534
No department stores anchor this mall—just 130 eateries and retail outlets like Foot Locker and Kay-Bee Toy & Hobby. Several Afrocentric shops sell African clothing, decorations, and food. The mall also has a half-dozen CD stores and several beauty salons. You can take the Baltimore metro to the mall, located on the subway line about halfway between downtown and Owings Mills. (Northwest)

OWINGS MILLS
10300 Mill Run Circle
Owings Mills
410/363-7000
This sprawling upscale mall is located in the northwestern suburbs, about a half-hour from downtown. Department stores include a Hecht's, JCPenney, Macy's, and a recently opened Lord & Taylor and Sears. A decent selection of women's fashion can be found at stores like Ann Taylor, Lane Bryant, Lerner, and Victoria's Secret. Jewelry is also a big sell here, with about 10 dealers. The food court includes an outpost of Little Italy's tasty pasticceria Vaccaro's, perfect for dessert after viewing a matinee at the 18-screen theater. Light-rail stops in Owings Mills, but you'll have to take a bus to the mall.

(Northwest)

SECURITY SQUARE MALL
6901 Security Blvd.
Woodlawn
410/265-6000
www.securitysquare.com
Hecht's, Sears, Wards, and a recently opened JCPenney Outlet Store (promising goods at 20 to 60 percent off regular Penney's prices) anchor this mall west of the city, just outside the Baltimore Beltway. The mall's additional 120 shops include Fashion Bug, New York Fashions, and Old Navy. (Southwest)

TOWSON TOWN CENTER
825 Dulaney Valley Rd.
Towson
410/494-8772
Here you'll find the upscale department store Nordstrom's, where a piano player provides the live soundtrack for your high-fashion purchases. If your wallet's playing a different tune, try Nordstrom's Rack, a bargain-basement outlet with slashed prices and Muzak in the background. Toy store FAO Schwarz is among the nearly 200 other retail and food offerings, which also include Rainforest Cafe, a kid-friendly chain restaurant with a jungle theme. (North)

WHITE MARSH
8200 Perry Hall Blvd.

© The Rouse Company

Towson Town Center houses upscale stores.

White Marsh
410/931-7100
Part of a booming suburban district 20 minutes north of Baltimore off I-95, White Marsh boasts five department stores—Macy's, JCPenney, Sears, Lord & Taylor, and Hecht's—in addition to its approximately 170 retail and food outlets, including enough shoe stores to please Imelda Marcos for months. The food court, called The Picnic, features almost 20 eateries and a spiffy carousel. Nearby is Baltimore's only IKEA, the hip Scandinavian furniture outlet that has supplied many a young adult's first few apartments

If you're staying north of town, check out the 10800 block of York Road in Cockeysville, which has a dozen or so interesting antiques stores and consignment shops, including one dedicated entirely to old jukeboxes. Take I-83 to Warren Road, Exit 17, and turn left on York Road.

with attractive, "semi-disposable" furniture. (Northeast)

THE VILLAGE OF CROSS KEYS
5100 Falls Rd.
Baltimore
410/323-1000

Hardly a mall, Cross Keys is instead a ring of upscale boutiques surrounding an impeccably landscaped courtyard. Among the 26 stores are a Bibelot Books, a Talbots, and a Williams-Sonoma, but the majority of the shops sell women's clothing—the kind of stuff you'd normally have to travel to New York to find. Try Octavia for designs by Nicole Miller, Calvin Klein, and St. John. Ruth Shaw carries Richard Tyler, Armani, Moschino, and more. The "food court" consists of Crepe Du Jour, a touch of Paris in northwest Baltimore. (Northwest)

Bob Grieser

10

SPORTS AND RECREATION

Baltimore's long love affair with professional sports dates to the 1880s, when local brewer Harry Vanderhorst started a baseball team, primarily to sell beer. By the 1890s, the team was known as the Orioles, and, under the tutelage of Edward "Foxy Ned" Hanlon, had won several pennants. The original Orioles were a scrappy bunch known for purposely hitting foul balls until opposing pitchers were worn out (foul balls didn't count as strikes back then) and for the wisdom of infielder Wee Willie Keeler, originator of the immortal baseball cliché, "Hit 'em where they ain't." Baltimore still loves its O's, even though they've been hitting them were they are of late.

In 1947, the city got its first professional football team, the Baltimore Colts. Behind players like Johnny Unitas and Artie Donovan, the Colts won championships in 1958, 1959, and Super Bowl V, forever endearing themselves to hometown fans. When Colts owner Robert Isray moved the team to Indianapolis in the middle of a wintry night in 1984, the city went into a deep mourning that lasted for 12 long years, until Art Model, owner of the Cleveland Browns, pulled a similar move and brought his team here. (It's okay when it happens to them.)

In addition to professional baseball and football, Baltimore also goes crazy for horse racing, though less frequently. Since 1873, Pimlico Race Track has been the setting for the Preakness Stakes, the second race of the prestigious Triple Crown. The city also has its own peculiar sports, like duckpin bowling, jousting (Maryland's official state sport), and lacrosse, which you'll see played more often than baseball or football on front lawns in certain areas of the city.

When Baltimoreans seek recreation, they tend to find it in and around Chesapeake Bay. Boating, fishing, and swimming are popular pastimes. Biking and hiking take place on several wonderful rails-to-trails projects and in neighboring state parks.

PROFESSIONAL SPORTS

BALTIMORE BAYRUNNERS
Baltimore Arena
201 W. Baltimore St.
Baltimore
410/332-HOOP or 410/481-SEAT
(Ticketmaster)
www.ib/hoops.com/teams/
bayrunners
Since the Baltimore Bullets packed up and moved to Washington (now the Washington Wizards) in 1973, Baltimore has been without a professional basketball team. That changed in 1999, when the BayRunners, part of the fledgling International Basketball League, started playing here. The team plays 32 games at the Baltimore Arena, beginning around Thanksgiving. Tickets $7–$25. (Downtown)

BALTIMORE BLAST
Baltimore Arena
201 W. Baltimore St.
Baltimore
410/732-5278
www.baltimoreblast.com

Baltimore's other "football" team plays 22 home games indoors at Baltimore Arena and draws about 5,000 soccer moms, dads, and kids to its matches. The team plays in the National Professional Soccer League from mid-October through April. Playoffs run April and May. Tickets, which go for $9 to $15, can be purchased at the arena box office before the game, via Ticketmaster, or by calling the Blast office. (Downtown)

BALTIMORE ORIOLES
Oriole Park at Camden Yards
33 W. Camden St.
Baltimore
410/685-9800 or 888/848-2473
(O's Ticketmaster Hotline)
www.TheOrioles.com
Since it opened in 1992, Oriole Park has been cloned throughout the country, both for its retro design and for its concept as the "downtown" ballpark. The baseball-only stadium was built on the site of an old railyard, and the 1,000-foot-long B&O warehouse—one of the longest buildings

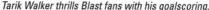

Tarik Walker thrills Blast fans with his goalscoring.

Bill Baughn

Oriole Park

on the East Coast—gives the stadium its distinctive profile beyond the right-field wall. Views from almost all of the 48,000-plus seats are decent. Getting tickets adheres to a classic supply-and-demand model of economics: When the Orioles are winning, expect a more difficult—and more expensive—time obtaining them. Face value for tickets ranges from $9 for bleacher seats to $35 for field-level box seats. & (Downtown)

BALTIMORE RAVENS
PSINet Stadium
1201 Russell St.
Baltimore
410/547-8100 or 410/481-7328
(Ticketmaster)
www.baltimoreravens.com
With the help of a high-tech, $220 million stadium that opened in 1998, Baltimore football fans—most of them, anyhow—are finally getting over the loss of the beloved Colts (to Indianapolis in 1984) and embracing the Ravens, named after the famous poem by part-time and now perma-

nent resident Edgar Allan Poe. (The team's trio of birdy mascots include Edgar, Allan, and Poe.) The stadium itself, while not approaching the classic design of Oriole Park, is nevertheless a great place to watch football, featuring twin 100-foot-long video screens and a bone-shaking sound system of 1,800 speakers. The upper deck rises steeper than a mountain road but manages to keep the 69,000 seats close to the action. Tickets average $35. & (Southwest)

BOWIE BAYSOX
Prince George's Stadium
4101 NE Crain Hwy.
Bowie
301/805-6000
www.baysox.com
The AA affiliates of the Baltimore Orioles play in Bowie, Maryland, about a 45-minute drive from downtown Baltimore. Prince George's Stadium is a fine ballpark, with both modern conveniences (food court, box seats) and minor-league charms (free hotdogs blasted from a giant slingshot in be-

Babe Ruth's father owned a saloon that, if it were around today, would be located in shallow center field at Oriole Park.

tween innings). Fireworks fill the sky over the ballpark after nearly every weekend-night home game. Ticket prices range from $4 to $12. (South)

FREDERICK KEYS
G. Richard Pfitzner Stadium
7 County Complex Ct.
Frederick
703/590-5900
www.frederickkeys.com
The Baltimore Orioles' single-A affiliate competes in the Carolina League in Frederick, Maryland, about a 45-minute drive from Baltimore east on I-70. The intimate stadium holds 5,300, not including the lush, grassy areas down by the left- and right-field lines, which are perfect for lounging on a blanket. Be sure to stick around until at least the seventh inning for a rousing rendition of "We Are the Frederick Keys," the team's theme song, accompanied by mass key-shaking.

Ticket prices range from $3 to $10. (Northwest)

PIMLICO RACETRACK
I-83 to Northern Parkway W.
Baltimore
410/542-9400
www.marylandracing.com
America's second-oldest racetrack (only New York's Saratoga is older) opened for racing in 1870 and held the first Preakness Stakes, the second jewel of horse racing's Triple Crown, in 1873. The venerable track's well-worn facilities have come under fire of late, but extensive renovations promise to return "Old Hilltop" to its original luster. Racing takes place Wednesday through Sunday from March to mid-June. Laurel Park (301/725-0400), about 35 minutes south of downtown, traditionally holds races January and February and July through December. To

If you're desperate for Orioles' tickets, try the team's supervised ticket-resale service, or "scalp-free zone," located at a north-facing gate beyond left field on Camden Street. Up to three hours before each game and one hour after the first pitch is thrown, the ticketless can add their names to a list and wait for sellers. Prices cannot exceed face value. Of course, if the scalp-free zone doesn't produce, you can always head to the *scalper-full* zones, usually near both Eutaw Street entrances.

Pimlico Racetrack, America's second-oldest, p. 161

purchase Preakness tickets, call 800/638-3811. (Northwest)

RECREATION

Biking (Rails-to-Trails)

BALTIMORE & ANNAPOLIS TRAIL
The B&A Line carried passengers and freight between Baltimore and Maryland's state capital, Annapolis, between 1887 and the late 1960s, before being transformed into a 13-mile recreation trail during the late 1980s. The well-maintained pathway cuts through residential neighborhoods and behind shops, skirting the park-

ing lot at Marley Station Mall. More than half a million hikers, bikers, and in-line skaters use the 10-foot-wide path annually.

To get there, take light rail to Cromwell Station. Or drive I-95 South to I-695 East to I-97 South. Get off at Exit 16, take Annapolis Boulevard (Rt. 648) south to Dorsey Road, and make a right. The trail starts across the street from the light-rail station. (South)

NORTHERN CENTRAL RAILROAD TRAIL

Along most of its length, a canopy of trees cover the packed dirt of the NCR Trail. Hikers and bikers make their way

T I P

Parks especially suited to mountain biking include the Avalon area of Patapsco Valley State Park, Loch Raven Reservoir, and Robert E. Lee Park. See Chapter 8, Parks and Gardens, for more information.

from sunlight to shade and back again and play peek-a-boo with the meandering Gunpowder River. The picturesque passage runs for 19.5 miles from its southern terminus at Ashland to the Maryland-Pennsylvania border (the Mason-Dixon Line), where it changes its name to the York Heritage Trail and continues for another 21 miles to York, Pennsylvania. The trail isn't just packed with beauty, it's also loaded with history. The NCR was one of the first rail lines when it opened in 1838, and Abraham Lincoln rode along its rails to deliver the Gettysburg Address; ironically, NCR trains also carried his body back to Illinois after his assassination. Rent bikes at a concession where the trail intersects Paper Mill Road or at the Bike & Hike shop at Monkton, where you'll also find a general store and park office. Rest rooms are available at Monkton and at port-a-potties along the route.

To get there, take I-83 North to Exit 20, Shawan Road East. Turn right on York Road (Route 45), then left on Ashland Road. Ashland turns right sharply into a housing development, where the road dead ends at a small parking lot. To get to Monkton, take I-83 North to Exit 27, turn right on Hereford Road, right on York Road, and left on Monkton Road, which you follow for several miles to the parking area. (North)

Boating

ANCHORAGE MARINA
2501 Boston St.
Baltimore
410/522-7200
Located near the popular neighborhood of Canton, Anchorage Marina charges a daily transient rate of $1.10 a foot. In addition to its 600 slips, other amenities include a swimming pool that's open on weekends, washer/dryers, and a nearby Water Taxi stop. (Southeast)

HARBORVIEW MARINA AND YACHT CLUB
1225 Key Hwy.
Baltimore
410/752-1122

Anchorage Marina

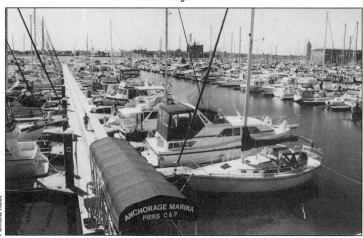

Pamela Root

Some of the biggest yachts (and the richest owners) dock their watercraft at this marina, near the towering Harborview Condominiums. Luxurious amenities include access to a health club and a floating swimming-pool barge. South Harbor Tavern serves up bar food in a casual atmosphere, with great happy hours along its waterside deck. Transient rates range from $1.35 to $1.50 per foot daily. Water Taxi service connects the marina with Inner Harbor tourist attractions. (South)

INNER HARBOR EAST MARINA
801 Lancaster St.
Baltimore
410/625-1700
This marina is in a good location, within walking distance of Little Italy and the Inner Harbor. Two-hundred slips accommodate boats year-round. Laundry and shower facilities are located on the premises. $1.30 a foot daily for transients. (Southeast)

INNER HARBOR MARINA OF BALTIMORE
400 Key Hwy.
Baltimore
410/837-5339
Located along the south side of the harbor wall, next to the Maryland Science Center, this marina's 158 slips fill very quickly in summer. Laundry and

showers are available, as is a small store supplying packaged goods and boating necessities. Transient rate of $1.15 per foot daily. (Downtown)

Boccie

LIBRA (LITTLE ITALY BOCCIE ROLLERS ASSOCIATION)
Between St. Leo's Parochial School and High St.
Baltimore
410/685-7013
The Italian version of lawn bowling is a blast to watch—and play—before or after dinner at a restaurant in Little Italy. During mild weather, you can find action nearly every night of the week at the twin packed-dirt courts. Tournaments are held every June during the neighborhood's St. Anthony Festival and again in August during the St. Gabriel Festival. (Southeast)

Bowling

SOUTHWAY BOWLING LANES
Charles and Hamburg Sts.
Baltimore
410/727-9263
Located above a drugstore in Federal Hill, Southway was the kingpin during Baltimore's duckpin-bowling heyday. Ask owner and former duckpin champ Ruth Brown to tell you about the alley's glory days, when

TRIVIA

The Preakness Stakes gets its name from Preakness, a three-year-old colt that won one of the first featured races at Pimlico in 1870. The storied horse went on to win several more important races before being shot by its last owner, the Duke of Hamilton, in a fit of rage—an incident that spurred stricter animal-handling laws in England.

Top Five Hikes Near Baltimore

by Bryan MacKay, author of Hiking, Cycling, and Canoeing in Maryland: A Family Guide *(Johns Hopkins University Press)*

1. **Soldiers Delight**: *A unique natural area west of Baltimore, harboring a variety of rare and endangered plant species. A network of trails laces through a broken landscape of pine forests and open grasslands. Look for the beautiful, sky-blue fringed gentian, which flowers in early October along streams.*

2. **Lake Roland Trail**: *Who would suspect that a small lake surrounded by suburbia, just north of the Baltimore city line, is one of Maryland's best spots for bird-watching? A heavily used trail runs along the lake, passing through mature forests and along reed-filled wetlands. A variety of warblers and several kinds of herons frequent the lake, especially during migration.*

3. **Northern Central Railroad Trail**: *An abandoned railroad right-of-way has been converted into a trail, which runs more than 30 miles north of the Baltimore suburbs. Extremely popular with hikers and cyclists, the trail follows the Gunpowder River and its tributaries. In autumn, the crimson of red maples contrasts sharply with the evergreen of Christmas ferns.*

4. **Patapsco Valley State Park**: *Maryland's premier mountain-biking destination features a variety of hiking trails as well, from level, paved paths along the river to narrow, leg-burning tracks over ridges and valleys. A swinging footbridge over the river is popular with kids, and several interesting ruins of old buildings lie scattered along the valley. Spring wildflowers here are both numerous and diverse.*

5. **North Point State Park**: *This pristine tract of forest and marsh is the last large chunk of undeveloped Chesapeake Bay waterfront on the upper western shore. An old road leads into vast Black Marsh, where huge old white oaks tower over a freshwater marsh. During the War of 1812, the area was in the British line of advance and retreat in the campaign that culminated in the Battle of North Point. The area was also home to the fondly remembered Bay Shore Amusement Park of the early 1900s.*

> Want to see jousting the way it's portrayed in King Arthur movies? Attend the Maryland Renaissance Festival, held every weekend from late August through October.

crowds used to pack Southway's second-level grandstands to watch city duckpin legends like Elizabeth "Toots" Barger bowl. Rock and bowl takes place every Friday night (seven dollars per person for unlimited bowling; reservations are accepted), and a small league plays on Saturday nights. There's a snack bar on the premises, but you're encouraged to bring your own beer—in cans only, please. (South)

Billiards

CHAMPION BILLIARDS CAFÉ
Perring Plaza Shopping Center
Joppa Rd.
Towson
410/665-7500
www.motorcade.com/champion/
champion.htm
This suburban pool hall offers about a dozen high-quality pool tables, which tend to fill very quickly during late-afternoon happy hours and weekend nights. The atmosphere is pure sports bar, with ample televisions tuned to local and national sporting events and a menu loaded with burgers, pizza, and plenty of fried appetizers. Hardcore hustlers and pool-sharks-in-training rack 'em up until 3 a.m. weeknights and 5 a.m. weekends. (Northeast)

EDGAR'S BILLIARDS CLUB
1 E. Pratt St.
Plaza Level

(adjacent to Hyatt Hotel)
Baltimore
410/752-8080
www.edgarsclub.com
Edgar's attracts mainly an after-work crowd and visiting conventioneers to its upscale environs. It has 17 regulation-size tables, plus two for snooker and one with a purple felt top that gets hauled outside on the plaza deck during summer months. The full menu ranges from nachos to roast duckling. A disc jockey spins tunes every Friday and Saturday night. Normal rates are $6.50 per hour per table before 6 p.m. and $11.50 per hour after. Women play for free every Wednesday. (Downtown)

Fitness Clubs

DOWNTOWN ATHLETIC CLUB
210 E. Centre St.
Baltimore
410/332-0906
This popular fitness club caters to the downtown worker, with daily aerobics, kick-boxing, and spinning classes. The sprawling warehouse facility also contains a complete weight room, an indoor pool, and racquetball courts. Technically, DAC is a private club, but they often allow guests staying at local hotels to use the facilities for a $15 fee. Free parking. (Downtown)

MEADOW MILL FITNESS CLUB
3600 Clipper Rd.

Top 10 Athletes from Baltimore
by John Steadman, *Baltimore Sun* sports columnist

1. **Babe Ruth**—Ruth was signed to his first contract by the Baltimore Orioles. He boasted a lifetime average of .342, 714 home runs, and (don't forget) 94 wins as a pitcher before he moved to the outfield. His birthplace on Emory Street is now a museum.

2. **Al Kaline**—Kaline graduated from Southern High School and went directly to the Detroit Tigers. At age 20, he led the American League with a .340 batting average. A member of 18 all-star teams, he also won 10 Golden Gloves for his defensive prowess.

3. **Pam Shriver**—The tennis standout was rated among the top 10 players in the world for nine years. With Martina Navratilova, she won five doubles competitions at Wimbledon, seven Australian Opens, and five U.S. Opens.

4. **Bob Williams**—Born in Cumberland but educated in Baltimore, Williams was only a teenager when he quarterbacked the Notre Dame football team to the national championship in 1949. He was a first-round draft choice of the Chicago Bears.

5. **Bob Garrett**—He paid his own way from Princeton University to the first modern Olympic Games, held in Athens in 1896, where he won both the shot put and discus competitions.

6. **Jack Scarbath**—He directed the University of Maryland football team to a 10-win season in 1951, plus a momentous upset of national champion Tennessee in the Sugar Bowl. A graduate of Baltimore Polytechnic Institute, he was a consensus all-American and first-round draft choice of the Washington Redskins.

7. **Tyrone "Muggsy" Bogues**—From Dunbar High School, the 5-foot, 3-inch Bogues went on to be a 10-year starter in the NBA. A brilliant playmaker and team leader in assists and steals, he spent most of his career with the Charlotte Hornets.

8. **Joe and Vince Dundee**—They were the first brothers to win professional boxing championships, Joe as a welterweight in 1927 and Vince as a middleweight in 1933.

9. **Gene Shue**—The all-American guard from the University of Maryland was a first-round draft choice of the Philadelphia Warriors. He played for 10 years, earning all-star commendations, and went onto a coaching career in the NBA.

10. **Tommy Byrne**—A product of Baltimore City College and Wake Forest University, the left-handed pitcher owned a devastating curveball. He won 85 games during his 13-year career and participated in four World Series with the New York Yankees.

Baltimore
410/235-7000
This friendly, unpretentious fitness club located in a historic mill has a complete line of free weights, Cybex equipment, and a daily roster of spinning, aerobics, and yoga classes. The 10 squash courts often host tournament play. The club is accessible via light rail's Woodberry stop. Walk-in guests pay $11 per day, which includes court time. (Northwest)

Golf

The Baltimore area has some fine courses for beginning and experienced duffers alike. Not surprisingly, the best courses are closed to the public—you must be either a member or a guest to play. The area has no semiprivate courses, either, so if you're in town for the day and don't know a fellow golfer, you'll have to bring your clubs to one of the city's municipal courses ($2 to reserve a tee time in person or $5 over the phone). Baltimore County has instituted a

helpful computerized system for reserving tee times at county-owned courses. Call 410/887-4653 (GOLF).

BULLE ROCK
320 Blenheim Lane
Havre de Grace
410/939-8887 or 888/285-5375
www.bullerock.com
Bulle Rock (pronounced Bully Rock) lies about 40 miles dogleg right of Baltimore, but it is included here because it's one of the best public courses in the country. (*Golf Digest* agreed, naming it the "Best New Upscale Public" course in 1998.) The Pete Dye–designed course, set on the gently rolling hills of an old horse farm, may be public, but it has all the sophisticated airs of a private course—right down to the mouthwash in the men's locker room. The pampering doesn't come cheap: It'll cost you about $140 to play here on a weekend. At 7,375 yards from the back tees, the sprawling course is ranked by the Maryland State Golf Association as the toughest in the

Bulle Rock Golf Course

Bulle Rock Golf Course

state—public or private. An additional course, resort, and conference center are scheduled for completion in 2001. (Northeast)

CARROLL PARK GOLF COURSE
2100 Washington Blvd.
Baltimore
410/685-8344
This quirky little course consists of just 12 holes, perhaps the only such golf course in America. With its wide-open fairways, generously sized greens, and limited number of sand traps, it's perfect for beginners. The location is less than scenic, but, with a greens fee of just $9 on weekends and $8.50 on weekdays, you can lose a few balls to the neighborhood kids and still come out ahead. (Southwest)

CLIFTON PARK GOLF COURSE
2701 Saint Lo Dr.
Baltimore
410/243-3500
This 18-hole bent grass course, designed in 1920 by Gus Hook, has several difficult doglegs and a few pesky old-growth trees that come into play. Not much water here—unless you

---

College Lacrosse

Baltimore enjoys an intensely competitive college lacrosse scene. The season takes place March through May; all games are open to the general public. Look for these top teams:

***Johns Hopkins University**—The perennial powerhouse, Hopkins has won a whopping 42 collegiate championships since its first in 1891. A 1999 addition to Homewood Field increased the seating capacity there to 10,000.*

***Loyola College**—A small college located in the heart of Baltimore's "lacrosse belt" gets big performances out of a small student body.*

***Towson University**—Part of the University of Maryland system, the Tigers are always ranked high in preseason polls.*

***University of Maryland, Baltimore County**—After a breakout season in 1999, this suburban college could be a force to reckon with in the future.*

***University of Maryland at College Park**—Under coach Dick Edell, the men's team has been a consistent contender for the national championship, but it's the women's team led by head coach Cindy Timchal that's the real dynasty. The Terps won an NCAA-record five straight championships in the 1990s.*

---

count the drinking fountains, which don't usually work. The course offers a pro shop with club and cart rentals, lessons, and a small grill. Weekend fees top off at $16.50. (Northeast)

FOREST PARK GOLF COURSE
2900 Hillsdale Rd.
Baltimore
410/448-4653
This basic but fun 18-hole course, built in 1929, claims to have the largest sand bunker on the East Coast. (Feel free to measure it yourself.) You won't have a lot of rough to contend with, just a few rocks and a wide-open back nine. The yardage is 5,815 from the white tees, with a par 71. A pro shop offers full amenities. $11.50 weekends. (Northwest)

GREYSTONE GOLF COURSE
2115 White Hall Rd.
White Hall
410/887-4653
One of the most scenic courses in the area, Greystone is located amid several huge farms, about 30 minutes north of downtown off I-83. You'll find water hazards on 7 of the 18 holes, including the course's signature number 4 hole, a 192-yard par 3, bordered by water on the left and woods on the right, with a pesky sand bunker in front of the green. In terms of difficulty, Greystone is ranked number two in the state, next to Bulle Rock, but it costs considerably less to play here. Greens fees range from $30 to $59, depending on day and time. (North)

MOUNT PLEASANT GOLF COURSE
6131 Hillen Rd.
Baltimore
410/254-5100
Built on scenic, rolling terrain, this course once hosted the old Eastern Open, at which Arnold Palmer won his first PGA tournament. (The course has the trophy on display to prove it.) It's still one of the nicest Baltimore munies—and also one of the busiest. The sloping terrain makes for some uneven lies and especially challenging shots. A well-stocked pro shop has carts, club rentals, and a snack bar. (Northeast)

PINE RIDGE GOLF COURSE
2101 Dulaney Valley Rd.
Towson
410/252-1408
This beautiful, well-maintained, and

What's a Duckpin?

Duckpin, Baltimore's take on tenpin, involves bowling balls about the size of softballs and pins as tall as beer bottles. Bowlers get three chances (instead of two) to knock down all 10 pins. The name duckpin most likely derives from the fact that pins scatter like ducks when knocked down. If the game sounds easier than tenpin, consider that no one in the history of the sport has ever rolled a perfect 300.

inexpensive course borders Loch Raven Reservoir. Water comes into play often, as does (less frequently) wandering wildlife such as deer and geese. The course can get crowded, and golfers complain of slow play. You'll find a full pro shop with lessons, lockers, and club and cart rentals, plus a lighted driving range. (North)

Ice-Skating

DOMINIC MIMI DIPETRO ICE RINK
Patterson Park
200 S. Linwood St.
Baltimore
410/396-9392
Named after an influential Baltimore city councilman, this indoor ice rink in Patterson Park accommodates a mixed bag of skating enthusiasts between October and March. You'll see all kinds of skaters, from teenagers showing off to senior citizens holding hands and making slow, lazy circles. $3 admission, $2 skate rental. (Southeast)

MOUNT PLEASANT ICE ARENA
6101 Hillen Rd.
Baltimore
410/444-1888
This indoor ice rink operates nearly year-round, except for August and most of September. You'll find a rental shop and a snack bar on the premises. Lessons are available. Admission costs $3.50 to $4.50; skate rental is $2. (Northeast)

NORTHWEST FAMILY SPORTS CENTER
5600 Cottonworth Ave.
Baltimore
410/433-2307
This popular year-round, indoor ice rink hosts a full roster of ice-skating, speed-skating, and hockey activities. Open skating sessions are held daily, but call for times, which vary seasonally. $5.25 per session, $1.50 skate rental. (Northwest)

RASH FIELD INNER HARBOR ICE RINK
Next to the Maryland Science Center
Baltimore
410/385-0675
www.bop.org
Baltimore's only outdoor rink also provides some great views. Skate during a crisp winter night and you'll be rewarded with vistas of the twinkling lights of downtown. Of course, the rink is less crowded—and cheaper—during the day. It opens around Thanksgiving and closes in March. $3–$5 per session, $2 skate rental. (Downtown)

Jousting

AMATEUR JOUSTING CLUB OF MARYLAND
410/557-9189
www.blackbox.psyberia.com
In one of the more creative acts of

the Maryland state legislature, jousting was declared the "state sport" by an overwhelming vote in 1962—giving Maryland the distinction of being the only state to even have a state sport. Why in the name of King Arthur was this done? Undoubtedly as a gesture to Maryland's founding family, the Calverts, who were great proponents of the sport. Although its popularity has waned since the seventeenth century, jousting nevertheless has been practiced continuously in Maryland. The local version of the sport involves charging a horse at full gallop toward three suspended rings. The rider, usually dressed in full medieval regalia, tries to spear the rings with a fine-tipped lance. Tournaments take place April through September at various area locations. Call for a schedule.

Rock Climbing (Indoor)

EARTH TREKS
7125-C Columbia Gateway Dr.
Columbia
410/872-0060 or 800/254-6287

The largest indoor climbing gym on the East Coast boasts 13,250 square feet of climbing space, including a 35-foot stalactite, an arch, and a variety of crags and overhangs. Handholds and footholds change every day to consistently challenge experienced climbers. Anyone who wants to climb must pass a belaying test or climb with an experienced climber. Three-hour introductory classes take place Thursday night and Saturday and Sunday afternoon. A shop rents and sells a full line of shoes, harnesses, and other gear. The gym is located in Columbia, about 30 minutes south of downtown. (South)

GERSTUNG GYMNASTICS AND MOVEMENT CENTER
1400 Coppermine Ter.
Baltimore
410/337-7781

Gerstung is a do-it-all physical education center that mainly caters to kids, but the 30-foot climbing wall and 60-foot bouldering wall are open to all climbers on Wednesday evening and Saturday afternoon. The walls are

A Day at the Beach—or the Pool

Gunpowder Falls State Park has a beach along the Gunpowder River at its Hammerman area, and several Baltimore County parks—Rocky Point, Miami Beach, and Oregon Ridge—offer beaches as well. Call the Baltimore County Beach Information Hotline at 410/887-3780.

You can also escape Baltimore's oppressive summer heat at one of the city's outdoor municipal pools, open mid-June through Labor Day. Most pools charge a modest fee for a day's use. Call 410/396-7931 for more information.

Gone Fishin'

Baltimore's anglers cast off from bridges, boats, and the shores of Chesapeake Bay. The bay's upper reaches hold catfish, yellow perch, fluke, and black bass. Rockfish or striped bass is king in the lower, saltier waters of the bay, along with bluefish, spot, flounder, and croaker. Inland, the Maryland Department of Natural Resources stocks lakes and streams with thousands of rainbow trout. They join native populations of small and largemouth bass, crappie, white perch, and other species of trout.

Some general rules for anglers: Maryland residents pay $10 for a non-tidal fishing license and $7 for a tidal license, which includes fishing in Chesapeake Bay and its tributaries. Those from other states pay $20 and $12 for non-tidal and tidal licenses respectively. Short-term licenses, valid for seven days, cost $7. Trout stamps cost $5, and striped-bass stamps cost $2. Licenses and stamps are available at most sporting goods stores or through the Maryland Department of Natural Resources at 410/260-2939. Licenses are not required for fishing from charter boats.

painted, not textured, and you must pass a test before climbing on your own. Beginning and intermediate climbers will do well at Gerstung; more experienced climbers should visit Earth Treks. (North)

Sailing

GETAWAY SAILING
Baltimore Marine Center at Lighthouse Point
2600 Boston St.
Baltimore
410/342-3110

You don't have to be a member of Getaway Sailing to charter one of its sailboats. Anyone who can prove a working knowledge of how to pilot a sailboat can rent one of the club's 22- or 23-foot sloops for a full or half day. Rental prices start at $95. Getaway also offers a variety of sailing classes, plus group sails Monday and Wednesday evenings and twice on Sunday. Boats go out from early April through early November, depending on the weather. (Southeast)

Amy Jones

11

Baltimore's active performing arts community mounts productions big and small every season. The Morris A. Mechanic Theatre and the Lyric Opera House host touring broadway shows, while Center Stage, a medium-sized performing-arts gem with its own repertory company, performs pretty much what they want to every season—usually with excellent results. Baltimore's smallest theaters, both amateur and professional, are real charmers in their surprising quality and ticket prices that top off at not much more than movie tickets.

On the concert stage, Baltimore's renowned symphony orchestra performs at Meyerhoff Symphony Hall, while rock, blues, and reggae fill the air at the Inner Harbor's outdoor Pier 6 Concert Pavilion. During the summer months, the free Friday-night concerts at the Harborplace amphitheater might be the best deal in town.

THEATER

ARENA PLAYERS
801 McCulloh St.
Baltimore
410/728-6500
www.dewinc.com/
arenaplayers/Home
Acting opportunities for Baltimore's African Americans in the early 1950s were just about nonexistent, until a group of community-minded individuals founded the Arena Players. Their first production was the prophetically entitled *Hello Out There,* and the Players have continued performing a busy schedule of cutting-edge social commentaries and classics ever since. Performances run from September through June at the 300-seat theater. & (Downtown)

AXIS THEATRE
3600 Clipper Mill Rd.
Baltimore
410/243-5237
www.axistheatre.org
Although it seats only 68, the tiny

theater has staged some big productions, including an ambitious showing of Tony Kushner's AIDS epic *Angels in America* a couple years back. The theater, housed in the refurbished Meadow Mill complex, is accessible via light rail's Woodberry stop. Tickets are just a couple bucks more than a movie. & (Northwest)

CENTER STAGE
700 N. Calvert St.
Baltimore
410/332-0033
www.centerstage.org
Center Stage grew out of the early-1960s regional-theater movement that spawned other resident professional theaters like Minneapolis's Guthrie, Washington's Arena Stage, and Boston's American Repertory Theatre. Center Stage presents four to seven dramas, comedies, and musicals a season in its 541-seat Pearlstone Theater as well as an anything-goes performance festival called Off Center in the smaller, ever-malleable Head Theater. Actors such as Samuel L. Jackson, John Goodman, Jimmy Smits, Mary Elizabeth Mastranonio, and Kyra Sedgwick have performed here. Tickets, already reasonably priced, can go for next to nothing during Center Stage's "Pay What You Can" days. & (Downtown)

ENCORE THEATER
4801 Liberty Heights Ave.
Baltimore
410/466-2433

TRIVIA

In 1934, the Vagabond Players staged Zelda Fitzgerald's *Scandalabra*, a horrific flop despite some doctoring by her famous husband. In the 1970s, the players performed the show again, and, according to theater denizen Tom Grahn, the show was equally disastrous. "We're probably the only theater in the country to put on the play twice," he says. "It shouldn't have been produced once."

Alfred Shriver's Strange Request

When Alfred Jenkins Shriver, a wealthy bachelor and early booster of Johns Hopkins University, died in 1939, his will revealed a strange request: To his alma mater, he left a gift of $650,000, to be used in building a lecture hall—but only if the university agreed to display in the hall the portraits of 10 beautiful women Shriver knew as a young man. Each was to depict how the woman appeared "at the height of her beauty." After some prolonged deliberations, the university honored his request, and today the likenesses of Shriver's 10 early crushes hang in the lobby of Shriver Hall.

Let your belly digest the preshow buffet while your mind works over the provocative themes presented on stage. This African American theater company performs comedy, drama, musicals, and original work by local playwrights in a caberet setting October through June. (Northwest)

EVERYMAN THEATRE
1727 N. Charles St.
Baltimore
410/752-2208
This 150-seat theater was founded in 1990 by Vincent Lancisi, a man on a mission to produce quality theater at affordable ticket prices. Apparently, he's succeeded: Performances re-

ceive steady praise from local theater critics, and no ticket to any show is more than $15. Professional actors perform four productions between September and June, usually consisting of two chestnuts like *The Glass Menagerie* or *Cat on a Hot Tin Roof* and two shows that never came near the lights of Broadway. ♿ (Downtown)

FELLS POINT CORNER THEATRE
251 S. Ann St.
Baltimore
410/276-7837
www.fpct.org
Located in a rehabbed antebellum fire station, Fells Point Corner Theatre

TRIVIA

Founded in 1916, the Baltimore Symphony Orchestra is the only major American symphony orchestra originally established as a branch of a municipal government.

sounds as if it would be tiny, and indeed it is. The primary, first-level theater holds 85, while a second-floor accommodates only 65. But the theater is a major neighborhood cultural asset and hosts a busy schedule of community acting and playwriting workshops and readings, as well as the Baltimore Playwrights Festival every summer. (Southeast)

MORRIS A. MECHANIC THEATRE
25 Hopkins Plaza
Baltimore
410/625-4230
www.themechanic.org

Built in 1967, this theater was called "Fort Mechanic" by some critics because of its hulking exterior design by architect John M. Johansen. The interior is decidedly less militant, accommodates 1,600, and makes a decent setting for a regular diet of big-budget, pre- and post-Broadway productions. *Rent, Art, Chicago, Titanic,* and other plays with multi-word titles have graced the stage in recent years. Tickets are available at the box office or through Ticketmaster. ♿ (Downtown)

SPOTLIGHTERS THEATRE
817 St. Paul St.
Baltimore
410/752-1225

Spotlighters gets the Cal Ripken award for longevity. This amateur

community theater has performed one play every month since 1962, repeating only seven (not including its annual holiday performance, *Scrooge*). The theater itself is located in the basement of the Madison Apartments and contains 94 seats around a 13-by-13-foot stage—call it theater-in-the-square. Tickets for the steady stream of comedies, dramas, and musicals top off at $10. ♿ (Downtown)

VAGABOND PLAYERS
806 S. Broadway
Baltimore
410/563-9135
www.jdjelliot.com

The Vagabonds have been putting on plays since about 1910, making them the oldest continuously operating small theater in America. In 1997, they found a permanent home in a former Fells Point watering hole, completely gutted it, and filled it with 107 seats and a proscenium stage. Amateur actors perform approximately six plays a year, including a healthy mix of comedy, drama, mystery, and musical. ♿ (Southeast)

DINNER THEATER

F. SCOTT BLACK'S TOWSON DINNER THEATER

The Baltimore Playwrights Festival, held each June through September, showcases never-before produced plays by Maryland playwrights on area stages. Call 410/276-2153 or the Fells Point Corner Theatre for information.

Top Ten Sights on a Hollywood Movie Tour of Baltimore

by Tom Kiefaber, owner, and Rebecca Jessop, director of special events, Senator Theatre

1. **Hollywood Diner** (400 E. Saratoga St.): The same diner seen in Barry Levinson's *Diner,* but in a different location.

2. **Garrett-Jacobs Mansion** (11 W. Mount Vernon Pl.): Ornate interior used in *12 Monkeys, Diner,* and *Her Alibi.*

3. **Woman's Industrial Exchange** (333 N. Charles St.): Where Meg Ryan eats a sandwich in *Sleepless in Seattle.*

4. **Video Americain** (Keswick Rd. and Coldspring Ln.): Roland Park video store seen in *Serial Mom;* also in *The Accidental Tourist* as the Bow-Wow Clippery.

5. **Senator Theatre** (5904 York Rd.): Seen in *Avalon, 12 Monkeys,* and *Cecil B. Demented*

6. **Mount Washington neighborhood**: The site of Shirley Maclaine's house in *Guarding Tess.*

7. **The Sun building** (501 N. Calvert St.): Newsroom scenes in *He Said/She Said* and *Sleepless in Seattle.*

8. **Hampden neighborhood**: The setting for John Waters' *Pecker.*

9. **PSINet Stadium**: Doubled for Washington's RFK Stadium in *The Replacements.*

10. **Union Square**: Used as a stand-in for nineteenth-century New York in *Washington Square.*

---

100 E. Chesapeake Ave.
Towson
410/321-6595
Come here for contemporary dinner theater right off the main drag in suburban Towson. You get a salad, dinner rolls, and a homestyle buffet with a choice of six desserts in addition to a show. Year-round performances Thursday through Sunday include a steady diet of mainstream hits such as *Fiddler on the Roof, Deathtrap,* and *My Fair Lady.* Chil-

dren's theater takes over during lunch on Saturdays and daily during summer months. ﬤ (North)

TIMONIUM DINNER THEATRE
9603 Deerco Rd.
Timonium
410/560-1113
This schmaltzy dinner theater offers weekend shows throughout the year. Catch the unique weekday matinees featuring the *Golden Girls Follies Revue,* a troupe of amateur perform-

ers all over 50 years of age. Dinner and a show cost $36. (North)

CONCERT MUSIC AND OPERA

BALTIMORE OPERA COMPANY
www.baltimoreopera.com
410/727-6000

Give the Baltimore Opera Company credit for its tell-it-like-it-is tagline: "Opera. It's better than you think. It has to be." The clever strategy has worked in attracting audiences who previously thought opera-going was an experience akin to root canal.

The company performs five fully staged productions, including family-friendly operas like *Cinderella,* each season at the Lyric Opera House. (Downtown)

BALTIMORE SYMPHONY ORCHESTRA
410/783-8000
www.baltimoresymphony.org

Music director David Zinman has helped establish the orchestra's international reputation via highly successful concert tours of Asia and the former Soviet Union. Russian-born Yuri Temirkanov, formerly of the St. Petersburg Orchestra, assumes the

Baltimore Opera performs The Pearl Fishers.

Jamie Facer

helm at the start of the 2000–2001 concert season. Tickets for the pops and celebrity concerts, Saturday morning family concerts, and al fresco summer concerts at Oregon Ridge Park are available at the Meyerhoff Sympony Hall box office, 1212 Cathedral St.

SHRIVER HALL CONCERT SERIES
Johns Hopkins University
3400 N. Charles St.
Baltimore
410/516-5473
www.shriverconcerts.org
Chamber music fills 1,100-seat Shriver Hall at least seven times per season at Johns Hopkins University. The series showcases both established and emerging performers; past guests have included the Emerson String Quartet, Murray Perahia, Dawn Upshaw, and Jean-Pierre Rampal. (North)

CONCERT HALLS

HARBORPLACE AMPHITHEATER
Inner Harbor Promenade
Light and Pratt Sts.
Baltimore
800/427-2671
www.harborplace.com
Check out a little free entertainment between visiting the sights. The amphitheater is simply a couple levels of concrete seats surrounding a makeshift stage, but the diversity of entertainment featured here is impressive. Elementary-school string bands; sword-swallowing magicians; jazz, pop, and rock bands; and more than a few unicycle-riding jugglers have all performed here. Some of the acts are really quite good and earn the tips they ask for at the end of each performance. Shows begin in late May and continue through Labor Day. Free. (Downtown)

Baltimore's Infamous Booths

Many well-known actors have performed on Baltimore stages, but none more famous—or infamous—than Abraham Lincoln's assassin, John Wilkes Booth. Booth made his acting debut in Baltimore as Richmond in King Richard III *and was much admired for his good looks and thespian talent. It seems that both acting ability and violent behavior ran in the Booth family. His father, Junius Brutus Booth, whose farmhouse still stands in Harford County northeast of Baltimore, reportedly got so caught up in his role as King Richard III that he chased his antagonist off the stage and through the audience with a prop sword. He also had a clergyman conduct funeral services for a pair of chickens in his hotel room—but that's another story entirely. Both Booths carry on their acts six feet under in Green Mount Cemetery (see Chapter 5, Sights and Attractions). On a side note, after Lincoln's assassination at Ford's Theatre, John Ford moved his playhouse to Baltimore, where it remained the city's premier showplace until its demolition in 1964.*

JOSEPH MEYERHOFF SYMPHONY HALL
1212 Cathedral St.
Baltimore
410/783-8000

You won't find a flat wall nor a 90-degree angle in the home auditorium of the Baltimore Symphony Orchestra. You will find copious and complex design techniques meant to dampen or amplify every sound in the place. Eighteen seven-foot-wide convex-curved plaster discs dangle above the stage and another 52 "concert clouds," mounted over the audience seating, work in concert to beef up the sound. Every one of the 2,462 seats has an unobstructed view of the stage, including those at the balcony levels, which look curiously like giant glove boxes hanging open over the orchestra seats. The hall was named for its benefactor, Joseph Meyerhoff, a successful developer and former president of the BSO. ⓖ (Downtown)

LYRIC OPERA HOUSE
140 W. Mount Royal Ave.
Baltimore
410/727-6000

Opera divas weren't the only performers in the early days of the Lyric. Built in 1894 and modeled after the Neues Gewandhaus in Leipzig, the Lyric accommodated

Peabody Conservatory

prize fights; speeches by William Jennings Bryant, Charles Lindbergh, Amelia Earhart, and Will Rogers; and the first demonstration of electric cooking in front of a Baltimore audience in 1905. In the 1960s, the Lyric was destined for the wrecking ball until a group of culture vultures raised the $14 million to save it. They preserved the regal interior, but the structure's exterior looks somewhat like an office building. Today the Lyric hosts performances by the Baltimore Opera Company and touring productions. ⅃ (Downtown)

MIRIAM A. FRIEDBERG CONCERT HALL

Peabody Conservatory
609 N. Charles St.
Baltimore
410/659-8124
www.peabody.jhu.edu/
concerts-and-events
See rising stars of the classical music world at the Peabody Conservatory's primary concert facility. Semiweekly performances feature the Peabody Symphony Orchestra, Chorus and Concert Singers, and numerous smaller groups of performers throughout the academic year. A guard at the North Charles Street entrance will direct you to the box office in Room 122 on the conservatory's lower level. ⅃ (Downtown)

TRIVIA

Shuffle Along, coauthored by Baltimore's own Eubie Blake, was the first Broadway musical to be written, produced, and performed by African Americans. In his 100 years, Blake wrote more than 300 songs, including his biggest hit, "I'm Just Wild About Harry."

TRIVIA

In 1924, Edna Ferber spent a week on Baltimore's James Adams Floating Theater, a barge that toured the Chesapeake presenting popular musical revues. The experience inspired her to write the hit musical *Show Boat*.

OREGON RIDGE AMPHITHEATER
Oregon Ridge Park
Shawan Rd. W.
Hunt Valley
410/783-8000
www.baltimoresymphony.org
The Baltimore Symphony Orchestra gives summer performances alfresco at this sprawling park about 25 minutes north of downtown. Bring a blanket and a picnic and watch the fireworks that often accompany or follow the show. Unfortunately, parking can be a hassle. Shuttle buses to the park depart from the Bell Atlantic parking lot, directly across Shawan Road from the Hunt Valley Mall. You can ride the shuttle bus for free, but parking at the park requires a permit paid for in advance at the BSO Ticket Office or from the Hunt Valley Mall. (North)

PIER 6 CONCERT PAVILION
Pier 6, Inner Harbor
731 Eastern Ave.
Baltimore
410/625-3100
www.concerthotline.com
Baltimore's outdoor concert pavilion sits right on the water west of the aquarium's marine-mammal pavilion on Pier 5. A sail-like roof covers the 3,338 seats as well as lawn seating for 1,000. In 1999, the pavilion received a welcome makeover of both its facility and its lineup of performers. The 1999 summer season saw diverse talents like Elvis Costello, B. B. King, Lyle Lovett, Patti LaBelle, and the Gypsy Kings play the intimate venue. Tickets are available at the Pier 6 box office Mon–Sat 12–6 or through Ticketmaster. (Downtown)

Craig Terkowitz

12

NIGHTLIFE

For many Baltimoreans, nightlife still means a trip to the corner bar. In fact, you'll find few cities with such an outstanding collection of neighborhood dives, shabby pubs, and shot-and-a-beer saloons. Many identify themselves simply as "Bar"; others don't even find it necessary to put a sign out front. Inside, if there's beer on tap, it's Bud, and perhaps there's a half-filled jar of pickled eggs or onions on the counter. The regulars resemble the cast of Cheers in that everybody knows one another's names, but they don't dress as well, and you'll never find Ted Danson behind the bar.

As it has since the city's inception, most of Baltimore's nightlife revolves around Fells Point. A hundred years ago, the area boasted nearly 100 pubs, a handful of brothels, and a couple of missions hoping to save the revelers' souls. These days, the count is down to about 50 bars—still more than enough to choose from—plus another couple dozen restaurants and cafes.

Other hot neighborhoods? Try the row of bars along East Cross and South Charles Streets in Federal Hill, surrounding O'Donnell Square and lining Boston Street in Canton, and along the 1000 block of North Charles Street in gay-friendly Mount Vernon. In these neighborhoods, you can walk from bar to night-club to café until you find a scene that suits your taste.

The Inner Harbor has its own form of nightlife. During the summer, live bands play at the Harborplace Amphitheater (see Chapter 11, Performing Arts), while many of the restaurants in the Pratt and Light Street Pavilions overflow into the sticky summer nights. It's all very touristy and family friendly—charming in its own way—but absolutely nothing like a corner bar.

Other stuff to remember: The legal drinking age in Maryland is 21, and for the most part it is strictly enforced. Clubs and bars start announcing last call at 1:30 a.m. and kick everyone out by 2 a.m. Hey, Baltimore ain't New York; this city sleeps.

DANCE CLUBS

Big Band and Swing Dance

BLOB'S PARK
Blob's Park Road
Jessup
410/252-4924

Maximillian Blob, who had a nose to match the name, established this Bavarian dance hall in 1933 to entertain his German immigrant friends. Located about 25 minutes south of Baltimore, the anachronism may be the only place in the area where you'll find dancers from age 2 to age 102 (literally). The house band—the Rhinelanders—plays mainly polkas, with some swing, cha-chas, and waltzes. The authentic German beers are as inexpensive as the food (side of sauerkraut, 75 cents), and fräuleins dressed in ethnic outfits wheel dessert carts of German chocolate cake between sets. The whole scene is something right out of a movie—made in 1954. Dances Friday and Saturday nights and on Sundays between 4 and 8 p.m. Swing dances are held every third Thursday. Cover ranges from $4 to $8. Take Rt. 295 south to Rt. 175 east; right on Blob's Park Rd. ♿ (South)

FRIDAY NIGHT SWING DANCE CLUB
various locations
410/583-7337
www.erols.com/hepcat

"Friday night" swing club is a bit of a misnomer. This social swing-dance club was founded in the early 1990s and saw its membership swell so much during the swing mania of the late 1990s that it now holds dances on Saturday nights, too. About 300 to 400 people of varying ages and skill levels dance to live music from 9 p.m.

to midnight. Latin music takes over some nights, and there's always a free beginner's lesson at 8 p.m. $10.

GRAND BALLROOM AT THE BELVEDERE
1 E. Chase St.
Baltimore
410/332-1000
www.ballroommusic.com

Ballroom enthusiasts of all ages cha-cha, rumba, waltz, fox-trot, and swing in an elegant ballroom at the Belvedere. The $14 admission covers four and a half hours of dancing to live music, a full buffet with a cash bar, and a one-hour lesson from the incomparable Helmut Licht. Wed 6–10:30 p.m. (Downtown)

SWING BALTIMORE
Avalon Dance Studio
624 Frederick Rd.
Towson
410/377-7410
www.swingbaltimore.org

Swing Baltimore holds dances every second and fourth Saturday of the month at a dance studio in Towson,

Boogie-woogie at Swing Baltimore

C.W. Alexander IV

about 20 minutes from downtown. You'll see more than a few hepcats in full vintage attire. Dance lessons start at 8 p.m., and live bands play swing, jump blues, or boogie-woogie from 9 p.m. to midnight. $10. (North)

Contemporary Dance Music

CLUB 13
13th floor of the Belvedere
1 E. Chase St.
Baltimore
410/332-1000
The elevator opens and suddenly you're standing in what appears to be the love nest of a 1970s Casanova, complete with leopard-skin carpet, moody red lights, and tables covered with black cloths. But as you investigate further, you'll realize that it's not what's on the inside that matters, it's the outside that's the real seduction. The view is incredible. From the 13th floor of the Belvedere condominiums, the city sprawls out below, a giant switchboard all lit up. It's a beautiful sight—one that goes well with the eclectic mix of rock, mambo, and reggae bands that play from a tiny stage above a tiny dance floor. Cover varies. (Downtown)

CLUB 723
723 S. Broadway
Baltimore
410/327-8800
Frenetic dance music plays at this club right along the strip in Fells Point. It attracts mainly a college-age crowd sporting big hair and tight clothes and looking for potential partners—for the dance floor or elsewhere. Ladies drink free Thursdays 9 p.m. to closing time. (Southeast)

HAVANA CLUB
600 Water St.
Baltimore
410/783-0033 or 410/468-0022
Fidel Castro would be appalled at the bedecked capitalist revelers who party at this swanky face place above Ruth's Chris Steak House (see Chapter 4, Where to Eat). Baltimore's

Club 13's 1970s decor

Owl Bar/13th Floor

Sip martinis at the Havana Club.

beautiful people—Latino or not—congregate here to dance disco, to sip martinis, or just to strike elaborate poses. Of course, being the Havana Club, the smell of expensive cigars permeates throughout. Wed night Latin dance lessons. (Downtown)

LATIN PALACE
509 S. Broadway
Baltimore
410/522-6700
Well-dressed Latinos come for the flashing dance floor, the cigar room, and Las Palmas, a restaurant within the club that serves excellent paella, black-bean soup, and caramel flan. The restaurant is open for lunch, but the dance floor doesn't start cooking until at least 11 p.m. on weekends. (Southeast)

PARADOX
1310 Russell St.
Baltimore
410/837-9110
Set in an industrial part of town not far from PSINet Stadium, the 'Dox features a steady line-up of Baltimore's best hip-hop DJs in a sprawling club with multiple rooms. Live music, discounts for college students, and other special promotions are frequent; call to see what's going on. (Southwest)

THE SPOT NITE CLUB
2314 Boston St.
Baltimore
410/276-9556
www.sunspot.net/citysearch/
thespotniteclub
Serious dancers frequent this Canton hot spot that bills itself as "two clubs in one." The "lounge side" features a tiny dance floor and '70s and '80s music on Friday and Saturday nights, while the larger "club side" has a frenzied light show and a lineup of competent DJs who keep the multiracial crowd bumping to techno music. Four dollars buys all the Miller Lite you can drink between 9 and 11 p.m. Sunday is actually one of the most popular nights at The Spot, with a cast of regular

dance-music crazies who can't get enough. (Southeast)

MUSIC CLUBS

Jazz and Blues

BERTHA'S
734 S. Broadway
Baltimore
410/327-5795
They're known for their mussels, but Bertha's also serves up some hot jazz on Tuesday, Wednesday, and Thursday nights in its compact front pub. Beat-up musical instruments hang from the ceiling, and friendly bartenders dispense a wide selection of imported and microbrewed beers. (Southeast)

BUDDIES PUB AND JAZZ CLUB
313 N. Charles St.
Baltimore
410/332-4200
The house band, the Bing Miller Quartet, jazzes up the joint Thursday through Saturday, while a New Orleans-inspired menu of po' boys, fat hamburgers, pastas, and seafood satisfies what the music can't. (Downtown)

FULL MOON SALOON
1710 Aliceanna St.
Baltimore

410/276-6388
www.fullmoon-saloon.com
Baltimore's self-proclaimed "Home of the Blues" hosts live music several nights per week in a friendly Fells Point bar. An unlikely mix of talent has graced the stage, including impromptu jams by Bruce Willis and hard-rocking Slash of Guns 'n' Roses fame. Call the blues hotline at the number above to find out who's playing when. (Southeast)

MAIN STREET BLUES
8089 Main St.
Ellicott City
410/203-2830
www.mainstreetblues.com
Main Street Blues gets some good national acts to go along with its New Awlins–inspired menu. Deanna Bogart, Charlie Byrd, and Cecelia Calloway all play here somewhat frequently. Other nights of the week, a steady influx of regional guitar pickers, blues harp players, and singers perform. Two shows—and two seatings—Fri and Sat at 8 and 10 p.m. (Southwest)

NEW HAVEN LOUNGE
Northwood Shopping Center
1552 Havenwood Rd.
Baltimore
410/366-7416
Baltimore's premier jazz club is stuck between a laundry mat and a nail

Want to know who's playing where? Check out Baltimore's free alternative weekly, *City Paper*. Every Wednesday it gives comprehensive listings of nightlife in Charm City.

Better Days on the Block

The Block, that infamous stretch of strip clubs and "bookstores of dubious intellectual appeal" along the 400 block of East Baltimore Street, didn't always have the sleazy rep it boasts today. Early in the century, the Block was practically family friendly and hosted a fantastic mix of vaudeville houses, movie theaters, restaurants, and bowling alleys. Entertainers like Jackie Gleason performed at the clubs and partied the rest of the night away. Burlesque moved in during the late '20s, and by World War II every serviceman who spent a weekend in Baltimore knew about the Block. In the 1950s, a West Virginian country girl named Blaze Starr blazed her way into the Two O'Clock Club and quickly became perhaps the number-one tourist attraction in the city. Starr went on to brag of an affair with John Kennedy when he was a senator, and she had a well-publicized tryst with Louisiana governor Earl Long, Huey Long's younger brother.

Meanwhile, the Block was becoming more tawdry than gaudy; in 1967 a Russian magazine article branded Baltimore a "city of sin" and told its communist readers that "its vices exceeded those things one can find in Paris or London." Talk of turning the Block into an "adult entertainment zone" with brick sidewalks, curbside trees, and Jazz Age street lamps never got off the ground. Nor did the idea of razing the Block for the Inner Harbor renewal, in part because other neighborhoods were fearful of inheriting its strip clubs. Besides, as then-mayor Schaefer told The Sun *in 1974, the Block "has value as a convention draw." These days, Baltimore has other amenities that draw conventions, but the Block keeps hanging on—and taking it off.*

salon in a nondescript shopping plaza in the northwestern part of the city. No matter, inside is a haven for jazz lovers. Homegrown pianist Cyrus Chestnut has played here, as have bassist Christian McBride and electric-organist Joey DeFrancesco. Jazz bands groove on Friday and Saturday nights, and the house blues band, Big Jesse Yawn and His Music Men, heat

> West Baltimore's Avenue Market (1700 Pennsylvania Ave., 410/728-1012) hosts live blues, jazz, and R&B acts every Friday night during warm weather. Bring a lawn chair and an appetite for crab cakes, fried chicken, and other good grub from the municipal market's vendors.

up the joint every Wednesday. (Northeast)

Rock

8 X 10
10 E. Cross St.
Baltimore
410/625-2000
No, it isn't really 8 feet by 10 feet—although the stage might very well be. This Federal Hill landmark attracts a diverse range of musical acts, from rock to folk, from ska to swing. It has surprisingly decent acoustics (depending on where you're standing), inexpensive beer, and, according to folkie John Wesley Harding, "some of the worst rest rooms in the United States." Really, what more could you ask for in a club? (South)

FLETCHER'S
701 S. Bond St.
Baltimore
410/558-1889
Regional rock, folk, and alternative acts with medium-sized followings invade this dark and smoky Fells Point club most nights. If you just want to feel the floor vibrate without seeing the show, a separate bar area has pool tables and a juke box. (Southeast)

RECHER THEATRE
512 York Rd.

Towson
410/337-7210
www.rechertheatre.com
First it was a movie theater. Then it was a pool hall. Now it's a concert hall with a proposed pool-hall annex. The Recher has seen a lot since it first opened for films in 1929. The space still looks like a theater with its seats removed, but the snack bar dispenses burgers and sandwiches, and a bar sells $3 rail drinks and $2.75 beers. The family-run operation can accommodate as many as 850 for its almost-daily lineup of rock, folk, and reggae acts. Don't miss the huge salt-water aquarium. (North)

Eclectic

CAT'S EYE PUB
1730 Thames St.
Baltimore
410/276-9866
Playboy magazine once named this pub "Best Bar in Fells Point." No small accomplishment in a neighborhood legendary for its nightlife. First and foremost, the Cat's Eye is an Irish pub with a good selection of microbrews as well as ales and bitter from the Old Country. It also features a regular lineup of bands that play everything from folk and blues to traditional Irish jigs. The crowd is a mix of tourists, bikers, and baby

boomers all united by a love of good music and Guinness. Things tend to get very crowded on weekend nights. (Southeast)

ROOTS CAFE
St. John's Church
27th and St. Paul Sts.
Baltimore
410/880-3883
Every other Saturday night from September through April, St. John's Church opens its doors and welcomes an earthy, nondenominational mix of folks who dance, eat cookies, and drink beer to live "roots music"—old-fashioned rock or blues, zydeco, reggae, or folk. This is one of the more unusual venues to see live music in Baltimore and one of the few places where you can bring your kids and dance to live "adult" music without going to a wedding. Call first to find out who's playing when. (North)

PUBS AND BARS

BALTIMORE BREWING CO.
104 Albemarle St.
Baltimore
410/837-5000
Fittingly located in what was once known as Brewer's Park for its plethora of German-owned breweries, Baltimore Brewing Company continues the tradition of tasty ales, lagers, and porter under the name DeGroen's. Try the Märzen, a tasty medium-dark brew with a malty aroma. Lunch, dinner. (Southeast)

BOHAGER'S
701 S. Eden St. at Aliceanna
410/563-7220
Baltimore
www.bohagers.com
The tiki-bar theme might be just the thing you're looking for on a hot summer night. Go for the thatch-roofed huts, giant aquariums, and fruity

Recommended Happy-Hour Spots

1. *Water Street*—Four bars overflow onto a cobblestone street. Just like college, but everybody's wearing business clothes. Live bands in the summer.

2. *Nick's Inner Harbor Seafood*, Cross Street Market—Oysters on the half-shell, three-dollar tubs of Bud. Need we say more?

3. *Tusk Lounge*, second floor of the Brass Elephant—Classy digs, two-for-one drinks. Great tapas, too.

4. *South Harbor Tavern*—Harborview Marina. The harbor breeze in your hair, three-dollar mixed-drink specials in your cup.

5. *The Wharf Rat*, Camden Yards or Fells Point—Three good pints of beer for three dollars until 7 p.m. every day.

drinks. During winter a giant tennis bubble covers the entire bar, sealing in the tropical air. (Yes, it looks as ridiculous as it sounds.) Nationally known bands entertain when the DJ isn't pumping out a Top 40 repertoire. Like many cold-weather clubs that adopt Hawaiian themes, Bohager's rates high on the meat-market scale. (Southeast)

THE BREWER'S ART
1106 N. Charles St.
Baltimore
410/547-6925
www.belgianbeer.com
Your ordinary brewpub? Hardly. How many beer halls serve fresh spinach and pumpkin ravioli with a hazelnut cream sauce? Yes, its menu is a little more upscale than the average hops house, but Brewer's Art attracts a crowd that's equally comfortable in suits or sweatpants. It's the only brewpub in Baltimore that specializes in "American-style Belgium beers," as co-owner Volker Stewart says. (Try the flavorful Resurrection Ale.) The stunning building itself dates from the Victorian age, and the interior is as diverse as the clientele: a hip front bar, an elegant dining room, and a dingy basement with a cement floor and orange-painted brick walls, popular with the dramatically dressed set. Definitely one of Baltimore's more unique haunts. (Downtown)

CLADDAGH PUB
2918 O' Donnell St.
Baltimore
410/522-4220
This neighborhood Irish pub packs 'em in on Friday and Saturday nights for excellent Black Angus burgers and cold Killian's. Located right on O'Donnell Square in Canton. (Southeast)

CLUB CHARLES
1724 N. Charles St.
Baltimore
410/727-8815
Club Charles is an old-school hipster's paradise, with red neon lights, murals of nudes on the walls, and Dave Brubeck on the jukebox. It's the place to go if you feel like lounging with the city's creative set. In addition to serving reasonably priced drinks, the bar shares an eclectic menu with Zodiac (see Chapter 4, Where to Eat) next door, and it remains the de facto watering hole after an artsy film at the Charles Movie Theater across the street. Oh, and that might very well be *the* John Waters on the lumpy red-vinyl barstool next to you—Club Charles is one of the movie director's favorite haunts. No cover. (Downtown)

E.J. BUGS
702 S. Broadway
Baltimore
410/563-0961
If you live in Baltimore and play in a

TRIVIA

Baltimorean William Fuld is credited with patenting the Ouija board, that kitschy game used to communicate with spirits. Befittingly, Fuld's original Ouija-board factory on North Central Avenue is now a funeral home.

Get the latest on downtown events, attractions, performing arts, and festivals by calling the Downtown Source at 410/342-SHOW, or check its Web site at www.baltimoredowntown.org.

rock band, you've probably played E.J.'s. This Fells Point dive is dark and smoky, and the bartenders sometimes talk back to you, but, hey, you gotta start somewhere, right? Cover varies. & (Southeast)

ESPN ZONE
Power Plant
601 E. Pratt St.
Baltimore
410/685-3776
www.espn.sportzone.com
Is it a nightclub? A restaurant? An arcade? It's actually all three, which makes ESPN's first venture into 3-D entertainment so popular. Call it a sports bar on steroids. There's a constant barrage of sports information thrown at you—from game updates and news printed on the paper place mats to famous plays etched onto the countertops at the bar. Television screens are everywhere—including the rest rooms. The restaurant side does its sports-bar food surprisingly well, but some of the items might cost you next year's signing bonus: $8.75 for a hamburger. The second-level arcade is a blast—wall-to-wall interactive games that simulate sports from basketball to tennis. Baltimore doesn't have too many hot, exclusive nightclubs with long lines of people waiting to get in—except here. Go early if you want to get a table. (Downtown)

EXPLORER'S LOUNGE
Harbor Court Hotel
550 Light St.
Baltimore
410/234-0550
A gong at the entrance, faux elephant-tusk lamps, palm-foliage wallpaper. The Explorer's Lounge is where people go to hunt old-fashioned cocktails in an environment that recalls the zenith of the British Empire. It's high class all the way from the impeccable service to the guy in the tux at the grand piano. Hot and cold hors d'oeuvres served Mon–Fri 5-7 p.m.; jazz trio Fri and Sat 9 p.m.–1 a.m. (Downtown)

GOOD LOVE BAR
2322 Boston St.
Baltimore
410/558-2347
Good vibrations fill one of Baltimore's sexiest bars. Candles glow throughout, while DJs serenade the crowd with jazz-infused techno music. The racially mixed twenty-somethings mingle on mismatched, retro couches and sip red wine or martinis in the near dark. Seventies love god Barry White would wholeheartedly approve. (Southeast)

JOHN STEVEN, LTD.
1800 Thames St.
Baltimore
410/327-5561
When debating Fells Point's best pub,

Live it up at Owl Bar.

John Steven is usually brought into the fray. It's got a lot in its favor: approximately 20 beers on tap; a chalkboard menu of steamed oysters, clams, mussels, and shrimp; and an easy-going cast of regulars that ranges from bikers and old salts to college kids. If the weather permits, opt for lunch or dinner in the serene redbrick courtyard. The pub and restaurant tend to get very crowded on weekend nights; you can make dinner reservations Mon–Thu only. (Southeast)

LEADBETTERS
1639 Thames St.
Baltimore
410/675-4794
The row house dates to the late eighteenth century, and it's been a bar almost as long. Aging hippies, Fells Point denizens, and young Turks raised on blues and classic rock stop by for inexpensive beer and an unpretentious atmosphere of exposed brick and well-worn bathrooms. A guitar-toting singer crammed into a nook by the entrance belts out traditional blues, old R.E.M, or Fleetwood Mac standards. Request "Freebird" and you just might get it. (Southeast)

MAX'S ON BROADWAY
735 S. Broadway
Baltimore
410/675-6297
Some bars have a dozen beers on tap. Max's has 65. And another 125 or so in bottles. It also has a few pool tables and an upstairs smoking lounge with high-backed leather chairs and a saltwater aquarium. The crowd (and it does get crowded) tends to be mainly twenty-somethings with an appreciation for good hops and fine cigars. If you forget your Macanudos, Max's runs the cigar store next door. & (Southeast)

OWL BAR
Belvedere
1 E. Charles St.
Baltimore
410/347-0888
H. L. Mencken used to enjoy a cold

one here back in the 1920s and '30s, and the Owl Bar is still one of the favored places in town to imbibe. The high ceiling, imitation stained-glass windows, and mounted animal heads hearken back to Mencken's day, but now the place isn't frequented by cranky newspapermen so much as by a post-college crowd, who come for the brick-oven pizzas and beers in yard glasses. A more mature crowd shows up for dinner but tends to clear out before the rock music starts blasting. (Downtown)

PISCES
Hyatt Regency Hotel
300 Light St.
Baltimore
410/605-2835
Located on the 13th floor of the Hyatt Hotel, Pisces is more than an upscale restaurant with spectacular views. It also has a mellow bar scene Tuesday through Saturday, with a half-price raw bar and two-dollar draft beer specials from 4 to 6 p.m. On Friday and Saturday between 10 p.m. and 1 a.m., a jazz trio plays mood music for the late-night tourist crowd. (Downtown)

SISSON'S RESTAURANT AND BREWERY
36 E. Cross St.

Baltimore
410/539-2093
Baltimore's original brewpub serves up to six microbrewed concoctions that vary by season, and its restaurant is one of the few places in town to specialize in food from the Bayou—jambalaya, seafood gumbo, and oyster po' boys. If you're the designated driver, stick with Sisson's excellent microbrewed root beer. (South)

SOUTH HARBOR TAVERN
500 Harborview Dr.
Baltimore
410/385-9987
Grab a table on the outside deck during the summer months and you'll be rewarded with a nice view of the water and warm harbor breezes in the shadow of Harborview—that somewhat out-of-place-looking skyscraper on the southern side of the Inner Harbor. Inside, the contemporary, hip restaurant offers burgers, crab cakes, and London broil. On Friday nights during summer, the outside deck gets packed with a thirsty after-work crowd. (South)

TUSK LOUNGE
Brass Elephant Restaurant
924 N. Charles St.
Baltimore

At the entranceway to the Owl Bar, take a look at the mounted photographs to get an idea of the variety of people who had business over the years in the regal Belvedere Hotel (now condominiums), built in 1904. Pictures of presidents Theodore Roosevelt, Taft, Franklin D. Roosevelt, Eisenhower, Kennedy, and Reagan, as well as entertainers from Al Jolson to Englebert Humperdink adorn the walls.

Top Ten Jazz Artists with Ties to Baltimore

by WEAA-FM (88.9) disc jockey and jazz historian John Tegler

1. **Eubie Blake**: Along with partner Noble Sissie, the marvelous ragtime pianist and band leader wrote many hit songs, including "I'm Just Wild About Harry," "Memories of You," and "Love Will Find a Way."

2. **Cab Calloway**: Actually born in Rochester, Calloway came to Baltimore as an infant. His 1931 recording of "Minnie the Moocher" brought him national fame.

3. **Cyrus Chestnut**: The Baltimore-born-and-bred pianist began playing piano in church at age four. He later studied at Baltimore's Peabody Conservatory. Since 1988 he has worked with Jon Hendricks, Wynton Marsalis, Betty Carter, Terrance Blanchard, and others.

4. **Ethel Ennis**: The well-known vocalist made her first national and international appearances with the Benny Goodman Band.

5. **Antonio Hart**: The brilliant young Baltimore-born saxophonist has worked with Mulgrew Miller, Christian McBride, Roy Hargrove, and others.

6. **Billie Holiday**: Holiday sang in Baltimore before moving to New York City in 1929. She sang with the Count Bassie and Artie Shaw bands in the late '30s, then went on to prominence as a solo artist.

7. **John Kirby**: The imaginative bassist is most famous for his sextet, John Kirby's Little Big Band, which brought a new element of ingenuity and finesse to small-band jazz.

8. **Ellis Larkins**: The Baltimore-born pianist graduated from Julliard in 1940. He worked with singer Mildred Bailey for many years.

9. **Hank Levy**: The Baltimore saxophonist, composer, arranger, and teacher is best known for his work with the Stan Kenton Orchestra. He went on to develop an outstanding jazz education program at Towson University.

10. **Chick Webb**: The great drummer led his group to Harlem as the house band at the Savoy Ballroom. Webb discovered and nurtured the talent of singer Ella Fitzgerald.

410/547-8480

If you want swank without paying for swank, come here. This second-floor lounge of the opulent Brass Elephant (see Chapter 4, Where to Eat) inherited the same culinary pedigree, with entrées at about half the price. Sample from a mix of soups, salads, and tapas—small appetizers like marinated grilled mushroom caps, escargot, or Caesar salad. Entrées are a success, too; try the fusilli with crab-and-shrimp sauce. All this in a romantic setting of chandeliers and Tiffany-designed windows and skylights. Come between 5 and 7 p.m. on weeknights for two-for-one drinks. (Downtown)

THE WHARF RAT–CAMDEN YARDS
206 W. Pratt St.
Baltimore
410/244-8900

Housed in a Civil War–era building with an iron facade, the Wharf Rat overflows before and after baseball games at Camden Yards. You can fight the crowds or go when the O's are away for a quieter evening of respectable pub food and a changing roster of 14 different microbrews. (Downtown)

THE WHARF RAT–FELLS POINT
801 S. Ann St.
Baltimore
410/276-9034

The Wharf Rat's Fells Point location is famous for its incredible beer prices: three pints of beer for three bucks all day until 7 p.m. (Also available at the Camden Yards location from 4 to 7 p.m.) It's a deal that's hard to beat, especially since they brew their own beer, under the name Oliver's. The space is dark, with beat-up wooden tables and a

raging fireplace in winter—a comfortable Fells Point atmosphere. (Southeast)

GAY CLUBS

CENTRAL STATION PUB
1001 N. Charles St.
Baltimore
410/752-7133

This sleek and modern bar crowds with mainly professional men for happy hour and weekend evenings. Diners get upscale bar food in a more sedate dining room or eat alfresco when the weather cooperates. (Downtown)

THE HIPPO
1 W. Eager St.
Baltimore
410/547-0069

With a huge dance floor, a great light show, and a sound system that would impress Liberace, the venerable Hippo (officially known as Hippopotamus) looks like it would be more at home in South Beach than downtown Baltimore. The space is divided into two sections: a mellow space with pool tables and a bar and another area with the aforementioned light show and pulsating music. The Hippo attracts all kinds—straights included—but drag queens rule on select nights. (Downtown)

PORT IN A STORM
4330 E. Lombard St.
Baltimore
410/732-5608

Port in a Storm has been a safe haven for the community's lesbian crowd for years. Pool sharks frequent on Thursday nights, and karaoke takes over on Sundays. Occasionally, live bands entertain, but more often couples dance to recorded music on a sizeable dance floor. (Southeast)

COMEDY CLUBS

COMEDY CLUB AT WINCHESTER'S
102 Water St.
Baltimore
410/576-8558
Two blocks north of the Inner Harbor, this comedy club has a regular line-up of regional comics who perform their schtick Fridays at 9:30 p.m. and Saturdays at 8 and 10 p.m. If you think you've got what it takes, attend open-mike nights, Thursdays at 9 p.m. Light menu and no drink minimum. $8 cover. Reservations are accepted. (Downtown)

COMEDY FACTORY
36 Light St.
Baltimore
410/752-4189
Above the ancient Burke's Restaurant, the Comedy Factory churns out a steady diet of belly laughs on Friday nights at 8:30 and 10:30 p.m. The jokes get recycled at the same times on Saturdays. $10 cover. (Downtown)

MOVIE HOUSES OF NOTE

THE CHARLES
1711 N. Charles St.
Baltimore
410/727-3464
Art-film fans rejoiced in spring of 1999 when this theater, located in an old trolley barn, expanded into four theaters. A main theater shows first-run productions while three smaller theaters with stadium seating showcase independent American and foreign films. The post-industrial lobby is unlike any you'll find in the suburbs: exposed brick and water pipes, glass-topped tables, and an art-deco concession counter offering espresso in addition to popcorn and Goobers. If you like art films and classics, this is the place to be. (Downtown)

MARYLAND SCIENCE CENTER'S IMAX THEATER
601 Light St.
Baltimore
410/685-5225
www.mdsci.org
Every Friday and Saturday night (and sometimes Thursday), the science center shows a double- or triple-bill on its five-story IMAX movie screen. Double features cost $7; triple features $10. On summer weekends, buy your tickets ahead of time from the main ticket window to make sure you get in. (Downtown)

THE SENATOR THEATRE
5904 York Rd.
Baltimore
410/435-8338
www.senator.com
The Senator is simply a great place to watch a movie. Built in 1939, the art-deco theater has 900 seats, the largest screen in the state, and a sound system that's worthy of a rock concert (in fact, several rock bands have played here). But the little things matter, too: the vintage "no smoking" alerts, the pre-show cartoons, and owner Tom Kiefaber's personal introductions to each film. Most of John Waters's and Barry Levinson's movies have premiered here, and the Walk of Fame out front is Baltimore's version of Hollywood's Mann's Chinese Theater. If

you're looking for dinner before or after your movie, try the Empire Cafe across the street or the vegetable dumplings at Cafe Zen (see Chapter 4, Where to Eat). No children under 5 allowed. (Northeast)

Harpers Ferry Nat'l Historical Park

13

DAY TRIPS FROM BALTIMORE

DAY TRIP: Washington, D.C.

Distance from Baltimore: 35 miles

Baltimore often gets lumped in with Washington, D.C., as in the "Baltimore-Washington Metropolitan Area," but in reality the two cities couldn't be more different. Baltimore is a town of aging row houses, crabs, and cheap beer. It's gritty and vibrant and suffers from a classic "second-city" complex. Washington (visitors bureau: www.washington .org) is a city of marble-columned buildings, expense-account steaks, and $8 martinis. It's sophisticated, international, self-important—and the center of power of the modern world.

Most visitors to Washington start at the **National Mall**, a three-mile expanse of prime real estate sandwiched between the U.S. Capitol and the Potomac River. Nine of the Smithsonian Institution's museums line this grassy quad, plus the **National Gallery of Art** and the **U.S. Holocaust Museum**. You could easily spend an afternoon at each site. The **National Air and Space Museum**, the most popular museum in the world with almost 9 million visitors annually, houses a couple of hangars' worth of famous flying machines, from the Wright Brothers' triumphant biplane to the *Apollo 11* capsule. The **National Museum of American History** has bric-a-brac reminiscent of a giant flea market, except everything is one-of-kind and definitely not for sale. Among the historic hodgepodge: Judy Garland's ruby slippers from the *Wizard of Oz*, Archie Bunker's chair from *All in the Family*, first ladies' inaugural gowns, and the original flag, stitched by Baltimorean Mary Pickersgill, that inspired the national anthem.

All Smithsonian museums are free—a very positive indication of your tax dollars at work. To witness your tax dollars being spent, visit the **U.S. Capitol**, both the symbol of and laboratory for American democracy. Tours of the massive structure and adjoining buildings—linked by its very own subway system—depart daily.

In the spirit of Jacksonian democracy and good public relations, the **White House** is also open for public tours, although the president would never make Boris Yeltsin wait the two-and-a-half hours it normally takes to get in after picking up a ticket. During summer tourist season, the masses start queuing as early as 6 a.m. for the 4,500 free admission tickets that usually disappear by 9:30. A far better option is to request tickets for a VIP tour (more rooms, no lines) from your state representative about a month before visiting. Tours run Tuesday through Saturday.

Architect Robert Mills did such a fine job on Baltimore's Washington Monument that the Feds hired him to design one in the nation's capital, as well. The **Washington Monument**, the tallest masonry structure in the world, might still be dressed in scaffolding by the time you visit, but a temporary visitor's center gives an education on Washington's life, the monument, and videotaped views from the top. The **Lincoln Memorial**, site of Martin Luther King Jr.'s "I Have a Dream" speech, lies west of the monument, beyond the stagnant **Reflecting Pool**, which mirrors Washington's obelisk in seven million gallons of illuminated water. When the **Jefferson Memorial** was being built, President Franklin Roosevelt ordered all the trees between the work site and the White House chopped down so he could view its progress. After protest by a small but vocal group of cherry-tree huggers, the memorial was completed in 1942.

Options for eating near The Mall are scarcer than budget surpluses. They include hot dog vendors; the massive cafeteria in the National Air and Space Museum; and dining with your senator in one of the U.S. Capitol cafeterias, where the house specialty is Senate Bean Soup, a concoction of navy beans and—what else?—pork. Gourmands should explore the neighborhoods of preppy Georgetown, gay-friendly Dupont Circle, and funky Adams-Morgan, where excellent restaurants abound.

Getting there from Baltimore*: Take either I-95 or the Baltimore-Washington Parkway (Hwy. 295) south. Or take I-95 to I-495 East, exit a mile later, and park at the Greenbelt Metro Station. If you're visiting on a weekday, you can take a MARC commuter train from the Penn or Camden Stations to Washington's Union Station.*

DAY TRIP: Annapolis

Distance from Baltimore: 35 miles

Maryland's 300-year-old state capital has more surviving colonial buildings than any other place in the country. And its location, where the Severn River meets the Chesapeake, gives the city an air of noble antiquity and a seafarin' ambience that lures old salts and landlubbers alike.

Maryland's **State House** dates to 1772, making it the oldest state

BALTIMORE REGION

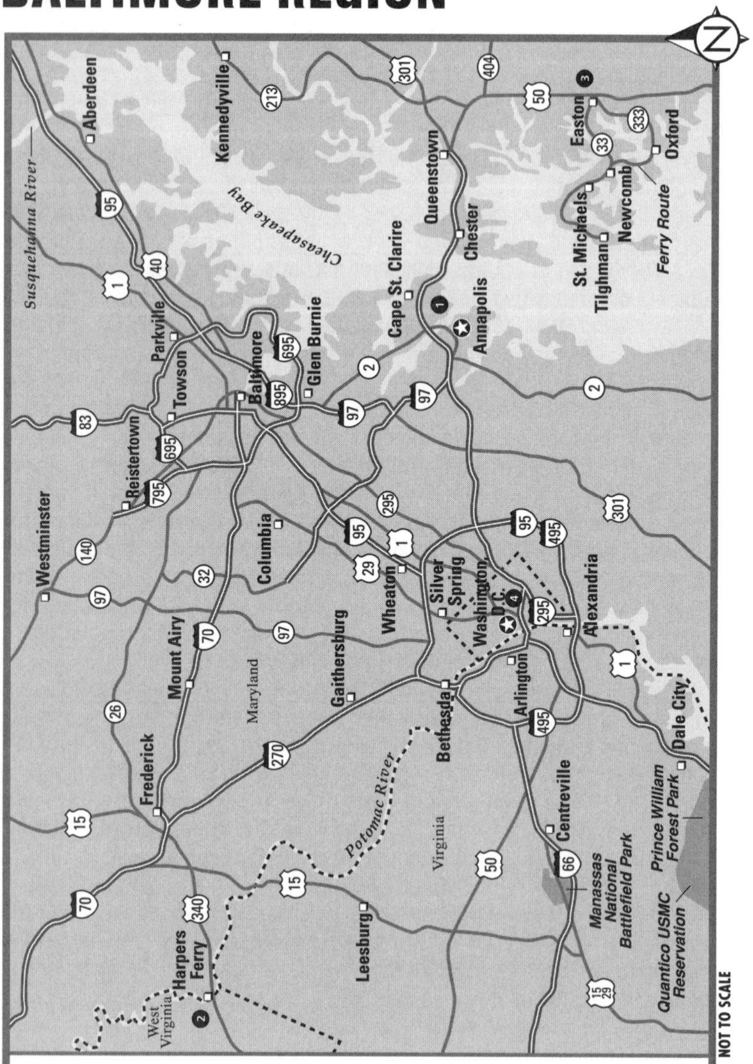

Day Trips from Baltimore

1 Annapolis
2 Harpers Ferry
3 Maryland's Eastern Shore/Easton
4 Washington, D.C.

NOT TO SCALE

Boats dock in the Chesapeake.

capitol in continuous legislative use. The Continental Congress met here from November 26, 1783, to August 13, 1784. After the American Revolution, George Washington resigned his commission as commander in chief of the Continental Army in the Old Senate Chamber. Free walk-in tours depart at 11 and 3 every day, but you may wander the historic hallways on your own.

It was President John Quincy Adams who first urged Congress to establish a naval academy "for the formation of scientific and accomplished officers." Initial attempts at training officers at sea met with disaster—three teenaged sailors were hanged for mutiny in 1842. Three years later, Secretary of the Navy George Bancroft pushed for the establishment of a land-based training facility at the site of 10-acre Fort Severn in Annapolis. There, the **United States Naval Academy** trained its first 50-member class of midshipmen. (The name midshipmen, or "mids," refers to the old British practice of training naval apprentices by positioning them in the middle of the ship to transfer orders fore and aft.) The Naval Academy is a military campus—or "yard" in academy parlance—and you'll have to drive or walk past a guarded gate to enter.

Begin your tour at the **Armel-Leftwich Visitors Center** (410/263-6933), which houses a small museum and theater. Excellent guided walking tours of the academy cover significant sights such as **Bancroft Hall** ("Mother B." to mids)—a sprawling structure where all 4,000 officers-in-training live. You'll also learn about academy traditions like the Herdon Monument Climb, during which the entire plebe, or freshman, class of 1,000 work together to remove a "dixie-cup" hat from atop the 21-foot monument, which has been greased with lard by upperclassmen. Legend has it that the plebe who reaches the hat will be the first in the class to make admiral. If you're touring on your own, don't miss the **U.S. Naval**

Academy Museum and its **Gallery of Ships**, a well-stocked museum of naval artifacts and home to a fine collection of model warships from the seventeenth through nineteenth centuries. Mids are forbidden to be married when they attend the academy, so many get hitched in the days after graduation at the academy's impressive chapel, which holds the **Crypt of John Paul Jones.** (The American Revolutionary War hero's body lay in an unmarked French cemetery for 113 years before it was shipped back to the United States.)

Shopping and dining opportunities abound along cobblestoned Main Street and City Dock. **McGarvey's Saloon** (410/263-5700), the favored watering hole of old salt Walter Cronkite when he's in town, has excellent seafood and microbrewed beer. **Middleton Tavern** (410/263-3323) has been serving up oysters on the half shell since 1740 and still charges only 95 cents for an oyster swimming in a shot of beer. (Although other delicacies are *a lot* more expensive.) **Cantler's Riverside** (410/757-1311), tough to find for first-timers, serves some of the best crabs in the state and offers a waterfront view to boot. **Chick and Ruth's Delly** (410/269-6737), open 24 hours a day, is an old-fashioned deli with orange walls and over-stuffed sandwiches named after local politicos. Diners and the kitchen staff recite the Pledge of Allegiance every morning. Chick and Ruth's also offers "bed and bagel" accommodations in a row house next door, but you'll do better by calling a reservation service such as **B&B of Maryland/Traveller in Maryland** (800/736-4667) or **Amanda's** (800/899-7533) to book a room at a B&B set in a historic house. To really experience Annapolis's nautical nature, book a bunk on a "boat and breakfast." Try the **Schooner Woodwind** (410/263-7837), a 74-foot schooner that offers nighttime cruises or **Harborview Boat & Breakfast** (410/268-9330), with its 50-year-old motor yacht, *Private Pleasure*.

Getting there from Baltimore*: Take I-95 south to I-695 east to I-97 south to Route 50/301 east to Exit 24.*

DAY TRIP: Maryland's Eastern Shore

Distance from Baltimore: 55 miles to Easton

Look at a map of Maryland, and you'll see a sizable hangnail of land, a peninsula really, separated from Maryland's mainland by the Chesapeake Bay and bordered on its eastern edge by the Atlantic Ocean. This is Maryland's Eastern Shore, distinct from the rest of the state in both geographic location and personality. For years, the Eastern Shore, Lower Delaware, and Virginia's Eastern Shore have threatened to secede from their respective states and to form their own duck-hunting, chicken-farming paradise. Former governor William Donald Schaefer, never one to phrase things delicately, didn't help matters when he once asked publicly, "How's that shithouse of an Eastern Shore?"

When the three-mile Chesapeake Bay Bridge united Maryland's eastern and western shores in 1952, it gave outsiders a better chance to experience the pleasures of Eastern Shore life: expansive water views, beautiful farmland, and a slower, more relaxed pace.

The town of **Easton**, located about 20 miles southeast of the Bay Bridge, is the unofficial capital of the Eastern Shore and the legislative and commercial hub of Talbot County. Its quaint shopping district of colonial, Federal, and Victorian buildings and its small-town atmosphere have attracted retirees and families fleeing big-city life. Every year in November, decoy aficionados and duck hunters flock to the town's renowned Waterfowl Festival.

Thirty minutes south of Easton lies **St. Michaels**, a historic watermen's hamlet known as "the town that fooled the British." As the story goes, townspeople prepared for a nighttime attack by hoisting lanterns to the masts of ships and to the tops of trees, causing British cannons to overshoot the town. The strategy proved ingenious, as only one house was struck.

Today St. Michaels's sleepy main drag, Talbot Street, makes for an idyllic stroll among antiques shops and cute boutiques. **Chesapeake Bay Maritime Museum** displays interesting exhibits about waterman history and culture and includes a charming 19th-century "screwpile" lighthouse. Across the street, the timeless **Crab Claw** (410/745-2900) serves up its namesake dish in various forms, and **Carpenter Street Saloon** (410/745-5111) provides the town with an oasis of nightlife and satisfying pub staples. Overnight accommodations top off at the pricey **Inn at Perry Cabin** (800/722-2949), a 41-room, circa-1820 mansion restored with Laura Ashley interiors and a four-star restaurant. The more moderately priced **Dr. Dodson House Bed & Breakfast** (410/745-3691) has just two rooms in a restored former tavern. A **Best Western Motor Inn** (410/745-3333) offers some of the least expensive rooms in town.

From St. Michaels, you can take a ferry to **Oxford**, home to several antiques shops and the venerable **Oxford Inn** (410/226-5220), whose crab cakes James A. Michener proclaimed his favorite during his two years of research on his Eastern Shore tome, *Chesapeake*.

Drive 10 miles south of St. Michaels and you'll be on **Tilghman Island**, a waterman's paradise and home of the last remaining fleet of sail-powered workboats in America. The oldest of the few remaining skipjacks is the *Rebecca T. Ruark* (410/886-2176), built in 1886 and now piloted by Captain Wade Murphy Jr., a third-generation waterman. On a two-hour cruise, he'll introduce you to a way of life that hasn't changed in more than 150 years. Murphy leads his sightseeing sails year-round, and during oyster season, October through March, he might even ask you to pitch in with his four-person crew. If you'd rather cruise in style, climb aboard the *Lady Patty* (410/886-2215), an expertly restored 1935 sailing yacht. Have your post-cruise meal of almond-crusted soft-shell crabs or stuffed rockfish at the sublime **Tilghman Island Inn** (410/886-2141). And if the island's peaceful rhythms lull you into spending the night, grab a hammock at the **Black Walnut Point Inn** (410/886-2452), set in a spectacular wildlife preserve where the Choptank River meets the bay.

Getting there from Baltimore: *Follow the directions to Annapolis (page 201), then continue on U.S. Route 301/50 over the Bay Bridge. Where 301 and 50 divide, follow Route 50 south to Easton.*

DAY TRIP: Harpers Ferry, West Virginia

Distance from Baltimore: 64 miles

Thomas Jefferson called the confluence of the Potomac and Shenandoah Rivers at Harpers Ferry "one of the most stupendous scenes in nature," and "worth a voyage across the Atlantic." You'll have to drive only about an hour and 15 minutes from Baltimore to enjoy the scenery—and the area's significant past.

If you recall your high school history, on October 16, 1859, abolitionist John Brown and his 21-member "army of liberation," believing they could free the slaves, chose Harpers Ferry's U.S. Armory and Arsenal and its 100,000-weapon cache as their starting point. Unfortunately, the raid was a miserable failure. Thirty-six hours after the siege had begun, with most of Brown's men dead or wounded, U.S. Marines led by Lieutenant Colonel Robert E. Lee captured Brown in the armory's firehouse. In nearby Charles Town, Brown was hanged for the crimes of treason, murder, and inciting slaves to rebellion. His raid had failed, but the martyr was correct in his final judgment that "crimes of this guilty land will never be purged away, but with blood." Civil war erupted two years later.

Today, the 2,300-acre **Harpers Ferry National Historical Park** (304/535-6298; www.nps.gov/hafe/home.htm) preserves the area as a monument to Brown and the Civil War. The most interesting attractions lie

Harpers Ferry

Nat'l Historical Park

in the Lower Town Historic District, a restored village of quaint shops, restaurants, and historically significant buildings, accessible via shuttle buses from the park's visitor's center on U.S. 340. Take the excellent ranger-led tours that detail Brown's siege or visit the **John Brown Museum** for a comprehensive look at the events leading up to his raid and its aftermath. The **Civil War Museum** covers the area's warring history, during which Harpers Ferry changed hands between North and South a very bloody eight times. The North suffered its most embarrassing loss here in 1862, when Thomas J. "Stonewall" Jackson surrounded and captured the town's 12,500-man Union garrison.

Visit the **Black Voices Museum** for an education on the town's early African American residents, who made up about 10 percent of the population at the time of John Brown's raid. After the Civil War, New England Freewill Baptist missionaries acquired several buildings and established Storer College, the country's first integrated school, designed primarily to educate former slaves but open to all races and genders. Frederick Douglas served as a trustee, and the college educated thousands of people until the U.S. Supreme Court ended legal segregation in 1954.

If you'd like to stay the night, the best views of the rushing Potomac and the Blue Ridge Mountains can be found at **Between the Rivers B&B** (304/535-2768). **Hilltop House** is homey and less expensive (800/338-8319), and the **Cliffside Inn** (304/535-6302) has views of the woods near the Park Service parking lot and free shuttles to Lower Town.

Getting there from Baltimore: *Take I-695 to I-70 to U.S. 15 South to U.S. 340 West.*

EMERGENCY PHONE NUMBERS

Police, Fire, Ambulance
911

Non-emergency Assistance
311

Poison Control
410/706-7701 or 800/492-2414

HOSPITALS AND EMERGENCY MEDICAL CENTERS

Greater Baltimore Medical Center
6701 N. Charles St.
Towson
410/828-2000

Johns Hopkins Hospital
600 N. Wolfe St.
Baltimore
410/955-5000

Maryland General Hospital
827 Linden Ave.
Baltimore
410/225-8000

Mercy Medical Center
301 St. Paul Pl.
Baltimore
410/332-9000

St. Agnes Hospital
900 Caton Ave.
Baltimore
410/368-6000

Sinai Hospital
2401 Belvedere Ave.

Baltimore
410/601-9000

Union Memorial Hospital
201 E. University Pkwy.
Baltimore
410/554-2000

University of Maryland
Medical Center
22 S. Greene St.
Baltimore
410/328-8667

VISITOR INFORMATION

Baltimore Area Visitors' Center
800/282-6632 or 888/BALTIMO
www. baltimore.org

CITY TOURS

About Town Inc.
410/592-7770

Baltimore Black Heritage Tours
410/783-5469

Baltimore Rent-a-Tour
410/653-2998

Concierge Plus Inc.
410/625-2585

Harbor City Tours
410/254-TOUR

Harbor Cruises, Ltd.
410/727-3113 or 800/695-2628

Schooner Nighthawk Cruises
410/276-7447

MAIN POST OFFICE

900 E. Fayette St.
410/347-4425

CAR RENTAL

Alamo
800/327-9633

Avis
800/831-2847

Budget
800/527-0700

Enterprise
800/736-8222

Hertz
800/654-3131

National
800/227-7368

Thrifty
800/367-2277

DISABLED ACCESS INFORMATION

League Serving People with Physical
Disabilities Inc.
410/323-0500
TDD 410/435-6589

Lifestar Response
410/665-0550

Parents' Place of Maryland
410/859-5300

MULTICULTURAL RESOURCES

Baltimore American Indian Center
410/675-3535

Baltimore Urban League
410/523-8150

Centro De La Comunidad
410/675-8906

Jewish Community Center
410/542-4900

OTHER COMMUNITY ORGANIZATIONS

Baltimore Community Foundation
410/332-4171

Gay & Lesbian Community Center of
Baltimore
410/837-5445

BABYSITTING AND CHILDCARE

Baltimore City Child Care Resource
Center
410/685-5150

Best Nanny Employment Agency
410/486-2135

The Nanny Network
410/321-1566

NEWSPAPERS

Baltimore Afro-American
410/554-8200

Baltimore Business Journal
410/576-1161
Baltimore Gay Paper
410/837-7748

Baltimore Jewish Times
410/332-1951

City Paper
410/523-2300

Daily Record
410/752-3849

The Sun
410/332-6000

MAGAZINES

Baltimore
410/752-4200

Maryland Family
410/366-7512

Style
410/332-1951

The Urbanite
410/366-0574

RADIO STATIONS

WCAO 600 AM/Christian
WCBM 680 AM/News/Talk
WBGR 860 AM/Christian
WOL 1010 AM/News/Talk
WBAL 1090 AM/News/Talk/Orioles
   baseball
WAVA 1230 AM/Christian
WJFK 1300 AM/Talk/Sports
WLG 1360 AM/Easy Listening
WJHU 88.1 FM/National Public Radio
WEAA 88.9 FM/Jazz
WBJC 91.5 FM/Classical
WWIN 92.5 FM/Pop

WPOC 93.1 FM/Country
WRBS 95.1 FM/Christian
WIYY 98 FM/Rock
WHFS 99.1 FM/Alternative Rock
WGRX 100.7 FM/Country
WWDC 101.1 FM/Rock
WLIF 102 FM/Easy Listening
WRNR 103.1 FM/Progressive Rock
WOCT 104.3 FM/Rock
WQSR 105.7 FM/Oldies
WWMX 106.5 FM/Pop

TELEVISION STATIONS

WMAR Channel 2 (ABC)
WBAL Channel 11 (NBC)
WJZ Channel 13 (CBS)
MPT Channel 22 (Maryland Public
   Television)
WUTB Channel 24 (UPN)
WBFF Channel 45 (Fox)
WNUV Channel 54 (WB)

BOOKSTORES

Adrian's Book Cafe
714 S. Broadway
Baltimore
410/732-1048

Atomic Books
1806 Maryland Ave.
Baltimore
410/625-7955

Barnes and Noble
Power Plant
601 E. Pratt Street
Baltimore
410/385-1709

Bibelot
The Village at Cross Keys
5100 Falls Road
Baltimore
410/532-8818

Bibelot
2400 Boston St.
Baltimore
410/276-9700

B Dalton Bookseller
529 Security Square Mall
6901 Security Blvd.
Baltimore
410/944-7733

B Dalton Bookseller
430 Gallery at Harborplace
200 E. Pratt St.
Baltimore
410/659-5846

Gordon's Booksellers
The Rotunda
711 W. 40th Street
Baltimore
410/889-2100

Louie's Café
518 N. Charles St.
Baltimore
410/962-1222

Waldenbooks
641 Security Square Mall
6901 Security Blvd.
Baltimore
410/944-7344

Waldenbooks
7749 East Point Mall
Baltimore
410/282-1077

INDEX

© Link Nicoll

ABOUT THE AUTHOR

Like most Baltimoreans, Joe Sugarman finds it hard to leave. Odd jobs have called him away at times, but he stubbornly endures lengthy commutes rather than choose relocation. A former senior editor for *Mid-Atlantic Country Magazine,* Sugarman has written for various national and regional publications such as Smithsonian's *Air & Space, Style,* and *Philadelphia* magazines, the *Baltimore Sun,* and the *Washington Post.* He has also written about Baltimore's quirky charms for Microsoft's on-line city guide, Sidewalk.com. Before he embarked on journalistic endeavors, you could find him performing in the city's annual parades dressed as T. Rex, the affable dinosaur mascot of the Maryland Science Center.

John Muir Publications and its City•Smart Guidebook authors are dedicated to building community awareness within City•Smart cities. We are proud to work with Baltimore Reads as we publish this guide to Baltimore.

Baltimore Reads aims to improve the quality of life for educationally disadvantaged adults, children, and families. As a local leader in results-based learning services, Baltimore Reads emphasizes the reading and life skills essential for learning, employment, and self-sufficiency. Other efforts include local and national collaborations, research, and consulting services.

For more information, please contact:
Baltimore Reads
5 E. Read St.
Baltimore, MD 21202
410/752-3595
www.baltimorereads.org